W9-AAT-655

D-DAY
— Minute by Minute —

# D-DAY

*— Minute by Minute —*

JONATHAN MAYO

MARBLE ARCH
PRESS

Marble Arch Press
1230 Avenue of the Americas
New York, NY 10020

10 9 8 7 6 5 4 3 2 1


Originally published in Great Britain in 2014 by Short Books.



First Marble Arch Press trade paperback edition May 2014

Marble Arch Press is a publishing collaboration between Short Books, UK, and Atria Books, US.

Marble Arch Press and colophon are trademarks of Short Books.

For information about special discounts for bulk purchases, please contact Simon & Schuster Special Sales at 1-866-506-1949 or business@simonandschuster.com.

---

Photo credits:

Cover
Getty Images, © John Cairns

Endpapers
Imperial War Museums ©IWM EA 25372

Pages 6-7
Normandy map by Two Associates

Page 10
Imperial War Museums ©IWM OWIL 44979

Page 14
Bundesarchiv, Bild 101I-719-0243-33 / Photo: Jesse

Page 18
Imperial War Museums ©IWM B 5103

Page 76
© Robert Capa © International Center of Photography/Magnum Photos

Page 274
Imperial War Museums ©IWM EA 29756

---

The quotation from Donald Burgett, US 101st Airborne Division on page 69 is taken from Burgett, Donald R, *Currahee! A Screaming Eagle in Normandy* (Dell, 2000)

The quotations from Anne Frank's Diary on pages 20, 184 and 228 are taken from Frank, Anne, *The Diary of a Young Girl* (Pan Books, 1954)



---

The 'Minute by Minute' format is applied to this publication with the permission of TBI Media

ISBN: 978-1-4767-7294-3
ISBN: 978-1-4767-7295-0 (ebook)

*For Hannah and Charlie*
*and the Normandy Veterans*

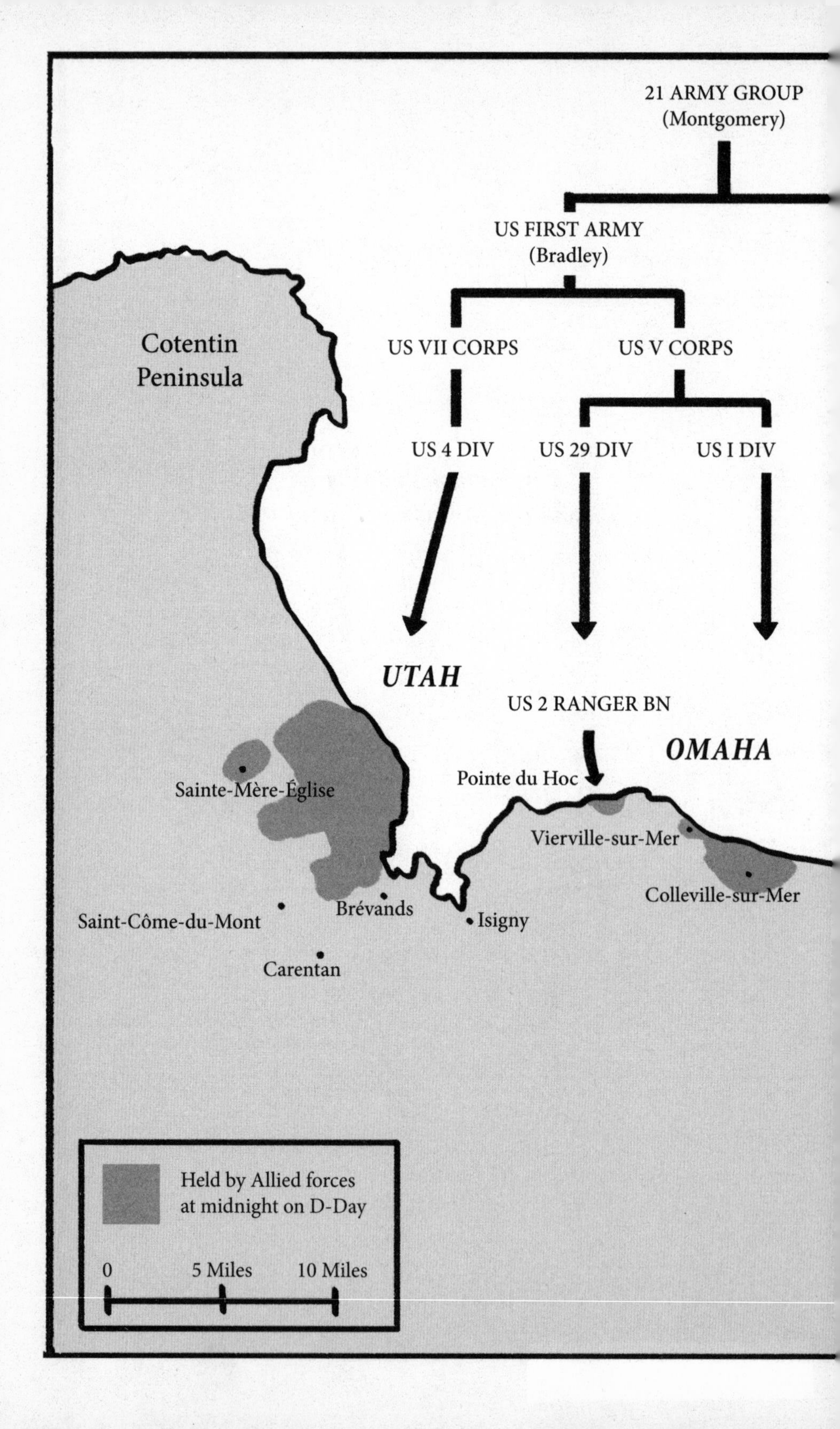

21 ARMY GROUP
(Montgomery)
US FIRST ARMY
(Bradley)
US VII CORPS
US V CORPS
US 4 DIV
US 29 DIV
US I DIV
Cotentin
Peninsula
UTAH
US 2 RANGER BN
OMAHA
Pointe du Hoc
Sainte-Mère-Église
Vierville-sur-Mer
Colleville-sur-Mer
Brévands
Saint-Côme-du-Mont
Isigny
Carentan
Held by Allied forces
at midnight on D-Day
0
5 Miles
10 Miles

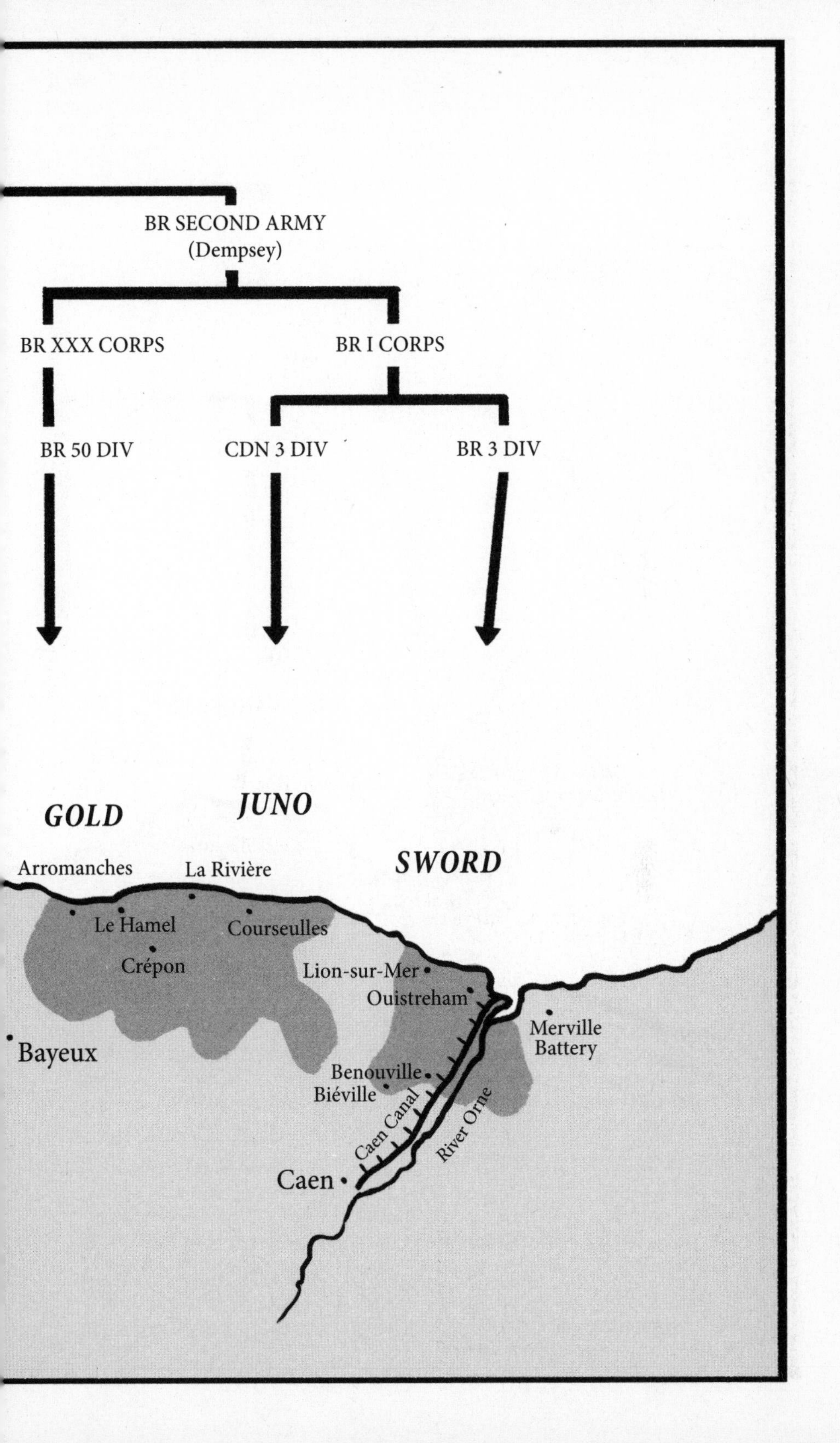
BR SECOND ARMY
(Dempsey)
BR XXX CORPS
BR I CORPS
BR 50 DIV
CDN 3 DIV
BR 3 DIV
GOLD
JUNO
SWORD
Arromanches
La Rivière
Le Hamel
Courseulles
Crépon
Lion-sur-Mer
Ouistreham
Merville
Battery
Bayeux
Benouville
Biéville
Caen Canal
River Orne
Caen

# Contents

*A dead US soldier on Utah Beach, 6th June 1944. The body has been given a label to ensure correct identification.*

# Introduction

The evening after D-Day, the naval shore base at Haslemere in Surrey held one of its regular dances. A young sailor, no more than 19 years old, slipped in and sat next to Wren Maureen Bolster. Just one look was enough to tell her where he'd returned from – his eyes were bloodshot and he was shaking all over. All the man could manage to say was, 'Make me forget it, please make me forget it – I've just got to.' A few days later, in another part of the country, a mother received a letter from her son serving as a lieutenant with the East Yorkshire Regiment. Although he too had witnessed the bloodshed of the Normandy beaches he wrote, 'I did not feel afraid, but rather elated and full of beans...'

This is not a book about military strategy – I'm not interested in explaining the movements of every regiment on D-Day – instead it's about those contrasting experiences that reveal a great deal about what it was like to take part in the largest invasion the world has ever known.

Just like my previous book *The Assassination of JFK: Minute by Minute,* this book has plenty of fascinating details that I feel bring history to life. For example Lord Lovat brushing sand from his brogues in the middle of the battle on Sword Beach; troops who have been blinded by flame-throwers being treated by medics while sitting in seaside deckchairs; General Montgomery's photos of enemy generals on a wall in his caravan, so he can get an insight into their character.

The variety of experiences of D-Day is reflected in the stories I've discovered. Sometimes the 6th June seems just like a 1950s war film with cockney corporals shouting, 'Come out and fight, you square-headed bastards!' Sometimes it's chaotic, especially in the first few hours. One commando veteran of Normandy said, 'War to the uninitiated is like a Marx Brothers film. Everything is a terrific balls-up, not from the generals' perspective, but from the soldiers' perspective.'

The chaos of war often meant that the participants had little sense of time. Captain Walter Marchand, a battalion surgeon on Utah Beach, broke off from treating patients to write in his diary, 'It is now noon – God, the five hours passed like lightning…' A Canadian chaplain wrote later, that in action, 'like a hospital patient, you lose all idea of time…' This means that sometimes I've had to estimate when events occurred or rely on statements such as 'just before sunset'; but more often than not I've benefited from the military obsession with logging events, either in diaries (with a surprising number being updated throughout the day at sea and even on the beaches), written accounts or regimental records. If there's no clue to exactly when an event took place, but I feel that it is worthwhile including, I have added 'about' before the time. Times are given as Double British Summer Time (GMT+2) unless stated.

In April 1942, the Admiralty, keen for information on potential invasion beaches in Europe, appealed over the BBC for the public to send them pre-war postcards or holiday snaps of France and the Low Countries. They were used to provide an incomplete, but vital 'photographic map' of the coast of Europe. This book is something like that – by telling the stories of some of the assault troops, airborne forces, sailors, politicians, civilians and medics, I hope to paint a picture of what D-Day must have been like – the chaos, the horror and the bravery.

### D-Day Acronyms

LCT: Landing Craft, Tank
LCVP: Landing Craft, Vehicle, Personnel (or Higgins Boat)
LCI: Landing Craft, Infantry
LCG Landing Craft, Gun
LCM: Landing Craft, Mechanised
PIAT: Projector, Infantry, Anti-Tank
AVRE: Armoured Vehicle, Royal Engineers

*Field Marshal Rommel, front, third from left, inspects beach defences in France.*

# May 1944

Two employees of one of the most successful toymakers in the world are arriving at a security checkpoint in the south of England. In their truck they have two gigantic plywood maps – one covering the coastlines of Scandinavia, Germany and Holland, the other covering Belgium and France. Each map is 15 feet high and 20 feet wide, and has been made by Chad Valley, by Royal Appointment 'Toymakers to HM The Queen' (her daughters Princesses Elizabeth and Margaret are known to enjoy playing with their dolls).

But it is the company's skills as makers of jigsaws – cut by hand with fret saws, ensuring that no two are alike – that has led to this unique commission.

The truck is at a checkpoint outside Southwick House, a stately home on the outskirts of Portsmouth, also the base of SHAEF (Supreme Headquarters, Allied Expeditionary Force). This means that Chad Valley, makers of jigsaws, teddy bears and train sets, has made the map on which the long-awaited invasion of Nazi-occupied Europe will be plotted.

The two Chad Valley men know that only one map is needed.

The other has been created as a decoy – no one must know where the invasion will take place. In the truck the men also have their suitcases. Once they've fixed the chosen map to a wall in Southwick House, neither of them will be allowed to leave the building until the invasion of Europe has begun.

> ***The peoples of Europe have suffered. Do everything you can to make them know that with your coming, their suffering is eased and may soon be over. Bear in mind continuously that the operation for which we have been assembled in Great Britain – the invasion of Europe – must be successful, or we have lost World War II.***
>
> ***Think that over.***
>
> ***Advice to US Troops in* Army Talks *magazine, May 1944***

*For more than two years, there has been talk of an invasion of occupied Europe by Britain, the United States and their allies. An invasion would ease the pressure on the Soviet Union, fighting a bloody campaign against Germany on the Eastern Front since June 1941.*

*There's growing optimism that the war is being won and that a Second Front will swiftly finish the Germans off. The changing mood in Britain is shown in the titles of the BBC's annual Christmas programme. In 1940 it had been* Christmas Under Fire*; in 1941* To Absent Friends*; in 1942* The Fourth Christmas *and in 1943 it was* We Are Advancing!

*In Britain, the slogan 'Second Front Now' has been painted on walls across the country (the majority allegedly done by pro-Russian firemen on night shifts) and its timing endlessly discussed in food queues, pubs and work canteens.*

*In the foreground Bill Millin with his bagpipes walks from a landing craft onto Sword Beach; Lord Lovat is wading in the water to the right of the column of men.*

# Monday 5th June 1944

## **'OK, let's go.'**

*4.15am*

In the Map Room in Southwick House, all attention is on the newly installed map of the coastline of northern France.

A storm is battering the building so fiercely that its walls seem to be shaking. In the old library on the ground floor, a tall, nervous 43-year-old Scottish meteorologist named Group Captain James Stagg is standing in front of some of the most powerful military men in the world. Stagg hasn't slept all night. D-Day was to have been today, but was postponed; for the invasion to be launched tomorrow, a decision has to be made by 5am.

Watching him intently, seated in armchairs and sofas, are the men who head SHAEF: General Dwight D Eisenhower, Eisenhower's chief of staff Major General Walter Bedell Smith, Air Chief Marshal Sir Arthur Tedder, Admiral Sir Bertram Ramsay, Air Chief Marshal Sir Trafford Leigh-Mallory and the man who is the senior ground force commander for the invasion of Europe, General Sir Bernard Montgomery. Everyone is in immaculate battledress, except Monty, who is sitting in the front row wearing a high-necked fawn pullover and light corduroy trousers.

Previous meetings with Stagg have begun with banter and pleasantries. There is none of that today. They want his weather forecast for the next 24 hours. What he's about to say will affect the lives of millions.

The whole of Europe is waiting.

*The Germans know that an invasion is imminent – they just don't know exactly where and when it will be. In November 1943 Hitler had told his chiefs of staff, 'All signs point to an offensive against the Western Front no later than spring 1944, and perhaps earlier...'*

*The Nazis occupy Norway, Denmark, Holland, Belgium, France, Poland, Serbia and Greece, and the peoples under their control are desperate to be liberated. The Nazis have introduced slave labour on a monumental scale. In Poland alone there are 5,800 different camps including forced labour camps, prisoner-of-war camps, concentration camps and death camps. The total number of Jews gassed at Auschwitz-Birkenau since 1942 is two million with a further 500,000 shot or starved to death. Hans Frank, the Nazi governor of Poland, said in 1943, 'Once we have won the war, then for all I care, mincemeat can be made out of Poles, Ukrainians and all the others who run around here.'*

*For almost two years, Otto and Edith Frank have hidden with their daughters Margot and Anne in a secret annexe on the top floor of an old building by an Amsterdam canal. In June 1942, Anne was given an autograph book with a red and white checked cover as a birthday present, and since they went into hiding has used it as a diary.*

*On 22nd May 14-year-old Anne wrote in it, 'All of Amsterdam, all of Holland, in fact the entire western coast of Europe all the way down to Spain, are talking about the invasion day and night, debating, making bets and... hoping.'*

*Those who are hoping will not have long to wait. In the Channel, some of the troops are already waiting in ships and landing craft. They have been there for several days in very cramped conditions. They were ready to set off on the 4th but the expedition was postponed because of the appalling weather.*

*Briefed with maps and photographs (including the holiday snaps of the Normandy coast sent in by the public in 1942), they don't yet know their destination as place names have been blacked out. However, some enterprising Royal Engineers in 82 Assault Squadron have worked out that if they wet a handkerchief and give a photo a rub, the names are decipherable. When one unit of Free French Commandos saw their map of Sword Beach with all the names covered, they recognised the beach straight away. One of them had even worked on the lock gates of one of the targets – the Caen Canal. Sadly for the Frenchmen, because of that knowledge, they were all confined to barracks until their ship sailed.*

*In May, one of the generals whose job it is to lead the invasion, American General Omar Bradley, was walking past Speaker's Corner in Hyde Park where a man on a soapbox was urgently calling for 'a Second Front now!'. Bradley wrote later, 'I thought of how little comprehension he had of what the Second Front entailed, of the labours that would be required to mount it.'*

*It is now two years since the millions of people who sent their holiday photos to the Admiralty each received a letter thanking them for 'their valuable contribution to the war effort'. People are getting impatient, especially as since January, German bombers have returned for night sorties over English cities, a campaign nicknamed 'The Little Blitz'.*

*Since mid-May, there has been so much movement of troops and trucks on the roads of the south of England that in Dorchester employers have given their workers an extra 15 minutes at lunch-time just to cross the streets. The narrow lanes of English villages in Hampshire, Sussex, Kent, Dorset and Devon have been clogged with jeeps and tanks, often knocking down gable ends and fence posts.*

*One hundred and fifty thousand troops are waiting in army camps across Britain, with vast amounts of ammunition and supplies hidden in woods and forests. Ten thousand firemen and fire-women have been moved to the south of England and south Wales to guard them. Eisenhower joked that it was only the large number of barrage balloons floating above Britain that kept her from sinking under the sea.*

*The army camps have signs to deter curious locals, saying, 'Do Not Loiter. Do Not Speak To The Troops.' In the past two years over 163 air bases have been built to cater for all the fighters, bombers, transports and gliders needed for the invasion. For weeks, docks from Essex to South Wales have been crammed with military and commercial shipping. In Southampton, ships are berthed eight abreast and its schools taken over by troops, and to store equipment.*

*Daytrippers have been banned from visiting the coast from East Anglia to Cornwall. Churchill had been unconvinced by the need for this plan and asked the things the public shouldn't be allowed to see to be written down for him on a single sheet of paper. Faced with a long list of construction sites, training areas, top-secret equipment, and embarkation locations, the prime minister relented.*

*Hospitals in the south of England have been cleared of civilian patients and scrubbed from top to bottom. The beds are ready for casualties – grey blankets have been spread on them to take men with dirty, bloody uniforms. Trolleys are piled high with towels, soap, flannels, razors and pyjamas for men who've lost their possessions. Cages have been built on the common at Portsmouth to hold German prisoners of war.*

*Over the past few days, Group Captain James Stagg has exasperated some of the top brass with his pessimistic forecasts. Yesterday, when Stagg walked in, Admiral Sir George Creasy muttered, 'Here comes six foot two inches of Stagg and six foot one inch of gloom...'*

*But General Eisenhower trusts the dour-looking meteorologist. He has been testing Stagg by getting him to make three-day forecasts, and then on the fourth checking the results.*

*When in 1943 Stagg had joined the planning staff for Operation Overlord (the code name for the invasion of France) the army, navy and the air force all gave him a list of the weather conditions they needed for a successful invasion. Their minimum requirements were for the paratroopers a late-rising moon, and for the navy calm waters for the landing craft, a low tide to expose beach defences early in the day to allow for 17 hours of daylight to land multiple waves of troops, plus an inshore wind to blow smoke away from their targets. Stagg worked out that they might have to wait 150 years before the perfect weather arrived to please all of them. However, he'd told them that a full moon and early low tide could be guaranteed on 4th, 5th, 6th and 7th June 1944.*

*Eisenhower grumbled earlier to his English driver Kay Summersby, (with whom he's been having an affair for over a year) that although military textbooks say that the weather is neutral, during his campaigns in North Africa and Italy the weather was always partisan in favour of the Germans. It seems the same is true now.*

*Last night, Stagg told Eisenhower there was in fact good news – there should be a brief break in the bad weather that had caused*

*D-Day to be postponed, from this afternoon until tomorrow afternoon the 6th June, but that he would know more in the morning...*

### *4.17am*

The rain is hitting the windows of the library in Southwick House hard. Eisenhower says, 'Now, go ahead, Stagg.'

Stagg manages a smile.

'Well, I'll give you some good news. Gentlemen, no substantial change has taken place since last time, but as I see it, the little that has changed is in the direction of optimism.'

The good weather he has predicted should last until tomorrow afternoon – 6th June. Visibility should be good and the winds no more than Force 4. Eisenhower has been pacing up and down, but now he stops and says quietly, 'OK, let's go.'

The room is full of the sound of cheering. Stagg thinks his audience look like 'new men... it was a marvel to behold'. Stagg fields a few questions and then the room rapidly empties, leaving Eisenhower alone.

Stagg heads to his tent in the grounds of Southwick House to try and get some sleep. A British general had said to him a couple of days ago, only half joking, 'Remember, if you don't read the runes right, we'll string you up from the nearest lamppost...'

> ***'In the middle of 1942... our commander came round and said they were looking for volunteers for hazardous underwater work; the qualifications were that you had to be able to swim and were single; as I qualified for both these things, I put my name down...'***
>
> ***Lieutenant George Honour***

### *7.00am*

Thirty feet down off the coast of Normandy, ten Royal Navy sailors are existing on a diet of baked beans, soup and tea. They are in *X20* and *X23*, two X-class midget submarines, and the same wind that's battering Southwick House has created a swell that's making them roll around on the bottom of the seabed and tug at their anchor ropes. The crews know that it must be stormy on the surface. Their fear is that they will be wrecked on the beach and Operation Overlord will be exposed.

*The subs have been there, still and silent, for two days. Their job, when D-Day comes, is to surface and erect an 18-foot telescopic mast fitted with navigation lights and a radio beacon to guide British and Canadian landing craft away from rocks and safely towards their invasion beaches.*

*They are so close to France that yesterday, through his periscope, one of the subs' commanders, Lieutenant George Honour, watched German soldiers swimming and playing with a beach ball. 'Little do they know what's coming their way,' he thought.*

*Each sub has a crew of five, crammed into a craft only 50 feet long, with barely five feet of headroom. The crews share a love of adventure. Sub Lieutenant Jim Booth, serving with Honour, wrote to the Admiralty two years ago complaining that the war 'wasn't exciting enough', and so they suggested he joined X-class submarines.*

*The crew sleep one at a time on four-hour rotations on a hard board in the battery compartment. The lack of oxygen and the smell of diesel from the engine (the same as a London bus) adds to the feeling of suffocation. The Americans declined the British offer to use these lightships for their invasion beaches, fearing if they were discovered, their intention would be all too plain, and months of planning would be wasted. The British have accepted that risk.*

## *7.30am*

In ports and at sea, naval officers are breaking open their sealed orders and discovering their D-Day destination.

*'D-Day' was first used by the US Army in the final months of the Great War, to indicate the day of the start of a military operation, keeping the precise date secret. 'D' simply stands for 'day'. By 1943 'D-Day' had come to mean the invasion of Europe. The landings on the Normandy beaches will start at 'H-Hour'.*

*The most obvious place for an invasion would be across the English Channel at its narrowest point – just 20 miles – at the Pas-de-Calais. The short journey would mean that there would be a greater chance of retaining the element of surprise and hence reducing the opportunity for a German counter-attack. However, the Pas-de-Calais is very strongly defended, for the simple reason that it's the obvious route. The Germans have concluded that for the invasion to succeed, the Allies must capture a port, to bring ashore the vast amount of supplies they'll need. In fact, a raid on Dieppe on the north coast of France in August 1942 taught the Allies that to attack a well-defended port would be suicidal – 3,000 troops were killed or captured.*

*SHAEF has identified a 60-mile stretch of coastline in Normandy as suitable. Although it's about five hours away by boat, and in places has plenty of cliffs and rocks, it has no major ports, its defences are weaker and its beaches are wide and have firm sand.*

*The Allies have chosen five invasion beaches between the villages of Vareville to the west and Ouistreham to the east. Each has been given a code name – the British and Canadians chose Gold, Juno and Sword at random from a list of names supplied by the British Army that could be clearly heard by radio operators in the heat of battle. The American names for their beaches, Utah and Omaha, were chosen by their generals. Winston Churchill had insisted that whatever names were chosen they should be dignified, as no mother would want to hear that her son was reported dead or missing on a beach named 'Bunny Hug'.*

### *7.45am*

The words 'Thank You' have been written in chalk on the pavement outside some of the houses of Southampton and Portsmouth, where troops and tank crews have been parked for the last few nights. Now the streets are empty.

Marjorie Box is standing in her street in Holbury on the outskirts of Southampton, tears streaming down her face as she waves goodbye to the soldiers who've been outside her house. In her kitchen she has a large number of ingredients given to her by their commanding officer, so she could bake them all a cake. Marjorie realises now that was just a ruse to give her and her family some scarce and badly needed rations.

> ***No Army Council Instruction has ever succeeded in stopping the British soldier from fraternising with children – especially if you're driving a 'duck' [amphibious vehicle] with a life-size painting of Donald on its side.***
>
> ***Alan Melville, BBC war correspondent***

### *9.00am*

The biggest invasion force the world has ever seen is mobilising. In all, D-Day involves over 6,203 vessels – 1,213 warships, 4,126 landing craft and 864 merchant vessels (liners, tankers and tugs) providing supply and support. They will all converge on an area south of the Isle of Wight code-named Area Z, but soon nicknamed 'Piccadilly Circus'. British and Canadian forces are concentrated around Essex, Sussex and Hampshire, American forces in Dorset, Devon and Cornwall.

General Eisenhower is on the South Parade Pier in Portsmouth watching the loading of British troops onto landing craft.

'Good old Ike!' they're cheering.

The landing craft are 350 feet long and can take up to 200 men. Others are designed to take tanks directly to the Normandy beaches; the tanks disembarking via large bow doors (modern day roll-on roll-off ferries are the direct descendants of these ships). Most of these ships have made a journey across the Atlantic to get here.

General Eisenhower is talking to some of the British troops, and his naval aide Captain Harry Butcher is watching. He can tell that the conversations are lifting his boss's anxious mood.

Ernest Bevin, the Minister for Labour, is watching the Durham Light Infantry embark at Southampton. A soldier shouts to him, 'Ernie, when we have done this job for you, are we going back on the dole?' Bevin's eyes fill with tears.

As the troops made their way through the ports, they'd been told by the commanding officers not to talk to civilians, but it's been difficult. War correspondent Alan Melville is travelling with a British regiment, and he can see in the faces of the people on the streets that they know this is no exercise.

Twelve-year-old Peter McElhinney is standing in a Portsmouth street watching the troops march by. A young GI empties all his money and cigarettes out of his pockets and pushes them into the astonished boy's hands.

'Here, kid, take this. I won't be coming back from where I'm going.'

Another soldier in a truck passing though Portsmouth throws a football to some boys in the street. On it was written, 'We have no further use for this and I hope it will give you a lot of pleasure.'

In nearby Gosport, one American GI marching past teenager Jean Charlesworth blurts out that he is afraid.

'You will be all right, I know it,' she says.

Margaret Woodhead is worried she's done the wrong thing. A few days ago she had been walking along Langstone Harbour near Hayling Island, past some army tents on a playing field. A soldier came up to her and said, 'Can you post a letter for me? We're not allowed out of here and I would like my wife to get this.'

Margaret had hesitated and wondered if he was a spy passing a message to the Germans, telling them where he's stationed. She'd posted it, but now she fears that D-Day might be affected because of what she's done.

A row of tanks from the Grenadier Guards has been parked in four-year-old Shirley Whittle's street in Bedhampton for the past few days. Her family has become quite attached to one of the crews, and has given them a Union Flag to fly from the turret of their tank. (The crew will fly it proudly through the hard-fought campaigns in France and Germany, and in May 1945, post it back to Shirley.)

*D-Day is the most closely guarded secret in British history. The few who know the date of the invasion receive top secret files with*

*'Bigot' stamped on them. (This is a reversal of 'To Gib' stamped on documents sent to Gibraltar.) 'Are you Bigoted?' is a question sometimes used in the corridors of power to determine who is in the know. It bewilders many people.*

*A plastic model of Omaha Beach has been created to brief the officers who will lead the assault. To ensure secrecy, individual parts have been made in different states of the US, and then assembled once in the UK.*

*Security around the date for D-Day has been tight, but there have been a few lapses. At a cocktail party at Claridge's (known as 'Little America' because of the number of US soldiers staying there) Major General Henry Miller, of the US 9th Air Force, complained about his supply problems but said that they would be over by D-Day, which would come 'before 15th June'. Even though he was an old friend, General Eisenhower demoted Miller to the rank of colonel and had him sent back to the States. Soon after, Miller retired.*

*At the moment, MI5 are concerned about the* Daily Telegraph *crossword. Number 5801 on 2nd June had contained the clue: 'Britannia and he hold on to the same thing.' The answer is Neptune, the code word for the amphibious invasion. Could it be just a coincidence? they wonder. They are suspicious, as in the past few weeks, four other code words have appeared in the crossword.*

*3rd May: 'One of the US' (Utah)*

*23rd May: 'Red Indian on the Missouri' (Omaha)*

*31st May: 'This bush is a centre of nursery revolutions' (Mulberry – the code name for floating harbours that have been built secretly over the past few months)*

*1st June: 'But some big-wig like this has stolen some of it at times' (Overlord)*

*Yesterday, two MI5 agents went to the Surrey home of schoolteacher Leonard Dawe, who since 1925 has been the* Daily Telegraph*'s crossword compiler. In August 1942 one of Dawe's clues, 'French port (6)', appeared two days before the disastrous Dieppe raid, leading to an investigation by the War Office. It was ruled to be a coincidence.*

*Having spoken to Leonard Dawe, MI5 are convinced that the appearance of the code words is, yet again, an incredible coincidence.*

*(However, in 1984, Ronald French, a former pupil of Dawe's, will claim that he had inserted the words into the teacher's blank puzzles; Dawe then came up with the clues. French said he heard the code words from troops stationed near the school.)*

## 'If you think you're going to get scared, you'd better get off this bucket right now'

### *About 9.45am*

At his dacha outside Moscow, Stalin is in full flow talking with Yugoslav guerrilla commander Milovan Djilas.

'Perhaps you think that just because we are allies of the English we have forgotten who they are and who Churchill is? There's nothing they like better than to trick their allies... And Churchill? Churchill is the kind of man who will pick your pocket for a kopeck, if you didn't watch him! By God, pick your pocket for a kopeck! President Roosevelt is not like that. He dips in his hand only for bigger coins.'

Stalin then mocks the invasion plans, saying that it will be called off 'if there's fog in the Channel'. He'd been promised in November by SHAEF that the invasion would take place by 1st May.

### *10.00am*

A small black tug named *Chokka* is steaming through Southampton Water. It normally supplies ammunition to troop ships, but right now it's on its way to rescue three landing craft that have broken down near the Needles. At the helm is Wren stoker Rozelle Raynes. She and two other Wrens had been woken up at 5am by having cold water thrown over their faces by their commanding officer Lieutenant Horace Sherwood. He'd told them their morning's mission and said, 'I know some of you would rather stow away on a ship that's bound for France, but the navy won't allow that, and this is the best I can do for you!'

On the *Chokka*, Rozelle is stunned by the huge armada of ships at anchor around her – minesweepers, destroyers, cruisers, trawlers and ocean tugs. A soldier is leaning over the stern of a landing craft, and above the noise of her tug's engine Rozelle can just make out what he's shouting.

'You're the last bit of Old England we'll see for a while, girls, and you sure look worth fighting for!'

> ***4th of June, I went to a party at a friend's house. As I stood there with people dancing all around me, I had this strange feeling that I was like a little god, because I could see into the future. I wanted to warn all my friends to go into hiding, but of course I couldn't say anything, not even to my parents, because I was sworn to secrecy. I stood there wondering how many of my friends would survive.***
>
> ***André Heintz, member of the French Resistance***

In Caen, the ancient capital of Normandy, 24-year-old schoolteacher André Heintz is tearing down posters that the

Germans have put up overnight mocking the Allies' victories in Italy.

*André is a member of the French Resistance, and this is a small act of defiance compared with what else he does to further their cause. André helps forge identity cards for those avoiding* Service de Travail Obligatoire *– forced labour in Germany – or Jews fleeing persecution. More often the identity cards are for Allied airmen who've been shot down. Their French is usually so terrible that he has to say on their card that they are deaf and dumb.*

*Heintz also gathers information on troop movements. One of his techniques is to join a queue at Caen bus station. If a garrison has moved out of a village, it is usually such a relief that it always comes up in conversation. When he gets to the front of the queue he pretends he's forgotten to buy a ticket, and joins a separate queue. Another method is talking to friends who do the laundry for German soldiers; they tell him the unit numbers that are on the inside of the soldiers' shirt collars.*

*Heintz's mother once overheard a German soldier tell a shop-keeper that if there were a landing he would 'behave like the mussels' – stay in his shell and not fight back. Another small but useful piece of intelligence he'd passed on to his contact by the coast, who then somehow sent it on to London. André is a firm anglophile. When he was 15 he spent six months at Bristol Grammar School to improve his English. They nicknamed him '57' after the varieties of the famous food company.*

### *10.30am*

On board the destroyer USS *Corry*, her officers are being briefed about their destination. They will be providing cover for the troops landing on Utah Beach. One of her junior officers, Ensign Robert Beeman, is shocked to see the chart shows Utah is overlooked by 77 large German guns. Where *Corry* is to drop anchor will be in range for almost all of them.

Two days before, Art Lindh, the communications officer, had appeared at Beeman's door, looking pale and shaken. He'd looked at him and said, 'If you think you're going to get scared, you'd better get off this bucket right now.'

Beeman had been mystified by what he meant, but now he understands.

Not everyone has been fully briefed. On an LCT heading away from Southampton, one of her crew says to Sergeant James Bellows of the Royal Hampshire Regiment, 'We're in a bloody hurry today, aren't we?' Where are we going this time – Hayling Island?'

'No, France,' Bellows replies.

'Don't mess about, mate. Where are we going?'

'France!' Bellows and his unit tell him, and to prove it they show the sailor their French currency.

### *11.00am*

The tug *Chokka* is heading back to Southampton with the three broken-down landing craft in tow. Wren Rozelle Raynes is looking at a thousand grey dots on the southern horizon with tears in her eyes.

A few miles from the Normandy town of Sainte-Mère-Église, 11-year-old Geneviève Duboscq is walking with her mother along a country road. In her mother's basket, under some dandelion leaves, is a pair of wire cutters. Every few yards they stop and cut a section out of a telephone cable running alongside the road and throw it over the hedge. It will now be harder for the German garrison in Sainte-Mère-Église to make contact with the outside world.

### *11.30am*

At the headquarters of the 22nd Panzer Division in Normandy, Captain Curt Fromm is answering the phone. On the other end is a Frenchwoman he doesn't know.

'Captain Fromm, all of us wish you the best of luck in the next few hours.'

The woman hangs up. Fromm is perplexed by the call – is this a warning? He starts gathering up his valuables to give to a fellow officer who's about to head to Germany on leave. Fromm is concerned they might get destroyed in an air raid.

*Many of the German troops in northern France have enjoyed a comfortable life, exchanging their cigarette rations for fine Normandy meat, cheese and butter. Many of the soldiers are very young and have had no experience of war. One infantry officer wrote, 'It is really sad to see these children's faces in grey uniforms.'*

*Many of the 7,800 soldiers manning the fortifications in Normandy are not German at all, but Poles and Russians who have been forced to fight for the Nazis. They were usually given the choice of conscription or being labelled 'politically undesirable', which meant imprisonment in a concentration camp.*

***Someone once asked me, 'What was that boat [a landing craft] like to drive?' I said, 'It was like driving a bulldozer in the water.'***

**Marvin Perrett of the US Coast Guard**

## *Midday*

General Eisenhower is in his large trailer hidden in woods close to Southwick House. It has a bedroom, living room and a study, plus a switchboard and a small kitchen. The General is playing a game of draughts with his aide Captain Harry Butcher. He is losing.

On the fortifications on the Normandy coast, those soldiers off duty are lying on their wooden bunks in the cramped dugouts, smoking, writing letters home, listening to the gramophone or (strictly against the rules) the BBC. Those on duty outside are seeking shelter from the wind and rain, or to ease the boredom, are taking potshots at homing pigeons that might be carrying messages to England from the French Resistance.

The heavy cruiser USS *Tuscaloosa* is sailing up the English Channel towards the Isle of Wight. On board is 46-year-old Colonel David Bruce – the London chief of the unremarkably named Office of Strategic Services. In fact, the OSS is the main wartime US intelligence agency, and will be a forerunner of the CIA.

*Bruce has been based in England since 1940 – first as a member of the American Red Cross and then from 1942 as a member of the OSS. A firm Anglophile, Bruce has believed from the outbreak of war that Britain's cause is also America's. At a Red Cross convention he described the British as 'that extraordinarily brave and gallant race'.*

*Travelling with Bruce is the head of the OSS, General William J 'Wild Bill' Donovan. They are on board the* Tuscaloosa *to observe the US landings on Utah Beach.* Tuscaloosa *will lead the shore bombardment. For the past few months the OSS has been training agents to operate in Occupied France – they currently have 13 agents sending vital information about German military strength. Donovan has asked Bruce to keep a diary during Operation Overlord – against OSS rules – but then Donovan doesn't care much for rules. He was forbidden by Washington to fly to England, let alone to be on a warship bound for France.*

The *Tuscaloosa* is sailing past two massive troop convoys; Colonel Bruce can count 67 barrage balloons flying above the ships. Above them, they have a reassuring escort of Spitfires. Bruce will shortly pass a four-row wide convoy of 350-foot Landing Craft, Tanks known as LCTs, which is a breath-taking five and a half miles long.

Bruce can't believe that a task force this huge won't be spotted by the Germans. The day before he'd written in his diary, 'Perhaps too much hope has been founded on the element of surprise...'

### *12.30pm*

At the last minute, General Eisenhower manages a draw in his game of draughts, which he sees as a good omen.

### *1.00pm/Midday European Time*

At the Berghof, Adolf Hitler's headquarters in the Bavarian Alps, his personal doctor Dr Theodor Morell is arriving for his daily appointment. Morell has been treating Hitler since 1936. Hitler is a hypochondriac and willingly takes the 28 different pills and injections that Morell gives him every day. Hermann Goering has nicknamed him '*Der Reichsspritzenmeister*', which loosely translates as 'Master of the Imperial Needle'.

*In March 1939 during a tense meeting with Hitler, the Czech President Emile Hácha had fainted after the Führer told him that the German Army was mobilised and about to crush his country. It was the ever-obliging Dr Morell's glucose injection that revived Hácha, allowing the reluctant president to give the order that his troops weren't to fire on the invading Germans.*

*But now Hitler is genuinely ill. He is 54 but looks older. His eyes are bloodshot, his hair is greying, his left arm trembles, and he has a worsening heart condition.*

At Downing Street, as usual, Churchill is having a large lunch with plenty of wine.

Fifty-one-year-old Field Marshal Erwin Rommel has travelled from his headquarters at La Roche-Guyon north-west of Paris, to be at his home in Herrlingen in south-west Germany, to celebrate his wife's birthday tomorrow. He's gathering some flowers in his garden for a birthday bouquet. As well as spending a few days' leave at home, Rommel has an appointment to see Hitler at the Berghof to ask for five extra panzer divisions to be brought close to the Normandy coast. The bad weather over the past few days in the English Channel has served the Allies well. Rommel, known as 'The Desert Fox' after his campaigns in North Africa with the Afrika Korps, is convinced that no invasion will take place in such conditions, hence his trip home. German forecasters have not spotted the break in the weather that Stagg and his team have.

*Rommel is a quiet man, who never smokes, has little interest in food and drinks only one glass of (watered-down) white wine a week. He is a man of habit who always goes to bed at 10pm and sleeps until 3am.*

*In the First World War, Captain Rommel was awarded Germany's highest award for bravery,* Pour le Mérite. *His commanding officer called him 'a commander of genius whom his troops followed with blind trust anywhere'. During the invasion of France in 1940, as commander of the Afrika Korps, Rommel proved himself to be a tactical genius, much respected by Hitler. Even after his defeat at El Alamein in 1942 at the hands of Montgomery, Hitler still trusts him. On 5th November 1943, Hitler gave Rommel the command of Army Group B and the task of inspecting Germany's defensive capacity on the north coast of Europe, the so-called 'Atlantic Wall'.*

*The army is Rommel's life and he can think of little else. His former chief of staff, Major General Alfred Gause, says of him that Rommel has no close friends, except one – the army. Once in North Africa, a staff officer pointed to a field of flowers growing in a valley.*

*'Isn't that a wonderful sight?'*

*'Yes,' agreed Rommel, 'it's a good place for 80,000 mines.'*

*The story has spread around the army, so now whenever an officer points out a spectacular view, someone else chips in with, 'Yes, it's a good place for 80,000 mines!'*

### *1.55pm*

Out in the Channel, on board the British troop ship *Princess Ingrid*, almost every soldier is on the upper boat deck waiting for a church service to begin. Suddenly a gust of wind catches the cloth covering a makeshift altar, and a small silver cross falls on the deck and breaks in two. The padre and the troops are distraught at the terrible omen. Ronald Seaborne, a naval telegraphist, thinks that now he knows exactly what the phrase 'fear of God' means. He wrote later, 'It is one thing to face up to the worst that human beings can do to one another, but it is much, much more difficult to cope with the thought that the wrath of God is about to strike...'

On another troop ship, Captain Arthur Rouse of the South Lancashire Regiment is listening to Lieutenant Colonel R P Burbury tell his men what their regiment expects of them. He then turns to Rouse and whispers, 'You say something now. Give them a bit of an uplift.'

'My God,' Rouse thinks, 'Henry V had more warning than this...'

LST *530*, destined for Gold Beach, is pulling out of her West Country port. Earlier, her American skipper Lieutenant Commander Tony Duke had been pondering what he should say to the 600 British troops on board by way of inspiration. Their British commanding officer came up on the bridge and said to him, 'Careful, young fellow, most of my men have seen the worst of desert warfare and a good many of them were in France and evacuated through Dunkirk. So I'd advise you to go easy, go quick, and don't get dramatic or emotional.'

*Before they left port, one of Duke's crew had come up to him and confessed that he had lied about his age when he joined the navy, he was in fact only 15, and didn't want to sail to Normandy. Duke had told him that he had to go.*

*'Well, Captain, I'm scared, and I want to get off – now!'*

*Duke suggested that the young sailor report to him on the bridge every hour.*

*'That way, I'll be able to see how you're doing, and you'll be able to see how I'm doing.'*

### *About 2.00pm*

Fourteen-year-old David Montgomery is at school at Winchester College. He's not far from Portsmouth, but his father, General Montgomery, knows that as the commander of the British and

US ground troops, if he went to say goodbye to his son, it would be obvious to everyone that D-Day was imminent.

Monty is writing a farewell note to David.

'When you get this, the second front will be well on its way. I am sending you a copy of my message [to the troops] and some photos. Goodbye and God bless you...'

*General Montgomery won't see David for another six months.*

*When Monty won the battle of El Alamein, church bells had rung out in celebration. At last Britain had a hero – a general who actually won battles. Montgomery, with his straight talking and unconventional uniforms, became a public idol. He admires Eisenhower.*

*'He is just the man for the job... I would trust him to the last gasp.' Although when they first met in May 1942 the meeting didn't go well.*

*'Who's smoking?'*

*'I am,' Eisenhower said.*

*'I don't allow smoking in my office,' Monty replied.*

*In his small caravan (captured in the desert from an Italian officer) in the grounds of Southwick House, Monty keeps photographs of enemy generals, including Rommel. It helps him decide what kind of person he is 'and how he was likely to react to any moves I may make against him.'*

*Montgomery has been touring army camps for the past few weeks to raise morale. In one camp he asked a young Welsh soldier, 'What's your most valuable possession?'*

*'It's my rifle, sir.'*

*'No, it's not. It's your life. And I am going to save it for you...'*

Most D-Day troops are writing or have written letters home. Private Sidney Verrier of the Oxfordshire and Buckinghamshire Light Infantry, who is taking off tonight from Tarrent Rushton airfield and parachuting into Normandy, has written, 'I'm off to the long-awaited "Second Front"... now then, Mum, if you don't worry, I won't be worrying, so keep your chin up... there is only one thing I wish, that is to have Dad on one side and Uncle Jack on the other side of me to tell me when I go wrong... remember me to all relations and folks. I love 'em all.'

In his tent in the woods near Southwick House, General Eisenhower is breaking the news to reporters from Reuter's, the BBC and NBC that Allied troops and planes attack Normandy tomorrow. Eisenhower is pretending to be relaxed. The reporters are pretending to be nonchalant at the news.

*Eisenhower has good relations with the press. In May he had assembled all the correspondents accredited to cover the Second Front at a club in London.*

*'I've been informed by the newspapers that an operation is pending...' (Much laughter.)*

*'Our countries fight best when our people are best informed. I will never tell you anything false... I have no doubts as to the outcome of the future but I have no illusions as to the magnitude of the task... it will be no basket of roses.'*

### *2.10pm/1.10pm European Time*

Having read the latest intelligence report on 'Allied Intentions', the man in charge of the army in France, 69-year-old Field Marshal Gerd von Rundstedt, is leaving his office to have lunch with his son Hans, at his favourite Parisian restaurant, the *Coq Hardi*. The intelligence report suggests that recent Allied bombing raids in the Dieppe area probably mean the invasion will be launched across the Pas-de-Calais, but 'imminence of invasion is not recognisable'.

*Born into an aristocratic family with a strong military history, von Rundstedt was responsible for the planning for the highly successful invasion of Poland in 1939. Although loyal to Hitler, in private he refers to the Führer as 'that Bohemian corporal'.*

*The report on von Rundstedt's desk is evidence that an Allied deception plan called Operation Fortitude is working well. The Allies have known that it is impossible to disguise their invasion preparations from the Germans, but what they can do is deceive them as to where the troops are headed. The Operation has two strategies – Fortitudes North and South. Fortitude South's aim is to convince the German High Command that the Normandy invasion is just a diversion for the main Pas-de-Calais attack.*

*The original plan for Fortitude South was to send six divisions to Kent to simulate a threat to the Pas-de-Calais. Montgomery vetoed the idea – he needed the men too badly. So a fake army was created, called the First US Army Group, and led by Lieutenant General George S Patton, whose high profile would serve the deception very well. The First US Army Group has its own signals unit to transmit fake radio traffic 24 hours a day.*

*Technicians from Shepperton Film Studios have built a fake oil storage depot near Dover; it was even visited by King George VI. Fake aircraft, inflatable tanks and lorries have been positioned in fields, and 255 landing craft made of canvas and wood moored in rivers on the Suffolk and Norfolk coast. The landing craft are moved around after two or three days to give the impression that they are being used for rehearsals. There is a whole army company – the 82nd Camouflage, devoted to leaving marks of tracks and feet in fields, as if they'd been used for military manoeuvres.*

*Fortitude North's aim is to make the Germans think that Norway will be the next target after the invasion of France.*

*Thanks to Bletchley Park's decoding of the German's Enigma code, the Allies know that Operation Fortitude is working, fooling von Rundstedt, Rommel, and Hitler himself. Almost a fortnight after D-Day, the Germans will still be fearful of 'the real Second Front'.*

*Field Marshal von Rundstedt and Field Marshal Rommel disagree strongly on how to defeat any invasion. Von Rundstedt has ordered that the main panzer regiments remain inland, away from the long range of naval guns and ready to attack the Allies if they should penetrate the coastal fortifications of Hitler's Atlantic Wall. Rommel, after his experiences in North Africa, knows that if you lack air superiority, then moving tanks across country is almost impossible. (The Germans have effectively surrendered the skies over northern France; their army has a joke: if you see a black plane it's British, if you see a white plane it's American, when you see nothing at all, it's the Luftwaffe.)*

*But for the moment, von Rundstedt's plan is backed by Berlin; it will play a major part in the outcome of D-Day.*

### *3.00pm*

A unit of Free French Commandos is getting on board their troop ship at Warsash, near Southampton. One smiles as he says to the military embarkation control officer on the gang-plank, 'No return ticket please.'

*Most of the commandos deserted the French Navy after France capitulated to the Germans, and made their way to England from fishing ports in Brittany. One even sailed in a rowing boat from Morocco.*

*D-Day is a truly international operation. Gearing up to drop into Normandy or land on the beaches, along with the French, British,*

*Americans and Canadians, are Poles, Norwegians, Belgians, South Africans, Australians and New Zealanders.*

### *About 3.30pm*

Lieutenant General George S Patton, the flamboyant and outspoken commander of the 3rd United States Army, is in the middle of addressing his men at a base in the south of England. Patton, wearing his trademark outfit of polished helmet, full dress uniform, riding boots and riding crop, intends to motivate them. His Smith and Wesson Magnum is hanging by his side. He dominates any situation; Marlene Dietrich (with whom he's alleged to have had an affair) said, 'He looks like a tank too big for a village square.'

The majority of his audience has never been in a battle and they are very nervous. Patton is famous for his plain speaking.

'I don't want to get any messages saying, "I am holding my position." We are not holding a goddamned thing. Let the Germans do that. We are advancing constantly and we are not interested in holding onto anything, except the enemy's balls. We are going to twist his balls and kick the living shit out of him all of the time. Our basic plan of operation is to advance and to keep on advancing regardless of whether we have to go over, under, or through the enemy. We are going to go through him like crap through a goose...'

Some of the soldiers are scribbling down what Patton's saying.

'There is one great thing that you men will all be able to say after this war is over and you are home once again. You may be thankful that 20 years from now when you are sitting by the fireplace with your grandson on your knee and he asks you what you did in the great World War II, you won't have to cough, shift him to the other knee and say, "Well, your Granddaddy shovelled shit in Louisiana." No, sir, you can look him straight in the eye and say, "Son, your Granddaddy rode with the Great 3rd Army and a son-of-a-goddamned bitch named Georgie Patton!"'

*Once asked about his colourful language, Patton said, 'It may not sound nice to some bunch of little old ladies at an afternoon tea party, but it helps my soldiers to remember. You can't run an army without profanity... an army without profanity couldn't fight its way out of a piss-soaked paper bag.'*

*Patton proved himself in North Africa and Sicily to be a ruthless and inspiring leader, but his mouth has a tendency to get him in trouble. Eisenhower once told Kay Summersby that Patton was like a time bomb.*

*'You can never be sure when he's going to go off. All you can be sure of, is that it will probably be at the wrong place at the wrong time.'*

*As if to prove Eisenhower right, a few weeks before D-Day, Patton spoke to a meeting of the Women's Voluntary Service in Cheshire.*

*'...it is the evident destiny of the British and Americans to rule the world...' The next day the* Washington Post *accused him of a blatant insult to Russia. Eisenhower told him to 'keep your goddamned mouth shut'.*

### 3.45pm

Twenty-two-year-old Sergeant Frank Murray of the US 18th Infantry is lying on a bunk of a troop ship pulling out of Weymouth Harbour; his best friend in the bunk opposite is reading out loud a letter he's just received from a former girl-friend back home. A few weeks ago he'd written to her to say that he'd met a Scottish girl and they were in love. She had replied, 'Instead of being a war bride, I hope your girlfriend's a war widow.'

Murray is shocked that anyone could write such a thing. Sadly, his friend will be killed in Normandy.

### *4.00pm*

General Eisenhower and Admiral Creasy have come to see meteorologist James Stagg in his office in Southwick House. They're concerned that the sky is still cloudy and the wind is still up – Stagg had told them that better weather was on the way. Stagg reassures them.

'They are coming along, sir; there'll be good breaks in the cloud by dark tonight and reduced winds.'

As Stagg bends to show the general the latest weather chart, Eisenhower puts his hand on his shoulder.

'Good, Stagg: keep it up a little longer.'

### *5.00pm/4.00pm European Time*

Hitler is having a late lunch. The Führer is a vegetarian, and at every meal says to his guests, 'The elephant is the strongest animal; he also cannot stand meat.'

A medical officer with the 24th Lancers sailing for Gold Beach from Southampton writes in his diary how he's taking a 'deeper than normal interest in these last glimpses of England... The girls look a lot more attractive when we know we won't see any for a long time to come...'

LCI 92 is pulling out of Portland Harbour in Dorset. Combat photographer Seth Shepard is taking pictures of the armada of ships around him. The other LCIs look top heavy with all their troops on deck. LCI *92* is only a year old but is already a veteran of the landings in North Africa, Sicily and Italy.

> ***When the vast invasion fleets moved out silently into the windy English Channel, it was as if a million trumpets began to blow again, a great heartfelt chorus of sanity and freedom, heavy with menace for the Nazis, thrilling with hope for those whom they had enslaved.***
>
> **Padre Iain Wilson, 1st King's Own Scottish Borderers**

### *6.00pm*

Albert Kings of the 1st Worcesters is on a troop ship pulling out of Newhaven docks. Someone by him kneels down to pray and others are joining in. Those with families at home are crying unashamedly. Albert is thinking of his wife whom he married in March and wondering if she will be a widow before the year is out. He wrote later, 'I tried to look ahead to better times but I knew it would only be brought about by our efforts. I was determined to do my best.'

The sound of bagpipes is echoing across the waters of the Solent. Standing in the bows of LCI *519*, first in a line of 22 ships, piper Bill Millin, dressed in kilt and full battledress, is playing stirring martial music, and it's being relayed over the ship's loudspeaker. Rupert Curtis, the flotilla officer for LCI *519*, is watching.

'The skirl of the pipes worked some strange magic that evening, for it set the troops in the waiting transports cheering from ship to ship...'

Millin has been asked to play by the commander of the

1st Special Service Brigade, Lord Simon 'Shimi' Lovat, the 25th chief of the Clan Fraser of Lovat. He is a soldier from a bygone age; his aristocratic leadership more in keeping with the Peninsular War of the early 19th century than the Western Front of the 20th.

*Scottish and Irish regimental pipers had traditionally played in battle, but by the start of the Second World War, the War Office had banned them. Lovat had told Bill Millin that he wasn't bothered what the War Office said.*

*'You are going to lead the biggest invasion in the history of warfare.'*

*Lord Lovat was once described by Winston Churchill as 'the mildest-mannered man that ever scuttled a ship or cut a throat'. In March 1941 Lovat was part of the successful commando raid on the German-held Norwegian Lofoten Islands, which resulted in the destruction of 11 ships, 18 factories and the capture of 216 POWs, parts of an Enigma machine and its logbook. When a telephone exchange was captured, the commandos took it in turns to send telegrams 'in basic English' to Hitler, Goebbels and Goering. Lord Lovat will prove himself to be one of the most memorable of all the D-Day officers.*

## 'The finest way to die is in the excitement of fighting the enemy'

### *7.00pm*

At No 10 Downing Street, Prime Minister Winston Churchill is dining with his wife Clementine. It's rare for the couple to eat alone; there is usually work that Churchill has to do while they're eating or someone of importance to be entertained.

Churchill is restless. The 69-year-old prime minister is desperate to travel to Normandy with his troops.

*In his lifetime Churchill has fought in the trenches during the Great War, and in 1898 even led a cavalry charge at the Battle of Omdurman in the Sudan. Since the outbreak of war Churchill has always refused to leave London – even during the heaviest bombing. Travelling to Washington in 1943 on the* Queen Mary, *he dismissed any fears about the threat of U-boats.*

*'The finest way to die is in the excitement of fighting the enemy,' he declared.*

*In the last week Churchill has received two blunt letters from King George VI telling him he must not go to France.*

*'My dear Winston... I am a younger man than you, I am a sailor, and as King I am head of all the services. There is nothing I would like better than to go to sea but I have agreed to stay at home; is it fair that you should then do exactly what I should like to do myself?'*

*Churchill has waited a long time for this moment. As far back as 25th July 1941, even before the US had entered the war, he had told President Roosevelt that Europe would be liberated by a huge number of tanks being landed onto beaches from specially adapted merchant ships when 'the opportunity is ripe'.*

At the Berghof, Hitler, Eva Braun, General Kurt Zeitzler and Joseph Goebbels are watching the latest newsreel with reports of the war. They are waited on by SS bodyguards dressed in white waistcoats and black trousers.

*The Berghof is safer than Berlin, which is constantly being attacked by Allied bombers, and Hitler has been based here for over four months.*

*Goebbels' wife Magda is happy to miss an evening at the Berghof.*

*'He can be Führer all he likes, but he always repeats himself and bores his guests,' she says.*

### *7.20pm*

Kay Summersby, a member of the British Mechanised Transport Corps, a former model, and Eisenhower's mistress, has driven the general to Greenham Common Air Base in Berkshire in his Cadillac staff car. Their affair began two years ago and Eisenhower takes Kay everywhere – she even attended the crucial conference between Roosevelt, Stalin and Churchill in Tehran in 1943. He's now talking, hands in pockets, with the American 101st Airborne Division, due to take off in a few hours. Reporters take notes and cameramen take pictures. Kay Summersby is getting a lot of attention from the paratroopers.

A soldier from Kansas named Oyler is telling Eisenhower that he's afraid.

'Well, you'd be a damn fool not to be. But the trick is to keep moving. If you stop, if you start thinking, you lose your focus. You lose your concentration. You'll be a casualty. The idea, the perfect idea, is to keep moving.'

Eisenhower will tell Kay later, 'It's very hard really to look a soldier in the eye, when you fear that you are sending him to his death.'

At this moment Eisenhower's wife Mamie is on her way to West Point Military Academy in New York, where their son is about to graduate as an army cadet.

Major General Maxwell Taylor has been in command of the 101st for only a couple of months. Having spoken to General Eisenhower, he is now walking away gingerly, trying not to show that he's injured his right knee that afternoon playing squash – he doesn't want the general to stop him flying. There is a parachutists' tradition that all officers jump into a combat zone with their men – this drop will only be Taylor's third.

*Twenty-four thousand paratroopers from the Allied airborne forces are a key part of Operation Overlord. The US 101st and 82nd Airborne divisions will parachute into drop zones near the town of Sainte-Mère-Église to protect the west flank of the troops landing by sea, while the east flank will be protected by the British 6th Airborne Division landing between Cabourg and the Orne River.*

*The parachutists got dressed for action a few hours ago. Their equipment includes a main chute, reserve chute, Mae West life jacket, M-1 rifle, .45 pistol, 4 knives, a cartridge belt, 4 blocks of TNT, an anti-tank mine, a first-aid kit, gas mask, canteen of water, 3 days' supply of rations, 7 grenades, a blanket, an overcoat, a change of underwear.*

*They have to be helped into their planes as they can barely walk.*

*Their dog tags have being taped together to prevent them making a noise. Some have bought commando knives while on leave in London. Some have cut-throat razors. Others have shaved their heads to make it easier for wounds to be treated by medics, while some have shaved their heads just to look like Mohicans. Faces are black with soot or boot polish. They want to look as invisible and as intimidating as possible.*

*Airborne forces are a new dimension of warfare. The first parachute regiment in the world was formed in 1936 as part of the Russian Red Army. The Luftwaffe 7th Air Division soon followed, and in 1940 proved itself in battle by helping to capture Belgium and Holland. The success of the 7th Air Division spurred the British and Americans to follow suit.*

*The US 101st Airborne was formed in August 1942 and became known as the 'Screaming Eagle Division', taking its number and name from a famous Civil War division.*

*The day after they were founded, the first commander of the 101st, General William Lee, declared, 'The 101st has no history, but it has a rendezvous with destiny.'*

*In tribute to their founder, the paratroopers shout 'Bill Lee!' when they jump from a plane.*

*The 82nd was formed about the same time as the 101st and took the name the 'All American Airborne Division'.*

*Both will play a key part in the Normandy landings.*

### *7.30pm*

'This is London calling with messages for our friends. Listen carefully, here are some personal items of information. It is hot in Suez... it is hot in Suez...'

In his cellar, Guillaume Mercader, the French Resistance chief for the stretch of coast between Omaha and Utah beaches, is listening to coded BBC messages on his radio.

Many are meaningless to Mercader; then the announcer says, 'The dice are on the table. The dice are on the table...'

That means the invasion is coming tomorrow. Mercader knows he has to get a message to the Resistance headquarters in nearby Caen about anti-aircraft guns he's seen being installed that afternoon. He runs up his cellar stairs four at a time.

### *7.50pm*

Admiral Don P Moon is on his flagship USS *Tuscaloosa*, relieving the anxiety he feels by hitting a punch bag he's had installed in his cabin. Moon is in charge of Task Force U – the ships heading for Utah Beach. He's ordered that a signal be flashed to all the ships in the Task Force U convoy, calling for the men to be 'brave and cheerful'.

*The men need encouragement. In April, Task Force U had a disastrous dress rehearsal at Slapton Sands in Devon, involving the 4th Infantry Division and the 101st and 82nd Airborne divisions. It was chaotic – air support never arrived and the beaches became gridlocked in the confusion. But confusion turned to tragedy when eight LCTs were attacked by German torpedo E-boats who had just happened to stumble across the exercise. Two landing craft were sunk, and 197 sailors and 441 soldiers died. The survivors were kept away from the public. No one knew about the deaths at Slapton Sands until after the war.*

### *8.00pm*

In the French port of Le Havre, E-boat skipper, 34-year-old Lieutenant Commander Heinrich Hoffmann is on the phone to his wife in their home in Marburg in Germany, talking about their young son.

Suddenly she says, 'Heinrich, I am restless tonight. Is there anything afoot?'

'Things are very quiet, darling. Nothing is going to happen tonight.'

### *About 8.30pm*

A coded telegram is being sent to Stalin from Churchill telling him about the departure of the armada.

'...tonight we go.'

### *8.45pm*

On board the troop ship *Empire Battleaxe*, the decks are crowded with hundreds of men. The soldiers of the 1st Suffolk Regiment have gambled away their English money and are starting on the French currency they've been given.

Albert Pattison is a platoon sergeant with the 1st Suffolk. In May 1940, at Dunkirk, aged only 17, he swam two miles out to sea, desperate to reach one of the small boats so that it could take him home to England. Now the *Empire Battleaxe* is taking him back to France.

Albert thought that Dunkirk was terrifying, but the waiting on the cramped ship and the prospect of the battle ahead is worse still.

*Some of the British soldiers heading to France have not been home for four years, but the vast majority had never faced a German soldier or panzer tank. Almost two-thirds of the troops destined for Normandy are either volunteers, have little combat experience or are conscripts called up since 1939.*

*Some of the American troops are veterans of the campaigns in North Africa and Sicily but most have never been in battle before. The typical GI is about 20 years old with only six months' training.*

*The British and American troops who have seen active service are understandably unhappy about being sent to the front line again. As General Omar Bradley said later of the men who had fought in two Mediterranean campaigns, 'Few believed that their good fortune could last them through a third...'*

**The Führer is continually praising Rommel's work. The Field Marshal has an old score to settle with the British**

> ***and Americans, he is burning with rage and has used all his cunning to perfect the defences. He is his old self again.***
>
> ***Joseph Goebbels' diary, 16th May 1944***

## 'More waves, Lieutenant Grant!'

*9.00pm*

Group Captain James Stagg is looking at the sky. To his relief he can see that there are breaks in the cloud over Southwick House. His prediction seems to be coming true.

Colonel David Bruce, the London branch chief of the US Office of Strategic Services, is on board USS *Tuscaloosa* to observe the assault on Utah Beach in the morning. The cloud may be breaking up over Southwick House but in the Channel the sea is rough. Bruce is concerned about the weather, but more concerned about what the troops sleeping, writing and gambling around him will face on the beaches. He knows in detail the defences the Germans have put in place.

*The RAF and USAAF have systematically photographed the whole coast from Spain to Holland – flying sometimes as low as 25 feet in a straight line for minutes at a time at considerable risk. A report in March 1944 by the 67th Tactical Reconnaissance Group stated simply, 'It soon became apparent that such flying is an anti-aircraft gunner's dream…'*

*Hitler is convinced that the Allied invasion will only succeed if they are able to capture a port on the Channel coast. So in 1942 he ordered that the ports of France, Belgium and Holland should be ringed by pillboxes that he himself designed. The Führer's rough sketches were then constructed, without any alteration, by the German Corps of Engineers. Armaments Minister Albert Speer overheard Hitler boast that his designs 'met all the requirements of a front-line soldier'.*

*Towards the end of 1943, Field Marshal Rommel had argued with Hitler that his plans were a mistake.*

*'We must repulse the enemy at his first landing site. The pillboxes around the ports don't do the trick. Only primitive but effective barriers and obstacles all along the coast can make the landing so difficult that our countermeasures will be effective.'*

*Speer noted that Rommel avoided saying the required courteous 'mein Führer'. He could get away with such disrespect, as Hitler admired him as a soldier.*

*To Speer's and Rommel's disgust, Hitler nevertheless ordered the defences to go ahead, leading to the construction of 17,300,000 cubic yards of concrete – costing 3.7 million DM and depriving armaments factories of iron they desperately needed.*

*As Speer noted, writing drily in his Spandau prison cell 20 years later, the Allies made Hitler's concrete coast irrelevant – by bringing their own port with them.*

*For the last two years, vast man-made floating harbours, code-named Mulberries, have been under construction at secret locations all over Britain (there is no significance in the code name; it was just the next on the official list). In Conway, North Wales, there has been lots of speculation about the concrete blocks being built along the River Morfa. Locals were told that it was a new jam factory. Once towed over to France in sections, they will create two harbours the size of Dover, able to handle 2,500 vehicles a day.*

*The idea of the Mulberries was sold to Churchill by Louis Mountbatten, then British chief of Combined Operations, when they were on board the* Queen Mary *on their way to a summit with President Roosevelt. In one of the liner's bathrooms, a Mae West life preserver was placed in the bath, to act as a Mulberry, surrounding 20 paper boats. The most junior officer present was handed a loofah, and told to make waves with it, to prove just how effective a Mulberry would be.*

*'More waves, Lieutenant Grant!' called Mountbatten.*

Tugs are on standby to start towing the first sections of the Mulberries over to Normandy later today.

Over dinner in his home in Germany with his wife and son, Rommel is talking about mines made of glass, and how they're effective because they're impossible to find with conventional detectors.

*In November 1943, Hitler put Rommel in charge of the defence of the whole European coast from the Spanish border to Norway. He'd used mines to great effect in North Africa (at El Alamein they became known as his 'devil's gardens') and so by the end of May, under his orders, six million have been laid in minefields along the coast. He's designed most of the defences himself – metal-tipped wooden spikes built on the sea floor on the approaches to the beaches, often with mines attached (if mines aren't available, they've been tipped with captured French artillery shells); 'Czech hedgehogs' 5-foot-high steel triangles, also with mines, tetrahedrons covered in barbed wire.*

*Behind the beaches, low-lying areas have been flooded, and in fields, stakes and tree trunks have been placed at intervals of 20 feet to deter parachutists and gliders, by a workforce of local conscripted labour and Italian prisoners of war. These defences have been nicknamed 'Rommel's asparagus' by the French.*

*Whenever Rommel came to inspect the defences, French workers were told by the Germans that they had to take their caps off in his presence. As a result, none of the French wore caps on inspection days.*

*Rommel's plan is that the more defences he has, the more the Allied troops will have to train to deal with them, giving him more time for his fortifications. He wants them completed by 20th June.*

## 'It may well be the most ghastly disaster of the whole war'

*About 9.15pm*

T Osbourne is a 15-year-old seaman serving on the rescue tug HMS *Assiduous*, anchored in Southampton Water. An American tug has moored up alongside *Assiduous*, and although her crew are being very generous with sweets and chocolate to the young sailor, he's shocked by their language.

Field Marshal Sir Alan Brooke, chief of the Imperial General Staff, is writing in his diary.

'I am very uneasy about the whole operation. At best it will fall so very very very far short of the expectation of the bulk of the people, namely all those who know nothing of its difficulties. At the worst it may well be the most ghastly disaster of the whole war. I wish to God it were safely over.'

*Churchill has his doubts too. At an Overlord planning meeting attended by the King on 15th May, he'd said that he was haunted by the prospect of the English Channel 'running red with the blood of British soldiers, extinguished like the soldiers of the Western Front, the men of Ypres and Passchendaele...'*

*General Eisenhower also fears a terrible defeat. In January he wrote a letter to his chiefs of staff.*

*'...this operation marks the crisis of the European war. Every obstacle must be overcome, every inconvenience suffered, every priority granted, and every risk taken to ensure our blow is decisive. We cannot afford to fail.'*

*For the past few weeks, to ease the stress he's under, Eisenhower has been reading paperbacks about the Wild West or playing golf in his office. He's smoking over 40 Camel cigarettes a day.*

*Earlier today he wrote a letter of resignation, which is now in his wallet.*

*'Our landings have failed... the troops, the air and the Navy did all that bravery and devotion to duty could do. If any blame or fault attaches to the attempt it is mine alone.'*

*The general is hugely popular in the States. A Hollywood studio has just offered him $150,000 for permission to make a film about his life. Earlier in the week Eisenhower wrote to his brother saying that the film should stress the 'initiative, effort and persistence' of the American family, and that the $150,000 should be used to help American students get to British universities.*

*Eisenhower served in the infantry and in tanks in the 1920s but made a name for himself as a member of the War Department's General Staff as someone able to grasp complex issues quickly and to get army, navy and air force leaders to work together.*

### *9.30pm*

The biggest invasion force the world has ever known is converging on the area south of the Isle of Wight code-named Area Z, or 'Piccadilly Circus'. Soon the 2,700 ships will make a ninety-degree turn out of Area Z and head for France down channels swept clear of mines and marked with buoys. There are five task forces: Force S to land on Sword Beach, Force G on Gold Beach, Force J on Juno Beach, Force U on Utah Beach and Force O for Omaha Beach.

Each task force has a channel, 40 miles long but only 400 yards wide, leading to the Normandy beaches. Closer to the coast, the five channels become ten – half for slow ships, half for fast ships.

None of the ships are receiving messages from the outside world, but in case the Germans should become suspicious at a reduction in wire traffic, meaningless messages are being sent from ship to ship. Vital signals are being communicated by carefully shaded spotlights. Overhead, Spitfires provide air cover.

It is an international fleet including ten warships of the Royal Norwegian Navy, 43 Norwegian merchant ships, three French, two Belgian and six Polish warships, a Dutch cruiser, and two more from the Royal Hellenic Navy, and 800 Danish sailors.

On USS *Tuscaloosa*, Colonel David Bruce is with Admiral Moon and the ship's officers, enjoying a dinner of steak and vegetables, with vanilla ice cream and chocolate sauce to follow.

On board LCI 92, combat photographer Seth Shepard is taking advantage of the fact that no-one else is in the head (ship's toilet) and is trying to shave. Shephard's cut himself only once, which he thinks is pretty good considering how rough the sea is.

HMS *Glasgow* is moving to the front of the line of ships forming Task Force O. *Glasgow*'s padre and the crew start to say Nelson's Prayer before the Battle of Trafalgar.

'May the Great God whom I worship grant to my country and for the benefit of Europe in general a great and glorious victory, and may no misconduct in any one tarnish it, and may humanity after victory be the predominant feature in the British fleet, for myself individually I commit my life to Him who made me…'

As they steam past the *Texas*, her ship's company hears the prayer over *Glasgow*'s tannoy, and take off their helmets.

### *9.50pm*

Churchill is in the underground Map Room in Great George Street, not far from No 10. Clementine comes in to wish her husband good night. The prime minister is anxious.

'Do you realise that by the time you wake up in the morning twenty thousand men may have been killed?'

### *10.00pm*

As they've done for the last two nights, *X20* and *X23*, the two Royal Navy X-class midget submarines, are braving the stormy weather and surfacing, so that the commando crews can listen for a radio signal. It may contain a message that will tell them if the invasion is on for tomorrow. The crews are grateful for the opportunity to get some fresh air and take it in turns to walk on the submarine's small deck. They pick up, very faintly, their call sign: 'Padfoot… Padfoot… Padfoot…'

### *10.15pm/9.15pm European Time*

'*Blessent mon coeur*
*D'une langueur*
*Monotone.*'
('*Wound my heart*
*With a monotonous languor*')

In a studio at the BBC's Bush House, an announcer is reading some lines of a 19th-century poem by Paul Verlaine. It's a coded message to the French Resistance that the invasion will begin within 48 hours and that they should start attacking targets on the rail network.

At the headquarters of the German 15th Army close to the Belgian border, intelligence officer Lieutenant Colonel Hellmuth Meyer is listening to the broadcast. He knows exactly what it means, because a member of the French Resistance on the payroll of German Intelligence has told them.

Meyer rushes into the office of the 15th Army's commanding officer General Hans von Salmuth, who is playing bridge with other officers, with the news.

'I'm too old a bunny to get too excited about this,' the general replies.

Meyer nevertheless sends teletype messages to the headquarters of Field Marshal Gerd von Rundstedt, Commander in Chief OB (*Oberbefehlshaber*) West, and to the OKW (*Oberkommando der Wehrmacht*) Supreme Command of the Armed Forces.

'Teletype No 2117/26. Urgent. Message of BBC, 21.15, June 5 has been decoded. According to our available records it means "Expect invasion within 48 hours, starting 00.00, June 6"'

Although German Intelligence is sure that radio messages on the BBC will be signals for the start of the landings, the German military are not so sure.

'What sort of general would announce a forthcoming invasion on the radio? You can forget it,' says General Blumentritt, Field Marshal von Rundstedt's chief of staff.

### *10.20pm*

The midget submarine commando crews have received a coded message that D-Day will commence in just a few hours. They must be in position by 4.30am, ready to erect their telescopic navigation masts to guide the landing craft.

Twenty-year-old Second Lieutenant Stuart Hills of the Sherwood Rangers is on an LCT as part of Task Force G. On her deck are six Shermans, securely fastened by steel hawsers and with chocks under the tracks to keep them from moving. The crew have stretched a canvas canopy over the tanks, but are still getting wet from the sea spray. Hills and his men are trying to cook a meal, but the vomit slopping around the deck is rather off-putting. A short while ago in the captain's cabin, they discovered their destination – Gold Beach.

Fussing around the convoys heading south are blue and white camouflaged corvettes and destroyers trying to keep their ships in position. Terse instructions over loud-hailers echo over the water.

> *The sun has only just set over the Channel. In June 1944, Britain is operating Double Summertime, two hours ahead of GMT, to maximise evening light. But for some it has disadvantages. An air raid warden in the south of England reported that a GI with a British girl on his arm and desperate for privacy said to him, 'Say, doesn't it ever get dark in this goddamn country!?'*

Percy Wallace is a coastguard on St Alban's Head in Dorset. All day he'd looked down from the high headland at the landing craft, tugs and warships sailing past. By now the sea is almost empty.

Percy is climbing into bed next to his wife Dora.

'A lot of men are going to die tonight. We should pray for them.'

> ***I couldn't go right off to sleep but the last thing I remember was the one shaded light hanging down over the mess table, swinging back and forth and sending its faint rays over the tiers of three bunks, most of them filled with sleeping forms, relaxed and trusting and not knowing what hell they would be facing in less than ten hours.***
>
> ***Seth Shepard, combat photographer***

### *About 10.30pm*

On a troop ship in Task Force J heading for Juno, 24-year-old Lieutenant James Doohan has won £3,600 playing craps. It's tucked safely in his uniform. Doohan volunteered within days of war breaking out, but after five years in the Canadian Army, the Normandy landings will be his first introduction to warfare.

On an LST heading for Juno Beach, Sergeant Kenneth Lakeman of the Royal Corps of Signals watches one of his men, clearly on edge, prising open a packing case with an unfamiliar serial number on it. The man goes pale. The box is full of white crosses.

'God, I don't mind going to my death, but to take my own cross...' he says, deeply upset.

Troop ship USS *Samuel Chase* flashes a signal to the ships around her, 'Mass is going on.'

On board the *Samuel Chase* is photographer Robert Capa,

described by the magazine *Picture Post* a few years before as 'the greatest war photographer in the world'. He's wandering around the *Samuel Chase* with his Contax camera. The ship seems to him to be divided into three groups – the gamblers on the upper deck playing poker with cards and money on stretched-out army blankets; the letter-writers hidden in corners scribbling last messages for home; and the planners down in the bowels of the ship scrutinising a model of Omaha Beach and pushing small boats towards the shore.

*Capa is certainly prepared to take risks for his pictures. In December 1943, near Monte Cassino in Italy, he was hit by shrapnel three times and the soldier next to him was killed.*

*His graphic photographs of the campaign in Italy for* Life *magazine provoked a strong reaction from readers; one wrote to the editor that America needed images like Capa's, '…to slap us in the face and keep us awake to realities'.*

### *10.35pm*

On all the large landing craft and troop ships, men are playing cards, reading, sleeping and praying. Two US Rangers are fighting – their commanding officer wants any disputes settled before they hit the beach. Some are unable to face the prospect of battle. On a ship transporting men from the Kings Own Light Infantry, a soldier has deliberately shot his own hand with his rifle. On another, a GI has stabbed his hand with his bayonet.

On LCI *519*, flotilla officer Lieutenant Commander Rupert Curtis, who has been hand-picked by Lord Lovat to land 4 Commando on Sword Beach, is listening outside Lovat's wardroom.

Curtis can hear cheerful laughter as Lord Lovat talks with his colonels Derek Mills-Roberts and Peter Young.

'There was no doubt in their mind about the outcome,' Curtis recalled.

In fact, fuelled by the discovery of half a bottle of gin, Lovat and his fellow officers are studying a paperback discovered below decks – *Dr Marie Stopes's Marital Advice Bureau for Young Couples.*

LCI *528* is sailing through heavy seas south of the Isle of Wight, her destination Sword Beach. On board, as part of the British 4 Commando contingent, are 177 of the Free French volunteers, men who have escaped to Britain and undergone rigorous commando training.

They've just been told they will be the first from 4 Commando on the beaches, a symbolic gesture the Free French have welcomed. One commando, Count Guy de Montlaur, is delighted that a former casino at Ouistreham, now a German observation post, will be his target.

'It will be a pleasure. I have lost several fortunes in that place.'

Another of the Free French, Corporal Maurice Chauvet, is at this moment writing his diary in a tiny cabin he's sharing with 24 other men in the bows of LCI *528*. He's relieved to know finally their destination – there had been rumours that they were headed for Norway or even Africa.

'It had not sunk in that we were actually landing in France. I needed to see those proper names on the map, then the operation meant something: liberation.'

Chauvet fled the French Navy in 1941 and as a result has been condemned is his absence to ten years' hard labour by the puppet Vichy government.

In a corner of the cabin, Chauvet can see a young boy who married his English girlfriend just before they sailed from Southampton. She's pregnant and the boy is convinced he will die in Normandy, and he wants the child to have his name.

The *Ben-my-Chree*, a former Isle of Man passenger ferry, is heading to Omaha Beach with over 200 US Rangers on board – an elite fighting force modelled on the British Commandos. The man who was to lead Able Company, Major Cleveland Lytle, is drunk. He's convinced that their mission is suicidal, and as a result he's already been demoted.

The Rangers have an extremely dangerous mission – to capture the gun emplacements at the western end of Omaha Beach on the 100-foot cliffs known as the Pointe du Hoc. Lytle has heard rumours that according to the Resistance the emplacements aren't operational as the guns have yet to arrive. He's claiming at the top of his voice to his fellow officers that their mission is pointless. Medical officer Captain Walter Block tries to intervene, and Lytle punches him. Other officers join in to restrain Lytle, and he is taken to his cabin.

### *10.45pm/9.45pm European Time*

At Rommel's headquarters at the chateau of La Roche-Guyon, 40 miles north-west of Paris, his chief of staff, Major General Hans Speidel is having a discussion with close friends about how to assassinate Hitler.

Having dinner with Speidel are his brother-in-law Dr Horst, war correspondent Major Wilhelm von Schramm, Rommel's naval advisor Admiral Friedrich Ruge and author Captain Ernst Jünger. Jünger has brought with him a 30-page blueprint for Germany and Europe once Hitler is dead, called 'A United States of Europe'.

*The army is at the centre of opposition to Hitler. In 1943 there were six attempts on the Führer's life by army conspirators, so now Hitler is suspicious of the army and constantly changes his itinerary at the last moment. The closest that army officers have come to success was in March 1943 when a bomb was placed in Hitler's plane, but the bomb failed to explode.*

*Although Speidel is taking advantage of Rommel's absence (he'd telephoned his friends saying, 'The old man has gone, I suggest you come over for dinner tomorrow so we can really have a night and discuss things...'), the field marshal is also part of the conspiracy. But rather than get rid of Hitler by assassination, Rommel would rather he'd be forced to make peace with the Allies and then tried in a German court of law.*

> ***Each paratrooper had to learn the whole operation by heart... We even knew that the German commandant of St Côme-du-Mont owned a white horse and was going with a French schoolteacher who lived on a side street just two buildings away from a German gun emplacement...***
>
> **Donald Burgett, US 101st Airborne Division**

### *11.00pm*

The American 101st 'Screaming Eagles' Airborne Division is taking off into the night sky above Greenham Common. General Eisenhower is on the roof of their headquarters, watching the planes disappear with tears in his eyes.

'Well, it's on. No one can stop it now,' he says.

Eisenhower knows that Air Chief Marshal Leigh-Mallory is convinced that the 101st and the 82nd Airborne divisions will be all but wiped out. He told Eisenhower the casualty rate could be as high as 80 per cent.

'Flap your wings, you big-assed bird!' Donald Burgett of the 101st shouts as their Dakota takes off. He's carrying so much kit that he's kneeling on the floor of the plane and resting his backpack and parachute on the seat behind him.

On a hill near West Woodhay in Berkshire a full-scale re-creation of a German gun battery made out of wood and hessian lies abandoned. Even the fields and farm tracks around have been remodelled. (The War Office had to pay £15,000 in compensation for the discarded crops.) For the past few weeks it's been the training ground, day and night, for the 9th Parachute Battalion, the Parachute Regiment. Tonight, all that training will be put into practice. The replica is a copy of the battery on a hill at Merville, which overlooks the beaches where the British and Canadians will land. It's essential that the battery is knocked out by 5.15am. At that point, if the 9th Battalion hasn't fired a flare signalling they've succeeded – the navy will start shelling it.

The Merville Battery is believed to have four 150mm guns contained in bomb-proof bunkers surrounded by two minefields and a 15-foot entanglement of barbed wire. Intelligence suggests that 200 men guard the battery, armed with cannons and machine-guns.

The plan is first for 100 RAF Lancasters to bomb Merville, then gliders will bring in equipment (including jeeps and flamethrowers) and assault troops. At the climax of the attack, a further three gliders will land on top of the battery itself. An ingenious touch is having two German speakers in the assault team, who will confuse the enemy by shouting out misleading commands. Everything must go like clockwork for the attack to succeed.

*The man behind this audacious plan is Lieutenant Colonel Terence*

*Otway. Only 29 years old, he already has ten years' service in the army. Otway demands a lot of his men and devises unusual ways to get the best out of them. Those who finish assault courses on time are allowed to go home on leave on the express train; those who lag behind go home on the slow one. Obsessed with secrecy, Otway once arranged for 30 members of the Women's Auxiliary Air Force to dress in civilian clothes and visit the pubs close to where his men were training. They were to woo the men and try and get information on the Merville mission. To Otway's great delight, the WAAFs failed.*

At RAF Broadwell, Otway's men are making their final checks. In 20 minutes the Merville mission begins. Otway has banned drinking in the run-up to the attack, but in his kit he has a bottle of whisky to pass round the plane.

### *11.25pm*

The Special Operations Executive's (SOE) youngest agent, 22-year-old Tony Brooks, works undercover as a mechanic in a garage in the town of Montauban close to Toulouse, under the code name Alphonse. His assignment is to set up a sabotage network on the French mainline railways.

German tanks in France are moved over long distances by railway transporter trucks, and Brooks has noticed that some of these trucks in a siding in Montauban stand unguarded. So for the past few nights he has sent sub-agents – two teenage sisters – after curfew to siphon off all the axle oil from the transporter cars' wheels and replace it with ground carborundum, a mixture parachuted in by the SOE especially that will glue up the wheels. Tomorrow when the order comes to move the crack 2nd Panzer SS Division *Das Reich* to Normandy, none of the transporters will be able to move.

The axle oil will also make the Resistance a lot of money on the black market.

*The SOE was founded by Winston Churchill in July 1940 to 'set Europe ablaze', as he put it. Its speedily trained agents have been dropped into Europe to encourage occupied peoples to engage in guerrilla warfare – with considerable success, thanks to the agents' remarkable bravery and the bizarre equipment they use. This includes exploding cowpats and guns disguised as cigarettes.*

*By June 1944, the SOE is an organisation that's feared by the Germans. The life expectancy of an SOE wireless operator in France is only six weeks.*

One hundred and twenty advance paratroopers known as 'pathfinders' are flying over the Channel in a fleet of Horsa gliders being towed by Halifax and Dakota aircraft. Their job is to fly 30 minutes ahead of the main airborne assault and mark drop zones for the paratroopers and landing zones for the gliders with flare paths and, electronically, with Eureka Radar Beacon Systems.

Ahead of them, three Halifax bombers, each towing a canvas and plywood glider, are approaching the French coast. Inside the gliders are men from the British 6th Airborne Division, led by 31-year-old Major John Howard of the Oxfordshire and Buckinghamshire Light Infantry. They are the first of the 156,000 about to take part in D-Day. The gliders are full of men singing and the smoke of Player's cigarettes. In the lead glider, Corporal Wally Parr is heading up the chorus. He chalked the name 'Lady Irene' on the side of the aircraft just before he boarded, in tribute to his new wife. Medical officer Dr John Vaughan is sitting shocked at how helpless he feels – one shell could end their lives in an instant.

The men in the gliders have a unique and audacious mission – to capture two adjacent bridges linked by the same road over the River Orne and the Caen Canal at Bénouville and overcome the garrison stationed there. If they succeed, it will stop German tanks coming west from Calais to fight the invasion forces due to land on the beaches in seven hours. The British paratroopers must capture the bridges before the Germans blow them up – they are needed intact. Their orders state that their success depends on 'surprise, speed and dash...' None of these men have been in combat before.

In about 40 minutes, at a height of 6,000 feet, the tow-lines will be released and the gliders will begin their descent.

*On 3rd June Monty had visited their headquarters and his parting words to Major Howard had been, 'Get as many of the chaps back as you can.'*

*Just before they got into their gliders, one private had run off into the dark, having had a premonition of his own death.*

***Some Handy French Phrases:***

| | |
|---|---|
| ***1. Food?*** | ***Manger? (mahn JAY)*** |
| ***2. Water?*** | ***Boire? (bwar)*** |
| ***3. Show me?*** | ***Montrez-moi (mawntray-MWA)*** |
| ***4. Washroom?*** | ***Lavabo (la-va-BO)*** |
| ***5. Soldiers?*** | ***Soldats? (sawl-DA)*** |
| ***6. Germans?*** | ***Boches? (Bawsh)*** |
| ***7. Friend?*** | ***Ami? (ah-MEE)*** |
| ***8. How many?*** | ***Combien? (kawm-B-Yan)*** |
| ***9. Thank you*** | ***Merci (mayr-SEE)*** |
| ***10. Where?*** | ***Ou? (oo)*** |

***Advice to GIs, June 1944***

### *11.30pm*

Pierre Vienot, the ambassador for the French government in exile in London, is face to face with a furious Winston Churchill. General Charles de Gaulle, the leader of the Free French, is refusing to broadcast a D-Day message on the BBC and has forbidden his liaison officers to take part in the landings. De Gaulle has seen the text of Eisenhower's speech that'll be broadcast at 10am tomorrow morning, and he resents the fact that it has no mention of himself or the Free French Committee, and talks about 'prompt and willing obedience to the orders that I shall issue'. Furthermore, de Gaulle dislikes the fact that French invasion currency has been issued to the troops. No one has told de Gaulle that the text of Eisenhower's speech is not a draft and that 47 million copies have already been printed in five languages.

De Gaulle's fierce patriotism (he once wrote a history of the French Army that didn't mention Waterloo) makes Roosevelt suspicious of him, but Churchill recognises that de Gaulle's involvement in the future of France is crucial. Nevertheless, the prime minister is angry and is telling Pierre Vienot that de Gaulle is guilty of 'treason at the height of battle' and that the sacrifice of the Allied soldiers is 'blood that has no value for you!'

Vienot replies, 'You have said untrue and violent things that you will regret. What I wish to say to you on this historic night is that in spite of everything France thanks you.'

### *11.45pm*

USS *Tuscaloosa* is now so close to France that Colonel David Bruce can see the flashes of guns on the cliffs firing at Allied aircraft.

### *11.55pm*

Nineteen-year-old WAAF Mary Babbs is about to start her shift as a 'plotter' at Fighter Command's Operations Room at Bentley Priory in Middlesex. Security had been tight when she arrived: two military policemen had checked her pass – normally Mary is simply nodded through. She walks into the Ops Room and looks at the large map table that dominates the room – it's covered in black arrows all pointing south, towards France. Mary knows it must be D-Day. She picks up her croupier-type rake, plugs in her headset and is immediately almost overwhelmed by the number of instructions she's receiving about the aircraft to plot.

Mary will work almost non-stop for eight hours, tracking the progress of aircraft that form a nose-to-tail stream across the Channel.

***Robert Capa's photo of Private Edward K Regan in the sea off Omaha Beach***

# Tuesday 6th June 1944

***The first 24 hours of the invasion will be decisive for the Allies, as well as for Germany, it will be the longest day...***

***Field Marshal Rommel***

*12.05am*

In the French section of SOE headquarters at 64 Baker Street in London, secretary Elizabeth Small is lying on her makeshift bunk. Major Gerry Morel, a former SOE agent and now head of air operations walks in.

'Come on, get up – I want you to type the "A" message' (the message that tells their agents and the Resistance the invasion of Europe has begun).

'O great – *great*!' Elizabeth replies.

'The airborne are en route and the boats have started. So that's something nice to tell your grandchildren.'

### *12.07am*

The Halifax bombers taking the men of the Oxfordshire and Buckinghamshire Light Infantry to the Bénouville bridges are releasing their towropes. The paratroopers stop singing and in the gliders the only sound is the air rushing over the plywood wings. The glider pilots can see nothing in the darkness, other than flames from Caen as the city burns in a bombing raid. Navigation is by stopwatch, airspeed and altimeter.

### *12.14am*

The pilot of the lead glider, Staff Sergeant Jim Wallwork, calls to Major John Howard behind him to get ready. The infantrymen link arms and raise their legs. Howard can see large beads of sweat on Wallwork's face. Wallwork must land the Horsa as close as possible to the bridge over the Caen Canal. Howard wants him to smash through its barbed wire fortifications as he does so. Landing gliders is extremely dangerous – there is good reason why Horsas have acquired the nickname 'Hearses'.

## 'We're here. Piss off and do what you're paid to do'

### *12.16am*

Jim Wallwork's glider thumps into French soil at 90 miles an hour. He can see the metal bridge rushing towards him. He shouts 'Stream!' and his navigator activates the glider's parachute. It lifts the tail and throws the nose into the ground. Sparks are flying past the open door of the glider – for a moment

Howard and his men think they're being fired on. After two seconds the parachute is jettisoned. The Horsa hits the barbed wire, and the glider stops violently. Jim Wallwork and his navigator are flung through the cockpit window still in their seats.

John Howard and his men are momentarily knocked unconscious. Howard's watch stops with the impact.

On the other side of the bridge, Georges Gondrée, the proprietor of the Café Gondrée, is being shaken awake by his wife Thérèse (they sleep in separate rooms as a way of preventing German soldiers, whom they detest, being billeted with them).

'Get up! Can't you hear what's happening? It sounds like wood breaking...'

Georges opens the window, but he can't make much out. Thérèse leans out and shouts to a German sentry on the bridge to ask what's going on. He turns, and Georges can see that the sentry's eyes are wide with fear. He stammers, 'Parachutists!'

In London, SOE secretary Elizabeth Small is typing out the signal to SOE agents in France telling them that the invasion is underway. She's taking great care. On her first day it was pointed out to her that someone's life may depend on her accurate typing.

### *12.17am*

'We're here. Piss off and do what you're paid to do.'

The second glider has crash-landed and its pilot, Oliver Boland, is encouraging the stunned passengers behind him to get out and fight. His Horsa has landed close to a pond and broken in half, and many of the infantry have been thrown out. Part of the glider has landed on top of a German trench and the soldiers in it already have their hands up.

Twenty-two of Major Howard's men are charging towards the Caen Canal bridge. The third glider lands behind them.

Private Helmut Romer is walking towards the east end of the bridge. Suddenly he sees a group of men, their faces blackened, running towards him. Terrified, he turns and runs towards the centre of the bridge, shouting, 'Paratroopers!'

Romer spots a sentry at the other end firing a flare into the air – before seeing him shot dead.

### *12.19am*

Howard's men open a door to a pillbox and throw in a grenade. After the explosion the door is opened again and a machine-gun fired inside. They move on over the bridge towards the Café Gondrée. Inside, Georges Gondrée is taking Thérèse and the children to the safety of their cellar.

Meanwhile two other gliders have landed and secured the pathfinders' other objective without firing a shot – the bridge over the River Orne.

Twenty-two-year-old Private Vern Bonck, a Pole conscripted into the German Army, is in a brothel in Bénouville with another soldier. They should be on duty at the bridge. Hearing gunshots, they pull on their uniforms and run out into the street, letting off all their ammunition to give the impression they've been in a firefight. They then run to report the attack on the bridge.

Most of the conscripted soldiers guarding the bridge have run away; the only returning fire is from Germans. Corporal Wally Parr is standing in the middle of the bridge shouting, 'Come out and fight, you square-headed bastards!'

### *12.21am*

Georges Gondrée is peering through a first-floor window. Two soldiers are pointing their guns at him.

'*Vous civile*?' one says.

'*Oui, oui.*' Georges replies. He worked as a clerk for Lloyd's Bank in Paris for 12 years, so speaks good English, but he's still not sure of their nationality. One of the soldiers puts his fingers to his lips and motions to him to close the shutters. Georges does what he's told.

Platoon commander Lieutenant Dennis Fox (suffering from a broken arm) has found three Germans fast asleep in their dugouts, their rifles stacked neatly nearby. When he tries to wake them, they swear at him, thinking it's a joke, and go back to sleep.

Corporal Wally Parr steps on a metal grate outside the Gondrées' café, and looks down to see Madame Gondrée and her two daughters, Georgette and Arlette, staring back at him. Parr is concerned that a grenade might fall down the grate and kill them.

'Madame, go in, for God's sake! Tommy Atkins! Liberators!'

They don't move. He kneels down and gives the elder girl a bar of chocolate, and moves on.

Madame Gondrée is convinced that Parr is a German pretending to be British, and she throws the chocolate away in case it's poisoned. (Every Christmas, for the rest of his life, Wally Parr will send the girls chocolate, and they in return send him champagne.)

### *12.26am*

Lance Corporal Edward Tappenden is sending out the coded success signal for the capture of the two bridges.

'Ham and jam… ham and jam… ham and jam…'

Their mission is over in ten minutes. Two men from their unit have been killed and 14 wounded. With the bridges held, any German traffic over the River Orne will now have to go via Caen, which is a six-hour detour.

Air Chief Marshal Leigh-Mallory will call it the greatest flying feat of the Second World War. Their job now is to defend the bridge until reinforcements arrive.

German sentries Helmut Romer and Erwin Sauer, both 18, are hiding in some thick bushes by the edge of the Caen Canal. They are too scared to move. They'll remain hidden for another 36 hours before they finally give themselves up to the British troops.

### *12.35am*

Seven thousand British and 13,400 US paratroopers are now on their way to Normandy. Some of the US 101st and 82nd Airborne divisions are in Dakotas, others in gliders heading for their drop zone to the south of the Cotentin Peninsula. The aim of the 101st is to capture the town of Sainte-Mère-Église and its surrounding areas, while the aim of the 82nd is to seize the causeways across the flooded marshes behind Utah Beach, thus throwing a protective cordon around the American invasion beaches.

British paratroopers are headed to their drop zone east of the River Orne, in Horsa gliders towed by Dakotas. Piloting one of the Dakotas is 24-year-old flying officer Jimmy Edwards. A few days ago, he and the other aircrew of 271 Squadron were ordered to have their moustaches shaved off, the logic being that they would be identified too easily as RAF officers if they were shot down.

*Black and white stripes have been painted on the wings and fuselage of all D-Day aircraft to prevent friendly-fire accidents. Ten thousand planes have been painted in the last 24 hours. It had to be last minute, so that the Germans couldn't copy the markings. Twenty thousand paintbrushes and 100 gallons of paint were ordered by the War Office – factories had to work over the Whitsun holiday to get the work done.*

*At airfields around Britain, all aircrew had to muck in, officers included. Jimmy Edwards ended up covered in paint, much to his commanding officer's disapproval, but he said nothing. As Edwards wrote later, 'This was hardly the time for bullshit.'*

*After the war, Jimmy Edwards will become a famous radio and film comic actor, known for his trademark moustache. The moustache is to cover facial injuries he sustained when he was shot down in September 1944.*

In a fortification called *Widerstandsnest 5* (Strongpoint 5) on top of the dunes at the beach at Pouppeville, Second Lieutenant Arthur Jahnke is looking up at the sky. Jahnke is only 23, but he's a veteran of the Russian Front, where he won the Knight's Cross – the highest award for bravery in the German Army. Jahnke is wearing it around his neck tied with a shoelace (its nickname is the *Blechkrawatte* – the tin necktie). After being wounded in Russia, Jahnke was posted to Hitler's Atlantic Wall.

The drone of aircraft for the last hour has made him uneasy. He rings Strongpoint W2 further down the beach. Lieutenant Ritter replies.

'I have a feeling something's up.'

'But nothing that concerns us,' Jahnke says.

'I hope you're correct.'

'I'll come and have a tot of your cognac tomorrow, just to prove I was right.'

*As the tide is going out, Jahnke is convinced that the Allies won't invade this morning. Rommel himself had told him when he inspected the Strongpoint on 11th May that they would strike at high tide, so they can float over the beach defences, and avoid an 800-yard dash across the exposed beach.*

*Rommel had been unimpressed by the defences he'd seen and had questioned Jahnke about how he was using barbed wire. Jahnke said that all the wire he could get hold of was used on the beach. Rommel asked to see Jahnke's hands. Astonished, Jahnke took off his grey suede gloves and held out his palms. They were scratched and still bloody.*

*'Well done, Lieutenant. The blood on an officer's hands from fortification work is worth every bit as much as that shed in battle.'*

*For the last month, inspired by the field marshal, Jahnke has been building more beach defences in front of Strongpoint W5. The Allies have given the beach a code name: Utah.*

### *12.40am*

The Lancaster bombers have dropped a total of 382 bombs over the Merville Battery. But they have all missed their target as the markers had been dropped in the wrong place. Lieutenant Colonel Terence Otway's plan has gone wrong at its first stage.

'Hold your course, you bloody fool!' Otway is shouting to the pilot of the Dakota, taking them to the drop zone close to Merville.

'We've been hit in the tail!' the pilot protests.
'You can still fly straight, can't you?'

### *12.50am*

At the Bénouville bridges, Lance Corporal Edward Tappenden has had no acknowledgement of his success signal.

'Ham and jam... ham and jam... ham and *bloody* jam..!'

Lieutenant Colonel Terence Otway is at the door of the Dakota, about to jump. He notices that he has the half-empty bottle of whisky in his hand. He gives it to one of the RAF crew.

'You're going to need this.'

Otway jumps.

As he falls, the countryside below looks just as it does on his scale models, but he's heading straight for a farmhouse that he knows is the headquarters of a German battalion. Bullets are whizzing past him. Otway slams into the side of the building. A German soldier opens a window, only to be met by a brick thrown by one of Otway's men who's landed in the garden. The two paratroopers run away as fast as they can.

At Rommel's headquarters at La Roche-Guyon, Major General Hans Speidel's dinner party has broken up, and most of the guests have returned to Paris. However, Major Wilhelm von Schramm is staying overnight, as he plans to visit some divisions in Normandy in the morning. On his way back from the toilet he passes the desk of the adjutant Captain Ernest Maisch; lines of poetry German Intelligence had written down earlier catch his eye.

'*Blessent mon coeur*
*D'une langueur*
*Monotone.*'

Von Schramm knows that this is the signal German Intelligence has been waiting for, and he rushes to Speidel in a state of great excitement.

'Things are about to start!' he says and takes Speidel into the adjutant's office to show him the message. But the major general is unmoved. He turns to von Schramm and says, 'Well, that's the end of the evening. Now I'm afraid we must part.'

Speidel heads off to bed, but von Schramm stays on in the adjutant's office to see if any other reports come in.

*The previous night, Wilhelm von Schramm had been staying at the George V Hotel in Paris. He woke up in the middle of the night after hearing a voice saying clearly, again and again, 'The turning point of the war is coming... the turning point of the war is coming...'*

*Von Schramm had got out of bed and opened the door of his room to see if there was anyone there. The corridor was empty. The dream had deeply unsettled him.*

### *12.55am*

Sainte-Mère-Église is a small market town on the road between Cherbourg in the north and Caen to the south. The large swastika above its town hall is lit by flames. A house is on fire on the other side of the square, the Place de l'Église. Local people have been given permission by the German troops to break the 9pm curfew and put the fire out, and they've formed a human chain and are passing buckets from a nearby pump.

*In June 1940 German soldiers arrived at Sainte-Mère-Église, optimistically singing* 'Wir sind auf dem weg nach England!' *'We're on our way to England!' and ever since, the swastika has flown over the town hall. Many of the young people from Sainte-Mère-Église have been called up for* Service de Travail Obligatoire *– forced labour in Germany.*

*The locals have countered the humiliation they feel at being occupied with acts of defiance – joining the Resistance, listening to the BBC on banned radios and building Rommel's anti-glider defences in their fields as slowly as possible.*

*They are unaware that for almost a year, their little town has been central to the Allies' plan for the liberation of France. General Eisenhower himself has insisted that Sainte-Mère-Église be captured. As well as being a vital route to Cherbourg, a road from the town also runs straight to Utah Beach. That's why it's in the centre of the drop zone for the US 101st and 82nd Airborne.*

In their house three miles from Sainte-Mère-Église, 11-year-old Geneviève Duboscq and her family are celebrating what they are sure is the invasion. (Yesterday, Geneviève and her mother were cutting a telephone cable that ran from Sainte-Mère-Église.) Her father Maurice is about to go down into the cellar when the front door is kicked open and a paratrooper bursts in, holding a machine-gun.

'Friend or foe?' the man says.

Geneviève's little brother Claude steps forward.

'Friends, *monsieur* – we're all friends.'

'Friends. Really friends?' The paratrooper ruffles Claude's hair. Geneviève kisses his grimy cheek, and the paratrooper pulls out a map and says, 'Show me where the Germans are...'

***A padre gave us a sermon on board ship and at the finish we sang the hymn 'For Those in Peril on the Sea.' After that we began to move again and overhead there was a terrible noise of plane engines. Of course it was***

> ***dark – about one or two o'clock. I tried to sleep but it wouldn't come to me...***
>
> **Corporal Clifford Arthur Payne, 2nd East Yorkshires**

### *1.00am/midnight European Time*

218 Squadron and the 617 'Dambusters' Squadron are in the middle of an unusual mission. Well away from the invasion fleet, they are dropping aluminium chaff (code-named Window) over the Pas-de-Calais out of specially designed holes in the noses of their Short Stirling and Lancaster bombers. The plan for Operation Glimmer, as it's known, is that the falling chaff will fool German radar into thinking that a fleet sailing at eight knots is approaching the French coast near Dieppe.

It's a precise process – the planes must fly in a line at 180mph, exactly two miles apart, dropping the chaff at fifteen-second intervals. Most of the German radar stations have been destroyed by bombing, but enough have been deliberately left so that they can detect this 'phantom fleet'. (Intelligence sources have found that the German radars pick up signals once every 15 seconds.)

Lieutenant Nick Knilans of 617 Squadron, at the controls of Lancaster *R-Roger*, is getting precise, repetitive instructions from the navigator in his headphones.

'Tighten the turn, you're two seconds slow... You're three feet too low... On course, on course... Begin turn now! Ease up, you're three seconds fast...'

Once the chaff is dropped, the bombers turn away for exactly two minutes and ten seconds before coming round again. When one aircraft drops away to return to base, another must join seamlessly to avoid a gap that might give the game away. Beneath them, small boats are towing radar reflector balloons and simulating the radio traffic of a large fleet.

Operation Glimmer is working. The Luftwaffe has sent up reconnaissance planes to look for the enemy 'fleet' and the British bomber crews can see shore batteries firing into the sea where ships should be, convinced they are about to be invaded.

The bomber crews have no idea of the significance of what they are doing. Only when they wake up this afternoon, having returned to base, will they know that today is the long-awaited D-Day.

Paratroopers are also dropping objects from their aircraft. As they pass over Normandy one British paratrooper drops a stuffed moose's head he stole from a pub in Exeter; many US paratroopers are chucking away their cumbersome gas masks, and one is dropping a baseball with 'To hell with you, Hitler' written on it.

Thirty-four-year-old Lieutenant Commander Heinrich Hoffmann is in the cabin of his E-boat *T-28*. The phone rings; it's his commanding officer telling him that ships have been detected heading towards the Normandy coast.

'This must be the invasion!' Hoffmann says, but his chief is not so sure. Hoffmann has been uneasy ever since the conversation with his wife seven hours before when she'd asked, 'Heinrich, I'm restless tonight. Is there anything afoot?'

Hoffmann calls the commanders of the other five E-boats in his flotilla to meet on *T-28*.

> *Hoffmann is one of the German Navy's most successful E-boat commanders, having fought in battles defending their battleships the* Scharnhorst, *the* Prince Eugen *and the* Gneisenau. *He attacked British and Canadian forces during their disastrous Dieppe raid of*

*1942. There's a saying in the German Navy: 'When Hoffmann gets to a place, things start happening.'*

*That will be true today.*

On board USS *Tuscaloosa*, David Bruce is looking up at the sky and listening to the sound of planes heading back to England. He guesses they've just dropped the pathfinders. Bruce feels sorry for the paratroopers, who he fears will have been scattered by the strong wind he can feel on deck.

David Bruce is right. Many of the paratroopers have missed or are about to miss their drop zones, some by as many as 25 miles. Two British paratroopers have dropped onto the lawn of the headquarters of Major General Josef Reichert of the German 711th Division. They have been brought to him for questioning.

One of the pathfinders says coolly: 'Awfully sorry, old man, but we simply landed here by accident.'

After a pleasant evening around the fire at the Berghof reminiscing with Hitler about the early days of the Party, Joseph Goebbels is leaving for his quarters nearby in Berchtesgaden. A thunderstorm is beginning.

In Saint-Lô at the headquarters of the 84th Corps, there's a surprise 53rd birthday party for their commander, General Erich Marcks. Marcks, who lost an eye in the First World War and a leg in Russia in the Second, is a frugal man, so the celebration is low-key.

Once, when he saw whipped cream being served at dinner, Marcks declared, 'I do not wish to see this again as long as our country is starving.'

*Marcks is about to set off on the 100-mile journey to the town of Rennes. He and other army commanders are taking part in a 'Kriegspiel' to start at 10am. It's a war game that will test their readiness for an invasion. Using maps, the officers will have to respond to a scenario of an Allied invasion led by an airborne drop and followed by landings on Normandy beaches. In the war game, Marcks is playing the commander of the Allied forces.*

### *1.05am*

Geneviève Duboscq's mother and father are standing on the edge of a flooded field with the paratrooper who burst into their house just a few minutes ago. The night sky is throbbing with the sound of planes. The Duboscqs had thought he was alone but he's told them that he is just one of many paratroopers on the way.

'You've got to stop them! They'll all drown if they land here!' her mother says desperately.

The night sky is cloudy but the moon is breaking through, which means that as he looks over the port side of USS *Tuscaloosa*, David Bruce can make out scores of landing craft full of seasick troops. On most landing craft the sick bags ('Bag Vomit. For the use of') have already been used, and the troops are resorting to using fire buckets or even their helmets. Sick and seawater swills around the bottom of the boats.

### *1.10am*

Major General Josef Reichert is examining the maps the two captured pathfinder paratroopers were carrying. He's stunned by their accuracy – they show almost all of the German gun emplacements on the Normandy coast.

In his tent in the grounds of Southwick House, meteorologist Group Captain James Stagg is falling asleep to the sound of bombers overhead.

### *1.14am*

Donald Burgett of the 101st is hitting the soil of France hard. He's stunned for a moment, then as he lies on his back, he draws his pistol. Burgett looks at a night sky so full of tracer, it reminds him of the 4th of July.

Suddenly a Dakota flies overhead, chased by machine-gun fire. Burgett watches in horror as he counts 17 men jump from it. The plane is so low that as they hit the ground they make the sound of ripe pumpkins bursting.

'That dirty son of a bitch of a pilot! He's hedge-hopping and killing a bunch of troopers just to save his own ass. I hope he gets shot down in the Channel and drowns real slow,' Burgett thinks.

Burgett doesn't know it yet, but he is 12 miles from the drop zone and the rest of the 101st and 82nd are scattered all over the Cotentin Peninsula.

> ***Then the tank came down the road. We thought that was it, you know, no way were we going to stop a tank...***
>
> ***Corporal Billy Gray, Oxfordshire and Buckinghamshire Light Infantry***

## 'One up and two to go!'

### *About 1.20am*

About 25 American paratroopers have been captured in and around the Normandy village of Brévands, a few miles from the coast, and are being held in the headquarters of the 352nd Infantry Division (two paratroopers had the misfortune of landing right on top of its roof).

Twenty-eight-year-old Captain Ernst Düring, assistant battalion commander of the 352nd, is talking to one of the American officers, a man about his own age. Düring's English is quite good as he studied it at high school. The American is scared.

'Take everything, but please don't shoot me!' he keeps repeating.

### *1.25am*

At the Bénouville bridges, Major John Howard can hear the rumble of tanks approaching from the west. His men must hold these bridges to protect the British invasion beaches, so for the last 45 minutes he's been trying to assess what equipment he has available to repel the inevitable German counter-attack. The only tank-busting equipment to have survived the glider landings is a solitary PIAT (Projector, Infantry, Anti-Tank). Howard can now see two Mark IV tanks cautiously approaching the bridge.

Alexandre Renaud, the mayor of Sainte-Mère-Église, has rushed from his home above his chemist's shop to join the firefighters trying to put out the blaze in the Place de l'Église. There's a real danger that sparks will ignite the straw in a barn nearby.

From the west, wave upon wave of aircraft are flying low overhead, all with strange black-and-white markings he's never seen before. In the belfry of the church a machine-gun nest is taking shots at the planes. Its bell is tolling.

On most of the large troop ships in the Channel, the quarters are cramped, but not without their diversions. On one, the soldiers are watching a Mickey Rooney and Judy Garland film in the cafeteria. Most of the LCTs are open to the elements – their blunt bows send plumes of spray over the ship, soaking the men aboard, and their flat bottoms make them roll, in the words of one disgruntled soldier in the Kings Own Scottish Borderers, 'like a porpoise'.

### *1.30am/8.30pm US Eastern War Time*

At Bénouville, the Oxfordshire and Buckinghamshire Light Infantry's PIAT is in the hands of Sergeant 'Wagger' Thornton, and he's shaking like a leaf. The PIAT is unpopular with the infantry – it's heavy and most of the time its projectiles fail to detonate.

The first of the two German tanks is about to turn at a T-junction and head towards the bridges. Thornton is about 30 yards away from the tank – he can 'more hear it than see it'. He has only two projectiles with him.

Thornton fires, and hits the tank side-on. There's a huge explosion, which sets off the rest of the tank's ammunition, resulting in multiple blasts. Shrapnel and shells are flying everywhere.

President Roosevelt is broadcasting to the nation from the White House, informing them of the capture of Rome the day before. For the moment, D-Day must remain a secret.

'The first of the Axis capitals is now in our hands. One up and two to go!'

*The president is not a well man. He is 62 but looks as if he's in his seventies. For the last three months a cardiologist named Dr Howard Bruenn has been his full-time physician, seeing him every morning and evening, and with him on all his trips. On 28th March*

*Roosevelt underwent tests at Bethesda Naval Hospital and Bruenn discovered that he was on the verge of heart failure.*

*Another physician, Dr Lahey, was summoned to give a second opinion.*

*'Mr President, you may not care for what I have to say...'*

*'That will be all, Dr Lahey,' Roosevelt interrupted. That was the end of the consultation.*

*Not even FDR's wife Eleanor or their children know how sick he is. Bruenn is sworn to secrecy about his health, as Roosevelt plans to run for an unprecedented fourth term.*

*For the past two years the White House has had blackout curtains at every window and gun emplacements on the roof.*

In Gascony, deep in occupied France, SOE agent Yvonne Cormeau is reaching under a beehive to retrieve some weapons hidden there a few weeks before. Yvonne had reasoned that the bees would help hide the guns – the Germans would be unlikely to risk getting stung searching for them.

Listening earlier to a radio concealed in a hayloft in a barn, she had received the message from London that the armada had sailed, and had then headed to the hive.

*In November 1940 Yvonne's soldier husband had been killed in an air raid on London, and she decided that she would take his place on the front line. Her daughter is in a boarding school back in England.*

Lieutenant Colonel Terence Otway has arrived at the agreed rendezvous: a wood a mile east of the Merville Battery. One of his officers greets him.

'Thank God you've come, sir. The drop's bloody chaos. There's hardly anyone here.'

Just 120 paratroopers of the planned 650 have made it to the rendezvous. The majority of the 32 planes carrying the 9th Battalion had dropped the parachutists and equipment beyond the drop zone because visibility was poor due to a large dust cloud caused by the RAF bombs and a strong easterly wind. Some navigators had mistaken the River Dives for the River Orne and dropped them miles away. One paratrooper will take four days to be reunited with the battalion. One hundred and ninety-two men will never be heard of again – the majority drowning in flooded fields and marshes.

### *1.35am*

The German tank hit by Sergeant 'Wagger' Thornton's PIAT has finally stopped exploding. Now the men of the Oxfordshire and Buckinghamshire Light Infantry can hear a man screaming. It's the driver of the tank who's managed to get out of his hatch and is lying in the road. British Private Tommy Klare runs forward and scoops him up, puts him on his back and carries him to their first-aid post.

The second tank retreats, convinced that the British have a six-pounder anti-tank gun and must be a vast unit of men. For the next few hours, the wrecked tank blocks the T-junction, stopping German traffic north to the beaches and east to the bridges.

At Brévands, Captain Ernst Düring has accepted a Chesterfield cigarette from the terrified American paratrooper and offered him one of his. The two men are now quietly smoking. Watching him, Düring can see that the American had believed the propaganda that all Germans are mindless killers, but is now slowly recognising that the German Army captain is much like himself.

Later, Düring will realise that many Allied paratroopers were ill-served by propaganda saying that the Germans would shoot them if captured. Many in hopeless situations are refusing to surrender and are dying as a result.

### *1.45am*

Twenty-year-old Raymond Paris is part of the human chain trying to put out the fire in the house in Sainte-Mère-Église. He stops and looks up – he can see that the doors of the latest wave of aircraft are open. Men start jumping out.

'That's it, it's the invasion!' he shouts.

Private Ken Russell of the 505th Parachute Infantry Regiment is one of the men jumping. He can see the flames below him and to his horror the fire is pulling both oxygen and his parachute towards the burning house. He's fighting desperately to steer himself away. Ahead of him, Private Charles Blanketship is falling into the flames. Russell hears him scream – just once. Then Russell hits the church steeple, his lines snagging the top. He's dangling over the edge of the roof, fortunately in the shadows and away from the fire.

Twenty-two-year-old Private John 'Buck' Steele is parachuting from his Dakota. He can see that instead of heading to the drop zone to the north-west of Sainte-Mère-Église, he's also drifting towards the town square. Everyone on the ground seems to be looking at him. A bullet shatters his foot just before he too hits the steeple.

As he drifts towards Sainte-Mère-Église, Private Ernest Blanchard sees a man level with him explode as tracer bullets hit his ammunition. The empty harness continues to float down.

## *1.47am*

Private Ken Russell is watching from the church roof as a red-headed German soldier in the town square shoots Sergeant John Ray in the stomach. The soldier then looks up and spots Russell and Steele on the roof and lifts his machine-gun to fire. The dying Sergeant Ray pulls out his pistol and shoots the soldier in the head. It's one of the bravest things that Russell has ever seen.

Russell cuts his parachute lines and falls to the ground. He looks up at Steele hanging lifeless from the steeple and assumes he must be dead, and then runs for the safety of some trees at the edge of town. In fact, Steele is playing dead. He'd tried to cut himself down but accidently dropped his knife into the square. German machine-gunners are just a few yards from him in the steeple. All he can do is hang there and watch the killing below him.

By the town pump, Raymond Paris and some of the other men are trying to rescue an American who's fallen into the trees. Others are not so lucky and are being machine-gunned as they hang helplessly.

'Tommies – all kaput,' a soldier beneath the trees shouts at the mayor Alexandre Renaud. Renaud can see one dead paratrooper hanging, bent double, as if he's looking at the bullet holes in his stomach.

Private Don Davis is lying on the cobbles of the town square pretending to be dead. A German soldier rolls him over just to make sure. Davis waits a few moments for the soldier to move on – then makes his escape.

Close by, Private Ernest Blanchard is hanging from a tree in the town square and is hacking at his harness with a knife to release himself before he's spotted. He drops and runs. In a few moments he'll realise that he's cut off the top of his thumb.

### *1.55am*

Raymond Paris sees a German soldier raise his machine-gun to shoot a parachutist, and taps him on the shoulder to distract him.

'Don't shoot. Civilian!'

The soldier doesn't fire.

Raymond Paris will always remember the day the parachutists landed in his town, and the sound of the planes, the gunfire, the screams – and throughout, the tolling of the church bell.

Although about 30 US parachutists have landed in Sainte-Mère-Église, about a thousand have successfully made it to the drop zone and are regrouping with the intention of seizing the town.

### *2.00am/1.00am European Time*

Hitler is finally going to bed.

Below decks on the troop ship HMS *Empire Javelin*, Captain Schilling of 116th Infantry is giving his men a final pep talk before they climb aboard their landing craft. Most are sitting on the floor, listening intently over the roar of the engines.

'This is the real McCoy. The dry runs are over, the amphibious assault training is concluded. I am proud to lead this company into battle.'

He explains that the troops defending their sector of Omaha Beach around the Vierville gully are not first-rate soldiers;

many of them are conscripts from Poland and Russia or elderly German Home Guard.

'Cross the beach fast, gain the high ground and get into a perimeter defence. When I call the roll tonight at Isigny [their objective nine miles inland] I want everyone to say "Here!"'

On USS *Samuel Chase*, the ship's loudspeaker interrupts photographer Robert Capa's poker game – all the men going ashore must go to their assembly points. The players stuff their money in waterproof money belts. Capa will be going to Omaha Beach with E Company from the 16th Regiment from the 1st Division, a group of men he knows well from the Sicilian campaign last year.

At Grendon Hall, the base for the training of SOE agents destined for France, wireless operator Anne Ponsonby smiles as she picks up radio messages from the French Resistance, who are delighted the invasion has begun.

'*Vivent les Alliés, Vive la France, Vive la Grande-Bretagne*!'

Yvonne Cormeau's guns are now safely out from under the beehive and she's checking them over. They're all covered in thick soap to protect them from the elements. Yvonne will give the guns to people in the local village she can trust. Within hours bridges and railways in Gascony will be blown up, and trees felled to block roads.

A large proportion of the American paratroopers are well and truly lost in the Normandy countryside, having missed their drop zones. Pilots panicked at the amount of flak they encountered, and the weather was worse than expected – cloud cover made it hard for the pilots to see the drop zones, and electronic navigational aids such as Eureka Beacons were rarely used as the pathfinder paratroopers responsible for them weren't sure they'd landed in the right place.

Even General Maxwell Taylor, the commander of the 101st Division, is lost – for half an hour he has been unable to find any of the 7,000 men under his command. He's still limping from the squash injury he suffered yesterday.

The Allies know from air reconnaissance photographs that the Germans have flooded fields in Normandy to deter paratroopers, and safe drop zones have been chosen accordingly. But some of the drop zones are not all they seem. Photos had shown fields of long grass behind Utah Beach, but in fact, some of the grass is growing above floodwater.

Paratroopers are falling out of the sky, and landing in the dark, laden with heavy equipment, they are toppling backwards in five feet of water. Men who had to be helped onto their aircraft cannot get out of the flood.

Lieutenant Ralph De Weese is being dragged on his back through the water by his parachute, and is struggling to cut himself free. Later, he'll find small fish in his pockets, and he'll have swallowed so much water he won't drink for two days.

Some men succeed in cutting away their harnesses, but many don't. One who's survived is Catholic chaplain Francis Sampson, who managed to free himself of his equipment, including his Mass kit. He's now diving into the water to retrieve it.

Thirty-six men from the 82nd drown.

A few miles away, in Strongpoint W5 overlooking Utah Beach, Second Lieutenant Jahnke is calling his battalion headquarters. A patrol has captured some American paratroopers wading through the flooded fields to the south.

'Nineteen prisoners of the American 2nd Battalion, 506th Parachute Regiment...' Then the line goes dead.

For all the chaos and missed drop zones, the scattered paratroop drop is succeeding in paralysing the Germans. The paratroopers have resorted to guerrilla warfare – hindering German communications by cutting telegraph wires and shooting motorbike dispatch riders.

The German soldiers in the fields and villages of Normandy can hear strange 'click click' noises. To some they sound like castanets, to others like crickets. The US paratroopers have each been given two-cent toy clickers as a way of identifying themselves in the dark. One click must be met with two clicks. It's an eerie sound, and it's unnerving the Germans.

However, one German patrol north of Sainte-Mère-Église has managed to round up 20 US paratroopers by using a captured clicker. Every time an American responded to a single click, he was taken prisoner.

Task Forces U, O, G, J and S are making good progress in the Channel. The leading ships are less than an hour from the point from which they must launch their landing craft. The majority of troops are still seasick.

Captain Walter Marchand is a battalion surgeon on a transport ship heading for Utah Beach. He's writing in his diary.

'Had a very early breakfast – then I lay on my bunk for a while – I couldn't sleep and I can't sleep – I keep thinking of my wife and my family – I love you my Corinne.'

### *2.11am*

In Saint-Lô, at the headquarters of the 84th Corps, General Erich Marcks' surprise birthday party is over. It was well received, but now he would rather discuss the war games taking place later today in Rennes. The conversation is interrupted by a phone call. Marcks' intelligence officer Major Friedrich Hayn will always remember this as 'an unforgettable moment'. It's the commander of the 716th Division in Caen saying that reports are coming through of enemy parachute drops east of the Orne estuary and by the Caen bridges. Could it be the invasion?

General Marcks says they should wait and see.

### *About 2.15am*

In his trailer hidden in the woods near Southwick House, Kay Summersby is massaging General Eisenhower's shoulders. She's finding it hard to loosen the knots of tension in the base of his neck. Eisenhower's eyes are bloodshot, and his hands shake when he lights a cigarette.

They talk about the time they drove to Dover in 1942 and Eisenhower had looked over at France and talked about 'when we get over there'.

Kay says, 'I thought that we had a very slim chance of ever doing that. But now we have. You did it.'

'We'll see... We don't know yet whether we did it or not,' Eisenhower replies.

The sound of aircraft rumbles over Southwick House. It's the rear of a line of planes that stretches all the way to France.

On a ridge just south of the Normandy town of Carentan, a group of men from the German 6th Parachute Regiment, all feeling the worse for wear after a party last night, are standing by their mortars watching the planes and the flashes of anti-aircraft guns.

'Now the shit starts,' someone says.

Twenty-two-year-old Fritz Müller is a German medical orderly with a mobile artillery regiment, who is wandering through the dark woods of Normandy. He's looking for wounded soldiers – both German and American. Earlier he'd watched from a hill, horrified as American parachutists were machine-gunned even before they landed, and he'd seen others drown in flooded fields.

Müller's commanding officer had told him to go on his mercy mission unarmed, but Müller, who has experienced the violence of the Eastern Front, is taking no chances and has a revolver in a trouser pocket. He has a red cross on his arm.

> ***I got along to the RV [rendezvous] and saw Colonel Otway looking very peculiar indeed. The reason was that there was hardly anybody there... When he saw me he said, 'You're commanding C Company. Well, don't just stand there. Get on, go see your company!' My company was about five men. Gradually it dawned on us that something had gone frantically wrong.***
>
> ***Lieutenant Alan Jefferson, 9th Battalion, Parachute Regiment***

*2.30am*

'This is it – this is D-Day!' the briefing officer at USAAF Station 117 Kimbolton, Cambridgeshire shouts with a flourish. There are whoops and cheers from the assembled Flying Fortress bomber crews. At last they will be working to help their ground forces by attacking German infantry and tanks, instead of chemical and ball bearing factories. The crews no longer feel so tired.

At the rendezvous for the Merville Battery attack, Lieutenant Colonel Terence Otway says to the 150 men who've turned up that he'll wait another 15 minutes to allow others to arrive before they start their assault. His batman Corporal Wilson (a former valet) has made it, and offers Otway a small flask.

'Shall we have our brandy now, sir?'

Wilson had survived his landing, when he ended up going feet-first into a greenhouse.

'What the hell am I going to do, Wilson?'

'There's only one thing, sir.'

Walter Hermes is a 19-year-old motorcycle messenger for the 21st Panzer Division based at an airfield four miles from the coast. He was woken up in his bunk half an hour ago by the sound of gunfire and his sergeant major shouting, 'The English have landed! Are you mad? Still lying in bed when there's shelling!'

Now fully dressed, Hermes is reporting for duty in the sergeant major's office.

'Do you want to see our first prisoner? He's standing there right behind the door,' he says.

Hermes turns quickly and sees a half-size dummy of a man, covered in firecrackers.

'By God,' Hermes says, 'if the Allies expect to win the invasion with this sort of thing, they're crazy. They're just trying to scare us!'

*As part of an operation code-named Titanic, the British have dropped dummies dressed in boots and helmets called 'Ruperts', wired so that they explode on impact, simulating gunfire. Some play recordings of gunfire and exploding mortars when they land. It's all designed to make the Germans think that the parachute drops are part of a diversion for the main landing in the Pas-de-Calais.*

## *2.35am*

USS *Tuscaloosa* is dropping anchor 11,000 yards from Utah Beach. Closer to the shore, just 3,000 yards away, the destroyers from Task Force U are taking their positions.

German medical orderly Fritz Müller is still on his mercy mission looking for American and German wounded in the Normandy fields. He's walking underneath trees filled with parachutes. Some have harnesses that are empty, some hold corpses. Following a distant voice, Müller walks into a clearing where an American paratrooper lies motionless on the ground; he can't tell if he is dead or unconscious. Kneeling over him is a German soldier who's rummaging through his pockets, making crude comments about a picture of a girl he's found in the man's wallet. Müller shouts at him to leave the poor man alone and to stop making comments about the girl. The soldier refuses, pulls a ring off the paratrooper's finger and walks away.

Suddenly there's a gunshot and the German drops down dead. Müller freezes, then kneels by the American parachutist, who he can now see is alive. Müller gets out his medical kit and starts treating him as best he can.

Then, as Müller works, cigarettes start to fall around him. Preoccupied, Müller reckons that the Americans must be dropping them from aircraft. He doesn't smoke, but he puts some in his pockets, as his patients are always asking him for one.

Only later does Müller realise that the cigarettes were dropped by American parachutists still hanging in the trees. They had shot the German soldier, and were thanking him for defending, and then treating their injured friend.

## *2.40am*

At his headquarters in Paris, the man in charge of the army in France, Field Marshal von Rundstedt, is studying the numerous reports coming in from Normandy. Naval headquarters say that their radar screens are covered with hundreds of blips – at first the operators thought it must be something wrong with their equipment.

Von Rundstedt is unimpressed.

'Maybe a flock of seagulls?'

Furthermore, he's convinced that the paratrooper landings are a deception to cover the real invasion that will be at Calais. He doesn't consider the situation important enough yet to disturb Rommel at home in Germany.

However, at the headquarters of the 84th Corps, General Marcks has seen enough. He's ordered that the code word *Viebig* (signifying 'invasion') be sent out to all units.

Marcks wants to mobilise the only tank division close enough to do any good – the 21st Panzer Division. They have seen plenty of action, many men have fought with Rommel in North Africa. Marcks has contacted von Rundstedt in Paris, even the German High Command in Berlin, but each has refused permission. They too are not convinced this is the real invasion.

Although the German Army war games in Rennes have been cancelled, many of the key divisional commanders, taking advantage of a day away from base, are already in Rennes, 100 miles away.

### *2.50am*

Lieutenant Colonel Terence Otway's patience has been rewarded by the arrival of 30 extra men at the rendezvous. He takes stock of what resources he has to knock out a four gun battery defended by 200 men and surrounded by minefields and barbed wire. Otway has 150 men, one Vickers machine-gun, 6 Bangalore torpedoes (instead of 60), a signal flare to be fired in the event of a successful mission and a pigeon to send a message to England once the attack is over. All their mortars, anti-tank guns, radio and mine-detecting equipment are lost somewhere in the countryside around them.

None of the engineers or doctors has made the rendezvous, but six medical orderlies (all conscientious objectors) are awaiting his instructions. He has two and half hours to complete the mission before the naval guns open fire on the Battery. As his batman Corporal Wilson said, he has no choice. What's left of the 9th Battalion sets out in single file towards the Merville Battery.

## 'It's all right, chum'

### *About 2.55am*

The Allied gliders don't just carry men, they carry jeeps, even field guns and small tanks. This makes landing extremely dangerous. Many of the large gliders bringing in reinforcements for the paratroopers are crashing into walls and farm buildings. Pilots are being crushed to death as the equipment behind them catapults forward.

Twenty-three-year-old Sergeant John Wilson of the British Glider Pilot Regiment is lying in the wreckage of his Horsa glider. It had been carrying a jeep, a trailer, two motorbikes, ammunition and seven men. When the glider landed it had bounced hard, and then, when it was only a matter of yards away, Wilson saw they were heading for a house. His co-pilot was killed outright.

The paratroopers he was carrying try to get him out, but the pain is unbearable.

'Leave me, leave me,' Wilson says, 'I'll be all right when it's daylight.'

Wilson will be trapped in the glider for two more days before he is discovered by a unit searching for dead to bury. Wilson lives, but loses a leg.

The mayor of Sainte-Mère-Église, Alexandre Renaud, is in his bedroom overlooking the town square. He can hear the sound of engines pulling away. It's the German anti-aircraft battery leaving the town.

Ten miles from the beaches, in Caen, the ancient capital of Normandy, 24-year-old schoolteacher André Heintz, aka '57', is wide awake – he hasn't been to bed and is still dressed. The noise of the planes overhead has just woken his mother up. His father and sister sleep on.

'It must be the landing, André, don't you think so?'

'I don't know,' he replies. But André does know. He's a member of the French Resistance and has spent the whole evening watching dispatch riders come and go from German 716th Infantry Division headquarters 100 yards away. He's amazed there hasn't been more movement from there.

Although wirelesses are banned, Heintz has built a crystal radio set so small he can hide it in a tin can, with dried beans on top to disguise it.

Last night he picked up the messages from the BBC specifically for the Resistance in Normandy telling them that the invasion was happening.

André can hear his neighbours calling to each other from their windows, asking what's going on.

'Why are you dressed?' André's mother says, noticing his clothes.

Churchill is still awake and on the phone to Bletchley Park, the headquarters of Britain's code-breakers.

'Has the enemy heard we are coming yet?'

The assistant to the operational head, Edward Travis, tells the prime minister that he's just sent him via teleprinter the text of an intercepted German naval signal.

> ***XX COMUNICA QUE HA ESCRITO CARTA HACE TRES DIAS ANUNCIANDO DE NUEVO REPARTO RANCHOS FRIOS Y X VOMIT BAGS X ETC X A LA X THIRD CANADIAN DIV***
>
> ***Part of message sent by double agent 'Garbo', 3.00am, D-Day***

### *3.00am*

In a suburban house in Hendon, north London, a radio message to Madrid is being tapped out in code by a man named Charles Haines. It's warning that the 3rd Infantry Canadian Division has left their camp in Hampshire and is about to embark on ships. The information is true, but Haines is an MI5 officer and this message is all part of an elaborate plan to fool the Germans. Watching Haines send the message he's composed is a double agent whom the British have code-named Garbo (because he is such a superb actor) and whom the Germans call 'Arabel'. His real name is Juan Pujol and he is a Spaniard who fled Spain to fight fascism.

*For the past two years, Garbo has been sending stories to Germany via a German Intelligence officer in Madrid, suggesting that the Allied invasion will be in Norway and Calais, and that the attack on Calais would be preceded by a diversionary invasion in France. Garbo claims to have a network of 24 agents who send him his information, with intriguing code names such as No 2 The Widow and No 5 Commercial Traveller. If the Germans doubt Garbo's claims, then they only need to make one of their rare reconnaissance flights over south-east England where they could see the landing craft and planes. The fact that they are fakes is undetectable from 10,000 feet.*

*The German Intelligence service believe in Garbo completely, and the small details he sends them, such as how Allied troops have been equipped with vomit bags, only add to his authenticity. Together with his MI5 minders, Juan Pujol has made 'Garbo/Arabel' a volatile Catalan, given to flowery prose and outbursts of temper. Rommel himself is sent the most crucial information supplied by Garbo.*

*Some of the intelligence that Garbo has sent over the past two years has been accurate, but that's merely to boost his credibility. This 3am message being sent by Charles Haines is designed to warn the Germans that D-Day has arrived, but without giving them time to do anything about it.*

Many of the troops heading for Utah Beach on the troop ship USS *Barnett* are painting the names of their home state on their field jackets. William Jones of the 8th Infantry Regiment bumps into an old friend from Tennessee called Thurman Charlton. Charlton asks, 'If you don't make it, is there anything that you want me to tell the people at home?'

'Just tell them that we went down swinging,' Jones says.

USS *Samuel Chase* drops anchor off Omaha Beach.

### *3.15am*

A signal is being sent by General Max Pemsel of the 7th Army to its chief of staff Hans Speidel at Rommel's headquarters at La Roche-Guyon:

'Engine noises audible from sea on east coast of Cotentin. Admiral, Channel Coast, reports ships located by radar off Cherbourg.'

Just as he was unimpressed earlier with his friend von Schramm's excitement over the Verlaine poem, Speidel is unmoved.

Georges Gondrée, the owner of the café by the Caen canal bridge, is still unsure who the men outside his home are. Neither he nor his wife can identify their accents.

There's knocking on his door. Georges opens it and in front of him are two men with smoking Sten guns and blackened faces.

'*Est-ce-qu'il y a des allemands à la maison*?' they ask. Georges says there aren't, and invites them in and takes them down to the cellar – accompanied by plenty of reassurances – and shows them Thérèse and the two children hiding there.

There is silence for a moment, then one of the parachutists says, 'It's all right, chum.'

Georges bursts into tears. They are English! The Gondrées are the first French family to be liberated.

*For the past few years the Gondrées have been passing information they've overheard in sentries' conversations about the bridge to the Resistance in Caen, who in turn pass it to British Intelligence. The detailed information they have supplied is one of the reasons for Major Howard's success.*

*3.40am*

Major General Hans Speidel orders the following message to be sent to General Pemsel:

'C in C West, does not consider this to be a major operation.'

At the Merville Battery an advance party from Lieutenant Colonel Terence Otway's much-reduced 9th Battalion has cleared a path through the minefield with their bare hands and they are now marking the safe path by sitting on the ground and inching backwards, making two lines with their heels in the dirt.

Georges Gondrée is digging in his garden. He's retrieving 98 bottles of champagne that he hid in June 1940 when the Germans invaded. His wife Thérèse's face is grubby from hugging and kissing so many blackened British paratroopers. She will keep her face like that for three days afterwards, telling anyone who asks that the dirt has come from British soldiers and she's proud of it.

## 'The war is like an actress who is getting old. It is less and less photogenic and more and more dangerous'

*3.45am*

At Strongpoint W5 overlooking Utah Beach, medical orderly Corporal Hoffman is reporting to Second Lieutenant Jahnke. About two hours ago 19 American paratroopers from the 101st Airborne Division were captured and have been put in a troop bunker. Hoffman tells Jahnke that he's mystified why the paratroopers are so restless. They keep asking what the time is and when they're going to be moved.

'I wonder what the hurry is?' Jahnke says.

What the paratroopers can't tell their captors is that Normandy is about to be hit by the largest amphibious invasion the world has ever seen – and Strongpoint W5 is slap-bang in the way.

At Sainte-Mère-Église, Private John 'Buck' Steele is still hanging from the church steeple, pretending to be dead. The church bell is tolling. Below him, American parachutists are slowly beginning to infiltrate the town.

Most of the German garrison has pulled out, but Chief Corporal Rudolph May and a colleague are still manning a machine-gun post in the steeple just a few feet from Steele. They've assumed that the motionless American parachutist must be dead, then they hear him say something.

May's colleague wants to shoot him.

'Are you crazy? If you shoot we'll be discovered!' May says.

May hauls Steele onto the roof, cuts off his harness with a pocket-knife and takes him prisoner.

A few days later, Steele will manage to escape and rejoin his division. He will be deaf for weeks because he was so close to the loud ringing of the church bell.

The crew of the troop ship *Princess Ingrid* are trying to persuade the assault troops that to calm their nerves they should have some rum to go with their breakfast of tomatoes and bacon (known as 'train smash' because of the way it looks on the plate).

*4.00am*

Off Omaha Beach, on the boat deck of USS *Samuel Chase*, photographer Robert Capa is standing in silence along with 2,000 other men waiting to clamber aboard landing craft hanging from davits over the ship's side. He's thinking of 'all the good times' and how he's going to get the best pictures of D-Day.

As well as his two cameras, Capa has with him a gas mask, a shovel, an inflatable lifebelt, a supply of condoms to keep his film dry, a silver pocket flask, and over his arm, an expensive Burberry raincoat he bought in London a few days ago.

In early 1944 Capa said in an interview with *Life* magazine, 'The war is like an actress who is getting old. It is less and less photogenic and more and more dangerous.'

A landing craft full of US troops is being lowered over the side of HMS *Empire Windrush*, but it's become stuck directly under the outflow from the ship's head (the toilet). Despite the shouts and yells from the GIs, for half an hour they are covered in urine and excrement.

One American officer recalled, 'The bowels of the ship's company made the most of an opportunity which Englishmen have sought since 1776.'

For about an hour Sainte-Mère-Église has been quiet. The mayor, Alexandre Renaud, looks out of his bedroom window and underneath the trees in the town square he can see the flare of matches, and the glow of cigarettes. He can see the outline of soldiers who seem to be sleeping – but are they German or British?

In the small seaside port of Ouistreham, the Hôtel de Normandie is hit by an RAF bomb. As walls collapse and fire breaks out, the young owner Odette Mousset runs out of the back door and heads for some trees on wasteland nearby. She stands with some other shocked locals as the hotel burns; she and her husband Raoul have only owned it for six months. A few hours earlier some German soldiers who'd been drinking in the café came back to warn her that the British were coming and that she should flee, then headed off in their trucks.

Raoul had spent the night in Caen, but was woken by the sound of bombing in the direction of the coast. He's now driving back to Ouistreham as fast as he can.

Reports are coming in to General Erich Marcks (his birthday celebrations long forgotten) that enemy parachutists are landing between Rouen and Le Havre. In fact, they are more 'Ruperts', the dummy parachutists that are part of Operation Titanic, designed to pull German forces well away from the invasion beaches. Marcks orders the 915th Regiment to intercept them immediately.

> ***Where they have one, we have ten. We have more of everything, and by and large, our stuff is better. I'd say their messkit, motorcycle and helmet are better than ours. But so far none of us has been eaten, run over or crowned by the Jerries, so we can take them – but good!***
>
> ***US* Army Talks *magazine, 10th May 1944***

> ***We knew the invasion would come… We couldn't run and hide, we had to stay, what else was there to do? It***

***was not a very pleasant prospect, knowing you had a good chance to be killed.***

**Lieutenant Heinrich Fürst, 706/8 Festungsdivision**

*4.10am*

Off the coast of Utah and Omaha beaches, US soldiers are climbing aboard the landing craft hanging off the side of their troop ships. Voices can be heard in the dark as men call to friends in other boats – farewells and words of encouragement.

Some of the men, reassured by talk of a naval and air force bombardment, are confident that the landing will be just like any other exercise.

Sergeant Robert Bixler is running his hands through his blond hair and saying to Sergeant John R Slaughter, 'I'm going to land with a comb in one hand and a pass to Paris in the other...'

Twin brothers Roy and Ray Stevens are on the deck of HMS *Empire Javelin.* They are both privates in the 116th Infantry, 29th Division, and their mission is to capture the gully that leads to the village of Vierville-sur-Mer behind Omaha Beach. Their unit, Company A, will be first in. Ray says that he isn't afraid, but Roy admits he is. Ray puts out his hand, but his brother doesn't take it.

'I'll shake your hand in Vierville-sur-Mer at the crossroads there, in the night or the morning sometime,' Roy says. His twin drops his head.

Roy will always regret not taking Ray's hand, as he never saw him again.

*The D-Day planners know how exposed infantrymen like the Stevens brothers will be as they run onto the Normandy beaches, so the intention is that Allied aircraft and the Allied navies will pave the way first. The 600 troops believed to be defending the four-mile stretch of Omaha Beach will be bombarded from the air, and then from the sea. If the German pillboxes and strongpoints aren't destroyed, at the very least the defenders will be traumatised by the intense shelling. Then 35,000 US assault troops will move in, consisting of two divisions – the 'Fighting 1st' and the 29th 'Blue and Gray', who both served with distinction in the trenches of the Great War. There is considerable rivalry between the two divisions. When a regiment from the 29th passed men of the 1st loading onto landing craft back in England on the 5th June chanting, 'Twenty-nine, Let's Go!' they shouted back, 'Go ahead, Twenty-nine, we're right behind you!'*

*Intelligence reports suggest that almost half the German 716th Division are in fact Polish ex-prisoners of war captured on the Eastern Front and with little incentive to fight to the death for the Nazi cause.*

*By the end of D-Day, the Americans plan to have a bridgehead sixteen miles wide and five miles deep.*

*But the strategy for Omaha Beach is flawed from the start. In March, the German 352nd Infantry Division arrived on the Normandy coast to boost the defences. The 352nd are well equipped and well trained and have experience of fighting in Russia. The Allies discovered the presence of the 352nd two days ago, but by then it was too late to change the invasion plans.*

## 'Bastards! Bastards! Bastards!'

### *4.15am*

As it gets lighter, it seems to Alexandre Renaud that his town has been taken over by Hollywood gangsters. The mayor of

Sainte-Mère-Église can see that the soldiers under the trees are Americans with loose, scruffy uniforms, grimy faces and revolvers hanging from their belts.

There's a knock on his door and a paratroop captain offers him chewing gum, and asks where the headquarters of the German commander is. Renaud shows him. The Americans kick the door down, but the commander and all his men have gone.

For four years Alexandre Renaud has been the spokesman for the town. He has been bullied, shouted at, even threatened with execution, but he has always managed to defend the rights of his townsfolk. It seems their ordeal is over. Sainte-Mère-Église is the first French town to be liberated.

### *4.25am*

Lieutenant Colonel Terence Otway and his depleted 9th Battalion of 150 paratroopers are at the barbed-wire perimeter of the Merville Battery. Otway is looking to the sky as three gliders with 66 men and a team of explosives experts are due to land on top of the battery – an extremely dangerous and audacious move. Otway is supposed to send up star shells to guide them in, but they too have been lost.

Otway has divided the paratroopers into four assault groups. One company is led by Lieutenant Alan Jefferson who is rallying his men by telling them that in order to protect their wives and sweethearts, Hitler must be defeated. Two of Jefferson's men are terrified because they've lost their rifles and they've been told that anyone losing their rifle will be court-martialled. Jefferson reassures them that they'll soon be carrying German rifles. Looking at the grass-covered bomb-proof bunkers in the moonlight, Jefferson thinks they look like squatting toads, and 'somehow nasty'.

> ***The sea was rough and it was dark. The navy guys had remarked that they were glad they were navy at this point. I'm sure they were. We got V for Victory signs from them as they helped us over the side. Victory didn't seem possible at the time. Survival maybe.***
>
> ***Bruce Bradley, radio operator, 29th Field Artillery Battalion***

### *4.30am*

The two Royal Navy midget submarines *X20* and *X23* have surfaced a quarter of a mile off the British beaches. Each has a telescopic mast that is slowly extending to a height of 18 feet. These navigational aids for the landing craft approaching the British beaches make them vulnerable to friendly fire. The crew of *X23* plan to fly a large ensign to make it clear they are Royal Navy.

The American 116th Infantry are in their landing craft and starting their two-hour journey to Omaha.

Twenty-five miles out from his base at Le Havre, Lieutenant Commander Heinrich Hoffmann is on the bridge of his E-boat *T-28*. Sailing with him at a speed of about 25 knots are two boats under his command (he's decided that the other two aren't ready to do battle with an invasion fleet he's sure is heading their way). Above him he can see scores of Allied planes heading south; they are clearly not interested in him as they are flying so high. He reckons they're looking for bigger targets.

At the Merville Battery, right on time, two of the three expected gliders appear silently overhead. Then a German anti-aircraft gun opens up and a glider is hit in the tail and crash-lands about 100 yards away. The other disappears into the gloom (the third had crashed in England).

'Get ready, men,' Otway says, then, 'Get in! Get in!'

Alan Jefferson's unit of seven men are under machine-gun fire from the bunkers and watchtowers, zigzagging as they run for No 1 gun. The Germans are firing at waist height as they pour through a gap in the wire. One of the men, Private Sidney Capon, is shouting, 'Bastards! Bastards! Bastards!'

Jefferson is hit in the leg, and falls.

At No 3 gun, Sergeant Major Barney Ross's unit can see very little in the dark. They spot some air vents and drop grenades down them. By the time Ross and his men make their way round the front of the emplacement, the gunners have had enough and are easily taken prisoner. The Russian conscripts manning gun Nos 1 and 4 surrender soon after. Fierce hand-to-hand fighting is continuing in the trenches and dugouts.

Churchill is on the phone to Bletchley Park again.

'How's it going? Has anything gone wrong yet...?'

### *4.45am*

The assault on the Merville Battery is over. The urgency now is to let the navy know that the battery has been taken, otherwise HMS *Arethusa* will start shelling in half an hour. Otway sends a yellow signal flare into the sky and an RAF plane spots it and waggles its wings. As the signals officer's rather battered pigeon has somehow survived the assault, a victory message is tied to its leg and it is sent on its way.

### *4.50am*

Private Stanley Gardner is in a landing craft about to be lowered down the side of HMS *Empire Battleaxe.* He's looking at the French coast seven miles away – Royal Navy shells and RAF strikes have turned it into a blazing inferno. Then the order comes over the tannoy for the landing craft to be lowered.

Gardner wrote later, 'We made ourselves as comfortable as possible, some sitting, some standing but all singing. New songs and old – sentimental – patriotic and ballads – but we all sang.'

Outside the village of Saint-Côme-du-Mont about five miles from Utah Beach, men of the 6th German Paratroop Regiment are looking in amazement at fields covered in different coloured American parachutes. They get out their knives and start cutting them up to make silk scarves.

Back at their base, other members of the regiment are waking up to discover that all their French drivers (who'd been forced to join the German Army in 1940) have deserted. Rumours are spreading round the regiment that the drivers have been tipped off by the French Resistance that the invasion of Europe is imminent.

### *4.55am*

Lieutenant Colonel Otway needs to get his men out of the Merville Battery as quickly as possible, in case the *Arethusa* still decides to bombard it. He's gathered all his troops together, and as they don't know the safe route out of the minefield, Otway asks the German POWs to lead the way. They refuse, so Otway tries a different tactic.

'Well, OK, we're going to make you walk forward and if you don't show us the way through the mines, we're going to start shooting the ground and you're going to lose your feet – and maybe the mines will go up too.'

That does the trick.

*The landing craft destined for Utah Beach are starting their two-hour journey to shore. Utah is ten miles from Omaha and is the westernmost of all the Allied beaches. It is also the least intimidating; it has a gentle slope and its biggest obstacle is a sea wall that ranges from four to twelve feet high. The object is for the US 8th Infantry to push inland from Utah and make contact with the 82nd Airborne around Sainte-Mère-Église, who should be protecting them from a German counter-attack.*

*As with Omaha Beach, the assault will begin with an air and naval bombardment to deal with the German defences, then troops and amphibious tanks will arrive. Engineers will demolish the beach obstacles and blow holes in the sea wall to allow the tanks through. The plan is to land 21,000 men and 1,700 vehicles before it gets dark.*

*For the majority of soldiers, the meticulous planning for the assault on Utah Beach will prove to be a complete waste of time.*

Twenty-four-year-old Captain George Mabry is in 8th Infantry and therefore part of the first wave onto Utah. He's standing in the bow of his landing craft, so excited to see action he's oblivious to the fact that he's getting soaked from the spray. The men behind him have their heads well down below the gunwale. Mabry believes that as an officer he must lead from the front, never asking his troops to do something he wouldn't do himself. When he left the States in 1943, he told his wife that he wouldn't be coming back. Mabry is sure he'll be killed in France.

*The first wave consists of 20 LCVPs with a 30-man assault team in each. LCVPs are more commonly known as Higgins Boats, named after their designer and manufacturer Andrew Higgins. New Orleans-based Higgins made his money in the Prohibition era by designing fast, flat-bottomed boats for Louisiana rum smugglers – and then, with great cheek, selling the same boats to the US Coast Guard so they could give chase. It's said that Hitler himself admires the LCVP, calling Higgins 'the new Noah'. Because of German interest in his work, Higgins has an armed guard outside his house.*

*The first wave of Higgins Boats is supported by four LCTs carrying 32 Shermans. The second wave has another 32 Higgins Boats carrying engineers and demolition teams. The last two waves bring in bulldozer tanks and armoured vehicles.*

Mabry's vessel is what's known as a 'free boat': it can join any wave of the assault. It's making good headway and has already overtaken the second wave. Through the gloom, Mabry can make out some of the ships that make up the Utah naval bombardment – USS *Tuscaloosa*, USS *Nevada*, USS *Augusta*, USS *Quincy* and HMS *Black Prince*. They are due to start firing in 45 minutes.

In a landing craft not far from Captain Mabry is his divisional commander Brigadier General Theodore 'Ted' Roosevelt Jr, the oldest son of the 26th president of the United States and a distant cousin of the current president. In his office in England, George Mabry had spent hours pouring over the plans for the assault. General Roosevelt was unimpressed.

'What the hell are you up to, George? Quit worrying. Whatever you plan, the boys are just going right in there and will throw in all they've got. So what do you want with all this paper?'

*Roosevelt was born frail and with poor eyesight but distinguished himself in the First World War, being gassed and wounded twice in action. In 1941 Roosevelt re-enlisted and led the invasions of North Africa, Sicily and Corsica, carrying only a walking stick and a .45 calibre pistol. He is well loved by the troops who are used to his loud voice, once described as being 'a few decibels higher than a moose call'. At 57, Roosevelt will be the oldest soldier on the Normandy beaches.*

*Roosevelt typifies the spirit and arrogance of the 'Fighting 1st' Infantry Division, whose watchwords are 'No mission too difficult. No sacrifice too great'. The general has managed to lose four life preservers so far on the crossing from England.*

### *5.00am*

At Rommel's headquarters at La Roche-Guyon, in an anteroom where only a few hours before they'd been plotting the overthrow of Hitler, Rommel's chief of staff Major General Hans Speidel is having coffee with Major Wilhelm von Schramm, Rommel's naval advisor Admiral Friedrich Ruge, and intelligence officer Colonel Anton Staubwasser. They are discussing the reports of enemy paratroopers across the coastal region. Speidel is quiet and preoccupied.

'We must wait and see and find out the magnitude of all this before committing further forces.'

About 60 US paratroopers are being held in the small village church at Saint-Georges-de-Bohon, about five miles from the coast. The east end by the altar is being used as a first-aid station for both American and German wounded. First Lieutenant Martin Pöppel, a paratrooper with the German 6th Parachute Regiment, is watching the Americans, fascinated. With their shaven heads and 'beefy faces' he thinks they look like escapees from the New York prison Sing Sing. Could they really be the American elite troops? Pöppel is unimpressed by the standard of their weapons but is enjoying their cigarettes.

> ***After hours at sea we were suddenly aroused by what seemed to be all hell breaking loose, the Navy opened up with everything they had and the noise was terrific, and it seemed as if you could have picked the shells from the sky, and momentarily I felt sorry for the enemy, thinking they could not survive this sort of barrage (how wrong can one be...)***
>
> ***Sergeant R A White, the Hampshire 'Tigers' Regiment***

### *5.05am*

Ronald Seaborne is a Royal Navy telegraphist with 50th TT Division. His job is to land with the invading troops and send back situation reports to HMS *Belfast*, for example the positions of her targets and information on how accurate her gunners have been. Seaborne is in the first landing craft to pull away from the transport ship *Princess Ingrid*. It's turning in circles and soon everyone on board is regretting their breakfast of fried eggs and rum. In the middle of the landing craft is a jeep – the pride and joy of a brigadier who is sitting comfortably inside.

### *5.10am*

Lieutenant Colonel Otway has moved the British and German dead and wounded to a barn the other side of the minefield. There's relief that the operation is over, but it has been at a cost.

Sergeant Major Barney Ross is looking around thinking, 'My God, what's happened to all the guys?'

Two hundred Germans and Russians have been killed and 22 have surrendered. Of the 150 men in Otway's force that began the assault, 75 are dead or wounded.

*The Merville Battery is not what it seemed. It had been feared that its guns would be able to inflict great losses on the troops on the beaches. In fact, the bunkers contain 75mm First World War vintage Czech guns and not fierce 150mm guns at all.*

*And the men who captured the guns don't have the expertise to destroy them properly. Later today, once the 9th Parachute Battalion, Parachute Regiment moves out, they'll be retaken and repaired by the Germans. The Merville Battery will continue to be fought over for the rest of June.*

Ronald Seaborne, who is used to the sea, is watching with amusement as the vomit from seasick troops is spraying all over the brigadier and his jeep. The brigadier is shouting to the men that from now on they must throw up on the other side of the boat.

Although the British and Canadian troops have shorter journeys in their landing craft, as their ships have anchored closer to the shore than the Americans, for all of the thousands heading to the beaches, it's a miserable and demoralising ride.

The men are using their helmets not only to vomit into, but also to bail water out of their craft. Ten Higgins Boats heading for Omaha Beach will sink before they get there.

Most of the men on board the Higgins Boats are standing, as their heavy backpacks make it impossible to sit down. Most can't see anything, and those at the sides can only see the rising and falling waves. Spray has soaked their clothing. Some are using capes to protect themselves from the cold and wet. Some are bickering; most are silent. Many are thinking about what lies in store for them. In a Higgins Boat heading for Omaha Beach, a young soldier asks Private Paul McCormick, 'Mac, when a bullet hits you, does it go all the way through?'

On another Higgins Boat, the men of Company C of the 2nd Ranger Battalion are singing in honour of their colleague Sergeant Walter Geldon. Today is his wedding anniversary. He will be dead before the day is out.

> ***I am not proud of the fact, nor will I ever cease regretting that I did not take the tanks all the way to the beach.***
>
> ***Ensign R L Harkey, LCT 602***

## 'There are bound to be tremendous casualties'

*5.15am*

As the sun begins to rise, the troops in the landing craft destined for Omaha Beach are just able to make out its high cliffs and 50-yard-high bluffs.

Two men know these waters very well. Over 30 times in the past few months, British commandos Captain Logan Scott-Bowden and Sergeant Bruce Ogden-Smith have swum at night from midget submarines to take samples of the sand on Normandy beaches. It's vital work – the texture of the sand determines whether it will support tanks.

> *No one had believed that they could get on and off the beaches undetected, so a dummy run was arranged. Scott-Bowden and Ogden-Smith swam to a Norfolk beach at night from an LCT, while*

*sentries patrolled on the look-out for them. They collected sand samples and were never spotted.*

*But they have had some close shaves in France. On a visit to Omaha, then code-named Beach 313, a German sentry tripped over their equipment but they managed to escape undetected; the presence of the sentry proved that section of the beach wasn't mined.*

*In January, US General Omar Bradley had expressed concern about a stretch of sand on Omaha; that night Scott-Bowden and Ogden-Smith landed there and the next day presented the stunned General with a sample of the sand. But what the men had seen on Omaha disturbed them.*

*Scott-Bowden said, 'Sir, I hope you don't mind my saying it, but this beach is a very formidable proposition indeed and there are bound to be tremendous casualties.'*

*Bradley put his hand on his shoulder.*

*'I know, my boy, I know.'*

*What they had seen were high cliffs and bluffs at the top of the five-mile-long curved beach. Above the sand is a shingle embankment with a wire-covered sea wall behind. The US troops' job is to break through the obstacles on the sand and fight their way across 400 yards of beach to five gullies that provide natural exits. All five are heavily defended by 15 strongpoints that are designed to be almost impossible to detect out at sea. The Germans have an uninterrupted view of landing craft coming ashore. The aim is for 92 landing craft to land on Omaha Beach in the first three minutes after H-Hour. The largest number of landings will be in front of the defences protecting the exits from the beach.*

Eighteen-year-old Corporal Franz Gockel has been stationed at the defences at Omaha Beach since October last year. He was there when Rommel inspected their position in January. The field marshal was angry that they were unfinished and had warned, 'If they come, they'll come here.'

Gockel is sitting in his machine-gun position, shivering and looking forward to when the cook brings him some more mulled wine. His strongpoint has been told that a fleet of ships has been sighted coming their way.

Captain Logan Scott-Bowden and Sergeant Bruce Ogden-Smith, who in January landed on Omaha to reconnoitre the beach and then report its dangers to General Bradley, are in a pilot boat helping to guide the landing craft to shore. Today Ogden-Smith should be at Buckingham Palace receiving a Military Medal from the King. Yesterday his wife was about to leave their home in Wales for the ceremony when she was told that her husband was unavoidably detained (she has no idea what his secret missions involve).

One of the landing craft crew is pointing out to Captain Scott-Bowden that the 16 LCTs have stopped 5,000 yards out from the beach and are about to launch their Duplex Drive tanks. Some of the waves are now six feet high.

'It's far too rough – they should go right in!' Scott-Bowden exclaims.

*A key element of the plan for the assault on Omaha Beach is the landing at H-Hour (6.30am) of 32 Duplex Drive tanks developed by the British.*

*These tanks, if they do their job, will make the infantry's job a great deal easier and will shock the German defenders – these are tanks that can swim.*

*A modified Sherman tank is fitted with a canvas side that wraps right round it, containing tubes that when inflated with compressed air allows it to float. The Sherman's engine is connected to two propellers that give it a top speed of four knots. They look like floating canvas bathtubs.*

*The Duplex Drive tanks have great potential as a weapon of surprise, but the British Admiralty has declared them unseaworthy. They are vulnerable to being swamped by waves or by the wash of other craft (their canvas side only protrudes a foot above the water). The tank commander can see over the canvas but the rest of the crew remain in the tank. If it sinks, there is a real danger they go down with it. The decision whether to launch them at sea or take them to land is a crucial one.*

Eight LCTs have dropped their ramps and their Duplex Drive tanks are slowly entering the sea. Scott-Bowden watches as one by one the 30-ton tanks travel for 100 yards and are then swamped, sinking like stones. One tank commander and his gunner are bracing themselves against the side of the canvas to stop it collapsing. But they too are swamped by waves and rapidly disappear.

But still the tanks keep coming.

A naval officer on LCT *549* is advising Sergeant John Sertell to keep his tank on board as it has damage to its canvas side. Sertell insists that the Duplex Drive's bilge pump will deal with any water if it leaks. He gets in his tank and proceeds down the ramp. A patrol boat will recover his body later today and return it to LCT *549*.

Already, 27 of the 32 tanks that the 1st Infantry Division is expecting to help them take Omaha are at the bottom of the Channel. Over 100 men have drowned. The eight LCTs that are taking the Duplex Drives straight to the beach will do so without losing a single tank.

In a bunker overlooking the eastern end of Omaha Beach, Major Werner Pluskat of the newly arrived 352nd Division is looking out to sea with his artillery binoculars. He literally steps back in amazement at what he sees – the horizon is filled with ships. How could this fleet have got here without anyone knowing? Pluskat calls Major Block, an intelligence officer at divisional headquarters.

'There must be 10,000 ships out there. It's unbelievable! Fantastic!'

'Look, Pluskat, are you really sure? The Americans and British together don't have that many ships.'

'For Christ's sake, come and look for yourself!'

Pluskat throws down the phone.

### *5.25am*

Twenty-four-year-old Private Joseph Blaylock Sr is in an LCT heading to Utah Beach. He can see a transport plane returning from dropping paratroopers in France spiralling out of control, having been hit by a German battery. It crashes into the sea about 400 yards from them. The soldiers shout to the young navy coxswain at the helm to change course and look for survivors, but he carries on. Blaylock and his fellow artillerymen take a quick show of hands, and the coxswain is outnumbered. Reluctantly he turns the boat towards the rubber life raft with three grateful crewmen on board that's now floating among the wreckage.

### *5.27am*

HMS *Belfast* starts the bombardment of Juno Beach, which in less than two hours' time will be the destination of the 3rd Canadian Division. One of the crew describes the *Belfast* as looking 'like a broody hen with a swarm of landing craft round her'.

Aboard USS *Ancon*, anchored off Omaha Beach, Lieutenant Arthur Newmyer is wrapping up his briefing to the crew over the public address system.

'The naval bombardment is about to begin. H-Hour is fast approaching. The liberation of Europe is on the way!'

In his pocket, Major C K King of the 2nd Battalion, East Yorkshire Regiment has written out some lines from Shakespeare's *Henry V* to inspire his men in their landing craft.

'From this day to the ending of the world,
But we in it shall be remembered.
We few, we happy few, we band of brothers;
For he today that sheds his blood with me
Shall be my brother; be he ne'er so vile,
This day shall gentle his condition;
And gentlemen in England now a-bed
Shall think themselves accurs'd they were not here,
And hold their manhoods cheap whiles any speaks
That fought with us upon Saint Crispin's day.'

### *5.30am*

The BBC newsreader Stuart Hibberd has been sleeping in a dormitory at Broadcasting House for a number of days to be on hand for the start of D-Day. He is now wide awake – the sound of thousands of planes over central London is shaking the building. Hibberd knows that the wait is over. His colleague, newsreader John Snagge, has been assigned the task of reading the communiqué from SHAEF giving the official announcement. Snagge hasn't been able to leave Broadcasting House for the last ten days – even when he goes to the canteen or the toilet he has to let someone know where he's going. Snagge is already on his way to the Ministry of Information studio in Maddox Street, from where he will broadcast the communiqué.

*The BBC is well prepared. The Corporation has created a team of war correspondents to report from D-Day and the military campaign that will follow. These reporters will be equipped with a new lightweight midget portable disc recorder, which was tested in battle by the reporter Wynford Vaughan-Thomas at Anzio in January. It carries 12 double-sided discs giving a total of an hour's recording. The correspondent sends the report via either a field transmitter or a plane back to London. A mock battle called Operation Spartan had even been staged, designed to test the skills of the reporters. A new and innovative programme called* War Report *will start this evening after the nine o'clock news.*

News of the invasion has reached the Berghof – Adolf Hitler's headquarters in the Bavarian Alps, but no one wants to wake the Führer to tell him.

*Over the past few weeks Hitler has been very relaxed. Even the news of the fall of Rome to the Allies hasn't troubled him.*

*A few hours ago the Propaganda Minister Joseph Goebbels wrote in his diary, 'All in all, the mood is like the good old times.'*

*Yesterday afternoon Hitler and Goebbels had walked through the woods to the Berghof's tea house for pastries, and discussed the new V1 flying bombs (*Vergeltungswaffe Eins *or Revenge Weapon One, which will be nicknamed 'doodle-bugs' by the British). More than 50 launch sites have been built on the Channel coast. Hitler told Goebbels that the attacks on London will start in a few days, and that he has 400 at his disposal.*

From his house in Caen, French Resistance member André Heintz is still watching the headquarters of the German 716th

Infantry Division. A number of vehicles are now leaving and the noise of their engines has woken up his mother again. Once more she asks what's happening, and André again lies, and says that he doesn't know.

> ***Aboard the* Tuscaloosa *the air is acrid with powder and a fine spray of wadding comes down on us like lava ash. Everywhere there is noise. When we fire, the deck trembles under our feet, and the joints of the ship seem to creak and stretch. When a whole turret is discharged the teeth almost rattle in one's head.***
>
> ***Colonel David Bruce's diary, 6th June 1944***

## 'When Hoffmann gets to a place, things start happening'

*5.34am*

German E-boat *T-28* is travelling at 28 knots in a light sea under a cloudy but clear sky. The sun is slowly coming up. Her skipper, Lieutenant Commander Heinrich Hoffmann, is staring at a horizon that for some reason has suddenly become hazy. Then he sees a plane fly out of the mist. Hoffmann realises that it's no mist – it's a smokescreen.

'What is going on behind there?' Hoffmann wonders. He signals to the other two E-boats with him to get in single file behind *T-28*. His little flotilla is going to pierce the smoke.

*5.36am*

Eleven thousand yards from Utah Beach, USS *Tuscaloosa* is unleashing her eight-inch guns against the 30 German batteries on and around the beach. It's earlier than planned because the German shore batteries have already started firing at them. The landing craft are heading slowly to the shore under a canopy of Allied shells.

In Strongpoint W5 Second Lieutenant Jahnke and his men have their hands pressed to their ears against the sound of the barrage. Many are screaming in terror. Most of Jahnke's beach defences have been torn to pieces. He looks out to sea in disbelief at the Allied armada.

'Rommel's blundered!' Jahnke thinks. They have come at low tide after all.

In the villages around Utah Beach, French civilians are fleeing the bombardment.

### *5.37am*

The three German E-boats of Hoffmann's flotilla are bursting out of the smokescreen at 28 knots, and find themselves in the middle of about 20 Allied warships, six of them battleships, all poised to start the bombardment of Sword Beach. Hoffmann can see other ships in the distance.

'It's impossible. There can't be that many ships in the world,' says one of Hoffmann's crew.

The Allied fleet hasn't yet seen him. Hoffmann's flotilla is outnumbered and outgunned, but he doesn't hesitate – he gives the signal to attack.

'*Toni Dora Six*!' 'Fire six torpedoes!'

Eighteen torpedoes are now speeding through the dark water.

Two are passing between HMS *Warspite* and HMS *Ramillies*; one narrowly misses HMS *Virago*. HMS *Largs* is going full astern and a torpedo passes a few feet in front of her bows. Two hundred yards away on *Largs*' port bow, on the bridge of the Norwegian destroyer HNoMS *Svenner*, her captain, Lieutenant Commander Tore Holthe, gives the order for 'full ahead and full port rudder!' But the *Svenner* is stationary and Holthe knows that she won't be able to move in time. Next to him, Lieutenant Desmond Lloyd is looking through his binoculars at the torpedo heading straight for them.

'How high will I fly?' he thinks.

*Svenner* takes a direct hit amidships and oil explodes over her decks.

Massive columns of water are erupting around the darting E-boats as the fleet retaliates. Hoffmann's crew hit back with their guns but then *T-28* heads for the safety of the smoke-screen, weaving as she goes to make herself a harder target. The other E-boats follow. Hoffmann instructs his wireless operator to warn his headquarters at Le Havre about the fleet and especially the landing craft he saw – it's clear to him that this is the long-awaited invasion. The message never gets through as *T-28*'s transmitter has been hit.

Not far from the *Svenner*, 15-year-old seaman T Osbourne is sheltering in the gun pit of the rescue tug HMS *Assiduous*. He is terrified by the gunfire and the tracer flashing through the sky. Two older crew members have their arms protectively around Osbourne, as he is shaking so much.

### *5.40am*

The *Svenner* has broken in half and is sinking fast. Lieutenant Commander Holthe gives the order to abandon ship. Many of her lifeboats are destroyed, but some smaller life rafts have already been thrown overboard. The *Svenner* has a huge hole in her side and some of those who jumped overboard are being sucked into it.

British commando Captain Kenneth Wright is watching from a transport ship, appalled. The *Svenner*'s bow and stern are folding together; to Wright she looks just like a pocket-knife closing.

### *5.45am*

In Caen, André Heintz's mother is burying her jewels in the cellar. First the sound of aircraft had alarmed her, then it was the Germans' trucks in the street outside their house, and now there are explosions on the coast just ten miles away. She knows something terrible is happening. She's already boiled some potatoes in case the gas is cut off, and filled their bath with water in case that's cut off too.

Major Werner Pluskat is in a bunker at the eastern end of Omaha Beach and is realising with terror that the ships out to sea, which have sailed steadily towards them for the last hour, are getting themselves in a position to fire. He can see the massive guns elevate and swing towards him. For the second time in the past hour he phones Major Block at divisional headquarters for permission to fire first.

'No, no! We're too short of ammunition. No gun must fire until the troops are nearing the beaches.'

### *5.50am*

Lieutenant Commander Holthe has jumped from the bridge of the *Svenner* and is in the water clinging onto a piece of wreckage. He watches the stern of his brand-new ship sink slowly into the English Channel.

Although the *Svenner*'s stern sinks, her bow remains afloat, pointing to the sky for the next few days, a grim welcome for the hundreds of troops heading to Sword Beach. Forty-four of the *Svenner*'s Norwegian crew die.

USS *Texas* starts her bombardment of Omaha Beach using her 14-inch guns. She's joined by 17 other warships from both the US Navy and Royal Navy. The noise is extraordinary and the firepower of this mighty fleet impressive. Associated Press combat reporter Don Whitehead can see that the troops in his landing craft are shaking as they pass the battleships – not with fear, but as a result of the concussion from the navy's big guns. In the dim light of early morning it is hard for the gunners to see the targets, which are already well hidden in the cliffs and gullies.

*Whitehead and the other journalists on the landing craft prefer to call themselves 'combat correspondents' rather than 'war correspondents' because they get so close to the action. For Whitehead it's 'a step higher in the correspondents' caste system'.*

Captain John Gower of HMS *Swift* is ignoring his orders not to up anchor and pick up survivors, and is heading towards his sister ship the *Svenner*.

### *5.58am*

Major Gerden Johnson of the 12th Infantry asks the skipper of his landing craft what battleship it is they're sailing past. Just as he's told that it's USS *Nevada*, she opens fire just 800 yards away with a broadside. Johnson's landing craft heels over from the shock wave. The *Nevada*'s guns will soon get so hot the paint will peel off the barrels, revealing the blue steel underneath.

Nineteen ships from Task Force U are now firing on the German batteries on Utah Beach.

## 'That's a fat lot of use, all it will do is wake them up'

*6.00am*

The dawn is bringing problems for the men of the Oxfordshire and Buckinghamshire Light Infantry at the Bénouville bridges. German snipers have them in their sights. Even their first-aid post is being targeted. An orderly is hit in the chest. Medical officer Dr John Vaughan shakes his fist at the sniper and shouts, 'This isn't cricket!'

In what will prove too late for many, the BBC is broadcasting a warning from General Eisenhower to French citizens within 35 miles of the Normandy coast.

'The lives of many of you depend on the speed with which you obey. Leave your towns at once – stay off the roads – go on foot and taking nothing with you that is difficult to carry. Do not gather in groups which may be mistaken for enemy troops.'

HMS *Stork* is signalling to Lord Lovat's ship, which is heading for Sword Beach: 'Good morning, commandos, and bloody good luck.'

Lovat sends a reply: 'Thanks; think we are going to bloody well need it.'

Lord Lovat looks at Lieutenant Commander Rupert Curtis, the flotilla officer on the LCI carrying 4 Commando, and thinks that Curtis probably feels lonely after seven hours of straining his eyes in the darkness, trying to keep to the mine-swept passage. In fact, Curtis is feeling a sense of elation.

'How glad I am to have been in this; how glad I am to be alive and how I should like to be in England just for a moment to know what our people at home are thinking about Mr Churchill's electrifying news.'

Curtis hoists his battle ensign.

General Eisenhower is being woken to be told that Admiral Ramsay has phoned with news that the naval side of the invasion is going well so far.

'What's your course, coxswain?' Lieutenant Robert Anderson of the US 29th Division is shouting from the stern of a Higgins Boat heading to Omaha Beach.

'Two-twenty, sir.'

'Then steer two-twenty, damn it! Don't steer all over the damn ocean!'

Even though Anderson has experienced landings under fire at Sicily and Salerno, he's very nervous. For his men this is their first hostile action.

Watching them is the writer and war correspondent Ernest Hemingway. On his head is a large scar, incurred not in the war, but in a car accident on 24th May, in a blacked-out London street after a drunken 'End of the World' party at Robert Capa's flat.

In front of Hemingway is TNT wrapped up securely in life jackets, so it can float in water, and bazookas wrapped up in something waterproof that reminds him of ladies' raincoats. The weight of the equipment in the bow means that the craft is hitting the rough sea full on. Many of the men are seasick – all are drenched.

Those who aren't being sick are watching the battleship *Texas* fire her 14-inch guns at the German batteries. The shells have set fire to gorse on the cliffs and the smoke is hugging the ground as it drifts east. The shock wave from the guns punches Hemingway's head like a boxing glove. He discovers that if he opens his mouth it doesn't hurt as much. He looks at the troops around him. Under their round helmets they look to him like medieval pikemen going into battle. The sea is covered with landing craft.

*The British troops in their landing craft have been issued with 200 French francs, chewing gum, seasick pills, two 24-hour ration packs, a tin of Taverner and Rutledge boiled sweets, waterproof containers for watches and other valuables, and two condoms to protect their rifle barrels from the sand and seawater. Back at base they were given lectures on how to behave towards French civilians – 'do not mention their defeat in 1940' – and given a pamphlet to reinforce the point.*

*'There is a fairly widespread belief that the French are a gay, frivolous people with no morals and few convictions. This is especially not true at the present time.'*

*The GI newspaper* Stars and Stripes *has some helpful advice: 'Don't be surprised if a Frenchman steps up and kisses you. That doesn't mean he's queer. It means he's French and darn glad to see you.'*

On the cliffs at the eastern end of Omaha Beach, Major Werner Pluskat's bunker is being bombarded by shells from the US Navy and Royal Navy. The bunker is rocking with the explosions. All the gunners are lying on the floor covered in dust, and Pluskat is dazed and barely able to speak. The phone is ringing. It's divisional headquarters again, asking for updates.

'Please give an exact location of where the bombs are falling,' says a voice Pluskat doesn't recognise.

'For God's sake, they're falling all over! What do you expect me to do, go out and measure the craters with a ruler?' he shouts back.

### *6.05am*

High above Omaha Beach, B-17 Flying Fortresses and B-24 Liberators are coming in from the sea and releasing their bomb loads. Henry Tarcza, the bomb aimer in Flying Fortress 'El's Bells', can feel the plane bounce and shake as their bombs explode. This is the only time that Tarcza has experienced this, in the scores of missions he has undertaken, such is the concentration of bombs – more than 13,000 are dropped.

But they are all missing the German defences. The cloud cover is making it impossible for the bomb aimers to see their targets, and furthermore they've been briefed that their own troops will only be '400 yards to one mile offshore during the attack', so they're delaying the release of their bombs. Some of the bombs are falling as far as three miles away.

Watching from his pilot vessel, British commando Captain Logan Scott-Bowden says out loud, 'That's a fat lot of use, all it will do is wake them up.'

It's worse than that. Some bombs have fallen on Vierville-sur-Mer, hitting a number of houses and the village bakery, killing the baker's nine-month-old baby.

On Omaha, Corporal Franz Gockel is hiding underneath his machine-gun's wooden platform and praying throughout the bombardment. They are the same prayers he used to say when he and his family were being bombed by the RAF at home in the Ruhr. He can't believe that he and his colleagues have survived. Peering through the slit in the concrete overlooking the beach, Gockel can now clearly see the invasion fleet stretching into the distance.

'Hell, they've got more ships that we've got soldiers,' he thinks.

### *6.07am*

The air attack on German positions on and around Utah Beach is beginning. Three hundred and forty-one medium bombers called B-26 Marauders are approaching the area at a height of 4,000 feet. Their task is harder than the bombardment at Omaha, as the crews know that US paratroopers are in the countryside behind the beach so they cannot delay dropping their bombs, neither can they release them too early, or they'll hit the 856 ships and landing craft of Task Force U out at sea. So they're flying parallel to the shoreline and 10,000 feet lower than the bombers at Omaha.

*The Marauders were briefed just after midnight by Colonel Wilson R Wood. (If they'd been told any earlier, they could have been shot down over France, captured and forced to divulge D-Day secrets.)*

*'I don't care if any of your aircraft are not a hundred per cent. You'll fly them this morning, and you'll get over that beach whatever happens, and you'll take any risk to get right on your targets and give those boys in the boats every bit of help you can. You will go in at any altitude necessary to get the job done... Let's kick the hell out of everything Nazi that's left!'*

Strongpoint W5 is the German defence post at the centre of Utah Beach. It still has its 19 American prisoners, eager to be moved, as they know what's going to happen on the beach in less than two hours. In his headquarters (which is merely a bunker in a hole in the sand behind an anti-tank wall), Second Lieutenant Arthur Jahnke is granting extra rations for his men as they have plenty of food, enough to last them a week. Jahnke looks out to sea and spots a perfect formation of USAAF Marauders.

'They're going to cross the coast north of us,' he says out loud. But suddenly the bombers turn and make straight for Strongpoint W5. Jahnke can see the bombs tumble out.

There's an explosion and Jahnke is flung across the dugout.

### *6.09am*

'Everything is wrecked, *Herr Leutnant*! Everything is wrecked! We've got to surrender!'

On Utah, Strongpoint W5's elderly mess corporal's assistant is in a panic. But Jahnke has no intention of surrendering. He orders his men to shift the rubble and start digging trenches. Then another wave of Marauders appears, flying just feet over the sea.

> ***There was no time to think as I performed my mechanical task. Next cordite charge in hoist... bend... lift onto tray... rammed home... breech and interceptor closed... BANG! Recoil... casing ejected... air blast expels fumes... smell of cordite fills the turret... next cordite charge in hoist...***
>
> ***17-year-old Royal Marine Leslie Garrett, HMS*** **Diadem**

### *6.20am*

The naval bombardment of Sword Beach has been going on for half an hour. HMS *Diadem*'s captain has hit upon an ingenious way to increase her range. He has moved fuel and water from the port to the starboard side of the hold, thus tilting the ship away from the coast, giving the guns a longer range.

Second Lieutenant Jahnke in Strongpoint W5 has survived the Marauders' repeated attacks. Looking out to sea from Utah, he spots landing craft approaching. He has no communications, so he orders a soldier to cycle to an artillery regiment two miles away, with instructions that they start shelling the beach. Within minutes, the soldier, pedalling furiously, is spotted and pursued by an Allied fighter, and machine-gunned to the ground.

### *6.25am*

Four hundred yards from Utah Beach, Captain George Mabry, just behind the first wave, is looking at the shore. None of it looks as it did in the reconnaissance photos. Where are the high Varreville dunes? Where is the windmill? Something is seriously wrong...

Jahnke waits for the landing craft to get in range.

As the landing craft approach Omaha Beach it's remarkably silent. But then, just before the ramps come down, bullets start clanging off the steel ramps 'like rocks being chucked at a bathtub'. Now, artillery shells and mortar bombs are exploding around the boats as the German gunners find their range.

***The war will be won or lost on the beaches. We'll have only one chance to stop the enemy and that's while he's in the water, struggling to get ashore.***

***Field Marshal Rommel***

***Everybody went off the sides. From then on it was screams and hollering and people getting hit and fear. It was bedlam...***

***Sergeant John R Slaughter, D Company, 116th Infantry***

### *6.30am*
### *H-Hour for Omaha Beach*
### *H-Hour for Utah Beach*

In a bunker overlooking Omaha beach, a German infantry sergeant says, 'They must be crazy. Are they going to swim ashore right in front of our muzzles?'

The ramps of the first landing craft are kicked down.

A thousand feet above Omaha Beach in an RAF Mustang, Flight Lieutenant R H G Weighill is acting as a spotter for HMS *Glasgow*, judging the success of her bombardment. He's looking down at Omaha and can see the first wave of 1,450 men jumping into the water from 36 landing craft. To Weighill it's a 'wonderful moment' to think that he'll be able to report back that the Allies have landed.

The reality on the sands of Omaha is rather different.

The leading company of the 116th Regiment is Company A, whose target is the Vierville gully. Their plan is to move off the ramps three abreast – the centre running ahead first and the two others peeling off right and left.

A stream of bullets coming from two angles hits the first men on the ramps, who topple forward into the sea.

From then on it is a bloody chaos.

The ramps have dropped into waist-high and sometimes head-high water. Men are diving into the sea; others are scrambling over the side of the landing craft. Some are drowning under the weight of their equipment and are desperately shedding helmets and weapons to save themselves.

Some of Company A are crawling up onto the beach and hiding behind Rommel's obstacles of mined stakes and barbed wire. Others are frantically trying to dig holes in the sand.

To Captain Joseph T Dawson of the 1st Infantry, the bullets humming through the air make the beach sound like a beehive. To Private Elmer E Matekintis, the 'sip sip' sound of bullets hitting the sand is like someone sucking on their teeth.

Men in the water are pushing their injured comrades to shore; those on land are going back in to save others from drowning. The sodden soldiers are so heavy that they're having to be cut out of their assault jackets, to get them out of the water.

The Americans are being shot at by defenders reinforced by the crack German division Allied intelligence had discovered was on Omaha only a few days ago – the 352nd Infantry. Their machine-gunners and snipers seem to be targeting officers. (In the next few hours, they will remove badges of rank and telltale signs such as binoculars and pistols.) Lieutenant Edward Tidrick of Company A is hit in the throat as he jumps from the landing craft, but manages to stagger out of the water and falls down a few feet from Private Leo Nash.

Bleeding from the throat, Tidrick lifts himself up and manages to say to Nash, 'Advance with wire cutters!'

But then machine-gun bullets hit his head and body, killing him instantly. Nash has no wire cutters.

Many of the Duplex Drive tanks that have successfully made it to Omaha are preferring to stay half hidden in the surf, as it gives some cover and time to search for German targets. Some GIs are hiding there too and will slowly advance with the tide.

The majority of assault troops on Omaha are leaderless, confused and terrified. They are surrounded by men from other units whom they don't know. Most landing craft have beached in the wrong place – for some it's only a matter of 100 yards, for others it's a mile.

The official regimental account will state, 'Company A ceased to be an assault company and had become a forlorn little rescue party bent on survival and the saving of the lives of other men.'

Landing with the assault troops on Omaha are US Navy demolition units whose job is to clear sixteen 50-yard gaps through the beach obstacles, working in teams of eight. They've been given only half an hour to clear each route. Despite the chaos of the beach, the demolition units set about their difficult task with remarkable coolness, even though many of them are being killed. Removing the obstacles is made even harder by the fact that groups of soldiers are sheltering behind them, desperate for the slight cover they give.

When blowing up an obstacle, the demolition teams are placing their charges alongside the mines attached to the top of the structures – they don't want to risk having live mines flying off when the obstacles are destroyed. To achieve this, however a man has to stand on another's shoulders – making him a conspicuous target.

As Lieutenant Commander Joseph Gibbons of the demolition teams says later, 'All of those men who were killed died with their faces toward the enemy and as they moved forward to accomplish their objectives.'

Of his 272 engineers, 111 were killed, most within their first 30 minutes on Omaha.

The wounded on the sand are giving themselves morphine injections to ease the pain. Those unable to move will drown in a few minutes when the tide catches up with them.

### *6.31am*

One minute after Utah Beach's H-Hour, General Teddy Roosevelt is wading through the shallows on Utah Beach holding his walking stick and pistol. In his pocket he has a book of poems by English poet Winthrop Praed. Men are being shot around him; some fall silently, some are screaming. Like Captain George Mabry looking at the beach from the landing craft a few minutes ago, he knows something is wrong. There is a house by the sea wall where there shouldn't be one. Where have they landed?

Mabry is jumping into the sea from his landing craft. Never before in his life has he wanted so badly to sprint, but he can only wade slowly forward. As he leaves the shallows he still can't run as his uniform is so sodden and his legs are numb with cold. He can see relief on his men's faces – there is far less gunfire from the Germans than they'd expected. It's almost an anticlimax.

A mile off Utah, destroyer USS *Corry* is coming under sustained fire from the German batteries. To the horror of Ensign Robert Beeman, the Allied plane supposed to be providing a smoke-screen for the *Corry* to hide in has flown *behind* them. The ship is now sitting in front of a curtain of black smoke and is an easy target. Her skipper Lieutenant Commander George Dewey Hoffman gives orders for the *Corry* to get underway and start a series of sharp evasive turns – full speed ahead, left full rudder, right full rudder.

> ***Suddenly I was in midair, flying some ten or fifteen feet down the deck. I had a brief struggle to regain my balance, at the same time trying to dodge a shower of miscellaneous debris coming down from the flying bridge. I had several instantaneous impressions. My first was, 'So that's what it's like to be hit.'***
>
> **Ensign Robert Beeman, USS Corry**

On Utah the German strongpoints W5 and W2 are firing as best they can. Their mortars are working well, but their large 88mm guns are destroyed or jammed. They do have an old French Renault tank, captured in 1940. In the turret, Lance Corporal Friedrich, peering through thick spectacles, is using a machine-gun with great effect. The American engineers working on what remains of the beach defences are having to dive for cover; others arriving on landing craft are being cut down by Friedrich's bullets. Then, with a noise that to Second Lieutenant Jahnke sounds like a church bell being struck, the old Renault takes a direct hit. Friedrich scrambles from the wreckage.

Fifty-seven-year-old General Roosevelt is now running across the 400 yards of open beach on Utah.

'Grandfather puffed a bit…' he will write home later.

Private Edward Wolfe is running past a GI, sitting with his back against a sea defence. He's dead, but looks as if he's asleep. Wolfe has an urge to shake him awake.

Around the Utah infantry, Duplex Drive tanks are coming ashore and speeding across the beach. Twenty-eight of the 32 have made it – the seas are comparatively calm off Utah.

Sergeant William Clayton's landing craft has grounded just off Utah Beach. He jumps into the sea up to his chest. A shorter soldier next to him disappears under the water. Clayton and another of his squad lift the man up and say, 'Now you walk and we'll get you in.'

The soldier is coughing up water, but he makes it to the beach.

The scene in front of him looks to Clayton like the set of a big play – until they start shooting. But as Captain Mabry is also finding, the gunfire is not as bad as he feared.

Behind them, out at sea, a shell hits the *Corry* amidships, almost splitting her in half. She loses all electric power and her rudder jams; she starts turning in a sharp circle. Her skipper Lieutenant Commander Hoffman orders a flag to be hoisted saying, 'This ship needs help.'

Ensign Robert Beeman runs into the pilot house. He's faced with a chaotic scene – the ship's helm (a heavy metal disk about three feet in diameter) has come off in the helmsman's hands and he's looking at Beeman as if to say, 'What am I supposed to do with this?'

***6.33am***

Berlin Radio is announcing that Allied paratroopers are landing in France, that Le Havre is being bombed and that one of its E-boats has sunk an Allied destroyer.

The 225 US 2nd Rangers are at a crucial point in their dangerous mission to capture the gun emplacements on the 100-foot Pointe du Hoc cliffs at the western end of Omaha Beach. It's feared that the guns could be turned on the troops on both Omaha and Utah beaches. The Rangers have been trained in the style of the British Commandos and are going to take the emplacements from the sea, by climbing the sheer cliff face. The Rangers have already lost 30 valuable minutes after being taken too far east by their Royal Navy coxswain.

From the beach below they're using special mortars to fire grappling irons up the cliff, but the ropes are heavy with seawater and many are falling back.

***6.35am***

On the Pointe du Hoc, the German gunners are hanging over the cliffs to cut the Rangers' ropes and throwing rocks and grenades. But some are close to the top. It is like a scene from a medieval siege.

At Southwick House, BBC engineers are setting up their equipment to record General Montgomery's message to the Allied armies, for broadcast later today.

Monty is getting dressed, having slept well after his usual early night.

His message is already typed out. In it he's quoted the Scottish nobleman and Civil War soldier James Graham:

*He either fears his fate too much,*
*Or his deserts are small,*
*That dares not put it to the touch,*
*To gain or lose it all.*

Monty ends his address by saying, 'Good luck to each one of you. And good hunting on the mainland of Europe.'

Meanwhile, in his home in Herrlingen in south-western Germany, Montgomery's old enemy Field Marshal Erwin Rommel has come downstairs to fetch his present to his wife – a pair of hand-made grey suede shoes from Paris. Today, Lucie Rommel is 50 years old. Rommel plans a family lunch with Lucie and their 15-year-old son Manfred, who is home on leave from his anti-aircraft battery. Rommel is convinced that the Allies will never invade while the Channel is so rough, and so has taken a couple of days' leave. He plans to visit Hitler at the Berghof tomorrow.

*Rommel believes that Britain is in a poor state of readiness. On 26th April he wrote to Lucie from Normandy, 'In England morale is bad... There is one strike after another and the cries of "Down with Churchill and the Jews" and for peace are getting louder... These are bad omens for such a risky offensive.'*

*Three days ago he'd had a visit from an old friend in the Afrika Korps, Major General Hans Kramer. Kramer had been captured in Tunisia and taken to a POW camp in Britain. In May the Swedish Red Cross had arranged a prisoner exchange because Kramer was sick. As he was driven under armed escort through south-east England, Kramer noticed a large build-up of troops and equipment. This he eagerly reported to Rommel, and the two old friends agreed that the invasion of Europe was most likely to be launched at the Channel's narrowest point – the Pas-de-Calais.*

*What Major General Kramer didn't know was that although he'd been told that the military build-up he'd seen was in the south-east, he was in fact driving through Dorset and Hampshire in the south-west of England. The simple deception had worked beautifully.*

The telephone is ringing at Rommel's home, interrupting his preparations for his wife's birthday. It's Hans Speidel, his chief of staff, with news that enemy paratroopers have landed in Normandy and that there are reports of an Allied fleet bombarding the Normandy coast. Speidel says that he's put all units on battle stations. Rommel tells him to call back when he knows more.

Off Juno Beach, HMS *Belfast* begins putting men onto the landing craft. Her ship's log describes them as 'expectant and eager'.

Not far from HMS *Belfast*, Lieutenant James Doohan of the Winnipeg Rifles is watching his 34 men from D Company clamber down ladders into their landing craft. Doohan hasn't slept all night, but he's more worried about getting all his men in the boat without any of them falling into the water.

Doohan notices the coxswain of the landing craft. He'd been at the helm during their rehearsals in Dorset for Juno Beach, and he had repeatedly ignored Doohan's commands. All Doohan's resentment at the man's insubordination comes flooding back.

Doohan has two gifts from his brother Bill with him – a silver cigarette case and a pearl-handled .38 Smith and Wesson revolver. He makes his way to the stern, and gets out the revolver and calmly points it at the man's face.

'Look – you didn't obey any order I gave you in all the practices we had. You better believe you are going to do it now, or I will take over the wheel. I'm in charge of this boat, not you.'

The coxswain readily agrees, and Doohan puts his gun away.

### *6.40am*

Private Joseph Blaylock Sr is treading water in front of his landing craft, about 300 yards from Utah Beach. He's had plenty of experience in the creeks near his home in Mississippi. With his hands and feet he's feeling if there are any underwater mines. He can't find any, so he signals to the crew of the landing craft, and the ramp comes down, and 25 assault troops head for the beach. Blaylock realises that he's lost his gun in the water. He allows a jeep to pull him in.

Thirty-three-year-old Private 'Mac' McIntyre is staggering onto Utah Beach. He feels that he should be running like they do in films, but this is the best he can do. The first person he sees is a military policeman.

'How did you get here so soon?' McIntyre asks.

'I'm left over from the last war, Mac!' the policeman laughs.

The Rangers at the Pointe du Hoc have brought in London Fire Brigade ladders to help them climb the cliffs.

## 'We're going to start the war from here!'

*6.42am*

Air Chief Marshal Leigh-Mallory is reporting to Eisenhower about how the RAF and USAAF have fared overnight. The news is encouraging – only 21 of the 850 American C-47 Dakotas and only eight out of the 400 British planes are missing. Four gliders are unaccounted for.

Eisenhower had said to his troops before D-Day, 'If you see a fighter aircraft over you, they will be ours.'

His prediction has proved correct: so far only three Luftwaffe night fighters have flown over the Normandy beaches.

Two thousand miles away in a hotel in Cairo, Meyrick Clifton-James, an ex-actor working in the Army Pay Corps, is alone in his room. For the past five weeks he has been employed as Montgomery's double – arriving first in Gibraltar and then moving to Algiers and Egypt, to make the Germans think that an invasion of France is even less likely with Monty – the hero of El Alamein – so far away.

Clifton-James' time as Monty is coming to an end. At the insistence of the real Monty, Clifton-James is drawing a full general's pay while he wears his uniform.

On his LCT, Second Lieutenant Stuart Hills and his crew are checking that everything on their Duplex Drive is ready for whatever they may face on Gold Beach. Hill is putting his possessions inside a container behind the turret – shaving kit, underwear, cigarettes, whisky flask, wallet and a photograph of his Wren girlfriend.

Their LCT will be one of the first to hit the beach, and their tank is first on the ramp. Hills has a feeling of great vulnerability. H-Hour on Gold Beach is 7.30am – an hour after neighbouring Omaha.

### *6.45am*

On Omaha Beach:

Fred Bitsig and Bernard Nider are behind a wrecked landing craft, saying to each other, 'What are we going to do?'

Joe Spechler explodes as the TNT-filled satchel he's holding is hit by a bullet.

Sergeant Klaus is lying injured in the water and losing the will to live when First Lieutenant Robert Edlin kneels over him and tells him to think of his wife and children.

Harold Baumgarten is reciting a Hebrew prayer from Deuteronomy.

'Hear, O Israel: the Lord our God, the Lord is One. Love the Lord God with all your heart and all your soul and with all your strength...'

William Otlowski is arguing with a commanding officer who wants him to stay on their landing craft which is being shelled.

'To hell with you, Lieutenant. If you want to die, go ahead!'

Gilbert Murdoch is standing on the turret of a knocked-out

tank, angrily firing its machine-gun, but his glasses are so misted up with salt spray he can hardly see.

Cries of 'Medics, hey medics!' can be heard above the gunfire.

Bob Sales is watching a doctor from his home town get cut down by a machine-gun, his helmet flying off revealing flaming red hair.

The ramps of the landing craft carrying Company B of the 1st Battalion of the 116th Infantry are dropping into the water. Company A has already been very badly hit; they have lost about 100 men out of 215, and scores are wounded.

Three sets of brothers in Company A come from the small town of Bedford, Virginia. Roy Stevens, who planned to meet his twin brother at Vierville-sur-Mer, has been wounded, and Ray has been killed; two brothers named Parker are dead; Bedford Hoback has been killed, his brother Raymond is wounded and, unable to move, drowns when the tide comes in. Raymond's body will never be found, but his Bible will be. In it are his mother's name and address, and so the GI who finds it in the water posts it to Raymond's family in Bedford.

As a result of the tragedies in Company A, the American military will introduce a policy to remove from active service any remaining members of a family when two have been killed in action – the inspiration for the film *Saving Private Ryan*.

### *6.50am*

General Roosevelt is striding around Utah Beach with a map and his trademark walking stick and pistol. His radio is out of action (and will be for the next three hours) so he's giving out orders personally. 'Most of our work,' he wrote home, 'was done on foot.'

To Sergeant Harry Brown he looks as if he's inspecting some real estate. Roosevelt is almost the only person on Utah Beach who's not wearing a helmet – instead he's wearing a regulation olive cloth cap.

Utah is still being hit by German shells and mortar fire. A GI in front of Captain Mabry is blown to pieces by a direct hit. One of the man's thumbs hits Mabry in the stomach.

*Roosevelt had initially been refused permission by Major 'Tubby' Barton to make the crossing, but he wrote to him to convince him that he was needed.*

*'You should have, when you get to shore, an overall picture in which you can place confidence. I believe I can contribute materially on all of the above by going in with the assault companies. Furthermore I personally know both officers and men of these advance units and believe that it will steady them to know that I am with them.'*

*This is proving to be the case. Roosevelt has already been to the dunes at the top of the beach and confirmed what he had feared – they have landed in the wrong place, a whole mile too far south. Many patrol craft were lost before H-Hour and the only surviving one was carried south by a strong tidal stream, and as instructed, the Utah landing craft simply followed it.*

The issue for Roosevelt is what to do with the ever-increasing numbers of troops and equipment landing on the beach behind him. Should they be diverted to the original beach? After a consultation with his battalion commanders he decides that this section of Utah Beach will remain the entry point for Force U. He turns to Colonel Eugene Caffey and says, 'I'm going ahead with the troops. You get word to the navy to bring them in. We're going to start the war from here!'

Although Utah Beach has not been as bloody as feared, on the shoreline there is a distressing collection of flotsam – bodies, life preservers, crates, discarded clothing and haversacks.

> ***Oh yes, we were scared to death. But I'll tell you what, as a coxswain I could never show my fear to... those 36 troops, whether it be Army or Marine, because they were as frightened as I was...***
>
> ***Marvin Perrett, US Coast Guard***

### *6.55am*

Marvin Perrett of the US Coast Guard is the coxswain on a landing craft heading for Utah Beach. None of the 36 soldiers from the 1st Infantry he's carrying are looking ahead – they are all staring at him, not saying a word. Perrett is unnerved. Then one of the GIs pipes up.

'Look, cox, we landed at Sicily and Salerno a few months ago and the coxswain put us off in about three or four feet of water, and we're telling you, you better not do that today...'

'Oh man, you're not going to get an argument out of me. I'll give it my best shot,' Perrett replies. He's not going to antagonise a man with a loaded Thompson sub-machine gun.

BBC reporter Colin Wills is on a landing craft heading for Juno Beach with the 3rd Canadian Division, and just about managing to record a piece on his newly issued lightweight midget portable disc recorder.

'You cannot imagine anything like this march of ships, like soldiers marching in line. I have never seen anything so expressive of intent. It is a purpose shared among many hundreds of thousands of men, who are going in now to the coast of Europe, to do the biggest job they have ever had to do. I can't record any more now because the time has come for me to get my kit on my back and step on that shore, and it's a great day...'

Rommel and his wife are having breakfast. Sadly, although she likes the grey suede shoes from Paris, they don't fit.

### *7.00am*

USS *Corry* is now sinking and slowly jack-knifing into a V. With no power on the ship, Ensign Robert Beeman and Signalman Van Corp are hoisting a flag that says she needs 'Emerg. Tow'.

Beeman hears the captain order the ship's two 26-foot motor whaleboats to be lowered.

'I want to get out of here before we get hit again,' Lieutenant Commander Hoffman says.

One of the *Corry*'s deck torpedoes has fired out of its tube and has rammed the forward funnel, but miraculously it hasn't exploded.

In the city of Caen, the explosions and firing from the coast ten miles away, have resulted in large queues outside the food shops. However, German troops are seizing most of the supplies.

In the small port of Ouistreham, linked to Caen by a canal, and to the east of Sword Beach, Odette Mousset is still sheltering in a small clump of trees close to the ruins of her smouldering hotel. Her husband Raoul is trying to get to Ouistreham from

Caen, but has been turned back at a German roadblock. One of the soldiers has told him that Ouistreham is burning.

'Did you see the Hôtel de Normandie?' he asked.

'It isn't there any more; it's gone.'

Odette's been joined by 20 of her neighbours who are also seeking refuge and too scared to go to their homes. Suddenly a shell from one of the ships of Task Force S explodes in the middle of the trees. Thirteen citizens of Ouistreham are killed outright. Odette is severely wounded.

### *7.05am*

Some of the crew of the stricken *Corry* are putting lids back on three-foot-long powder cans from her guns and throwing them over the side to act as floats for men in the water.

Admiral Moon, in charge of Task Force U on his flagship USS *Bayfield*, has been shaken by the loss of the *Corry* and by reports of stiff German resistance on the beach. He's holding back any further waves of landing craft and even considering cancelling the operation altogether. Admiral Moon had been in charge of Task Force U's disastrous rehearsal at Slapton Sands in Devon in April. On 5th August, suffering from exhaustion, and pessimistic about an Allied landing in the South of France, the admiral will commit suicide by shooting himself.

In the woods around Southwick House, General Eisenhower's aide Captain Harry Butcher comes into his trailer. Ike is sitting up in bed smoking and reading a Western. After speaking to Butcher, he dictates a message for his boss in Washington, the army chief of staff General George Marshall, giving the latest updates. He informs Marshall that the airborne troops he met last night had 'the light of battle in their eyes'.

At the captured Bénouville bridges, some dishevelled conscripted Italian workers have turned up. A number of days ago they were ordered by the Germans to put up anti-glider obstacles in the fields around the bridges. Major Howard's men generously give them some of their rations, and then with much laughter, watch the men put up the anti-glider poles around the crashed British Horsas.

> ***This is the first time I shoot on living men, and I go to the machine-gun and I shoot, I shoot, I shoot! For each American I see fall, there came ten hundred other ones!***
>
> **Franz Rachmann, German soldier, Omaha Beach**

### *7.10am*

On Omaha Beach the bloodshed continues. The second wave of troops is arriving. In one sector there is so much smoke it's hard for the landing craft to see what's going on; they can hear firing, but don't realise it's from the Germans.

One officer who can see all too clearly what's going on in his sector of the beach is Lieutenant Ed McNabb Jr. He's telling the men in his Higgins Boat to keep their heads down so they won't see it 'and lose heart'.

Captain Albert H Smith's Higgins Boat is 500 yards from Omaha Beach, and only inches away from the craft on either side. Their gunwales clang as they hit each other. They scrape on hard sand and the navy coxswain moves to drop the ramp.

'Hold the ramp!' Smith shouts, as he can hear machine-gun bullets bouncing off the steel and the boat's mahogany sides. The German machine gunner swings round and starts aiming at the landing craft on Smith's left.

'Drop the ramp!' Smith yells. It falls and 34 men from 1st

Infantry leap out – then the machine-gunner swings back again and the last two men are shot dead.

D Company is landing on Omaha Beach about 30 yards out. The first man off Sergeant John R Slaughter's boat jumps from the ramp onto a sand bar, but then the bouncing surf makes the boat surge forward and it crushes him. The man is unrecognisable.

D Company is under heavy crossfire, and like the thousands of men who have landed before them, the troops are trying to get out of the landing craft by jumping over the sides and diving off the ramp. Behind Slaughter, some are scrambling to the stern to escape the bullets.

Slaughter had never imagined gunfire like this – he thought A and B companies would have wiped the Germans out by the time they arrived. Some of his men are crying; some are cursing; others are defecating.

Now it's his turn. Slaughter sits on the edge of the ramp which is still bucking up and down; he wants to time it right so the ramp doesn't come down on his head once he's jumped into the water. Slaughter waits for it to drop, and jumps.

On the cliffs of the Pointe du Hoc, after suffering many losses, the Rangers have finally reached the top, helped by the guns of USS *Satterlee* and HMS *Talybont*. Most of the Germans have fled.

The Rangers radio the message 'Praise the Lord', the signal that the mission has been a success. But they soon discover that their intelligence was flawed. They've struggled and died on the cliffs for nothing. The batteries aren't operational – the guns have yet to be installed. Telephone poles are sticking out of many of the emplacements, having done their job in fooling air reconnaissance.

Major Cleveland Lytle, who last night on board their troop ship had drunkenly tried to warn them their mission was futile, was right.

### *7.15am*

Lieutenant Commander Hoffman is diving into the sea from the *Corry*. She's settled on the bottom, with her masts poking above the waves, and is still being targeted by German shells. The gunners are also aiming at his men in the water.

Photographer Robert Capa's Burberry raincoat is floating away with the tide. Moments before, he'd been kicked off the landing craft ramp by the coxswain, after waiting too long to take a picture. Now Capa is crouching in the water behind a steel pole next to a soldier also desperate for protection from the relentless bullets. Capa has decided that a raincoat isn't necessary on Omaha Beach.

The first British landing craft are 15 minutes from their beaches. In Captain Hutchinson Burt's landing craft, his 4 Commando unit are singing 'Jerusalem'.

In Brittany, SOE wireless operator Gordon Tack is helping men from the French Resistance load rifles onto the back of two old trucks. He parachuted in earlier this morning with two other SOE agents as part of a so-called 'Jedburgh' team, whose orders are to carry out paramilitary activities with the Resistance. The rifles, secured in heavy containers, were dropped at the same time as the agents. Tack grabs his rucksack and looks inside. To his disgust he can see all his personal effects – clothing, cigarettes, anything worth stealing – have gone. The Resistance must have stolen them while it was dark. The other two SOE agents discover the same thing has happened to them.

Tack joined the SOE desperate to see some action. His father was a gunner on a Royal Navy ship that was torpedoed in April 1941. He'd managed to get into a lifeboat, but the U-Boat surfaced and machine-gunned the survivors. Tack is out for revenge.

### *7.20am*

Off Utah Beach, a sailor from the stricken *Corry* is swimming over the wreck of the sinking ship. To the amazement of the crew watching on nearby USS *Butler*, he takes down the ensign from her stern and then swims towards the centre of the ship and runs it up the mainmast.

Meanwhile, Ensign Robert Beeman's life jacket won't inflate. He's swimming in desperation towards one of the *Corry*'s airtight powder cans that were thrown over the side a few minutes before.

The first wave of British landing craft is almost on Sword Beach – the most easterly of the invasion beaches. Sword is dominated by the small port of Ouistreham, where the River Orne meets the sea, and is heavily defended by a number of German strongpoints. Many of the houses that run along this stretch of coast have been turned into fortifications. The flat countryside behind Sword is heavily mined.

> *Lord Lovat, commanding officer of the 1st Special Service Brigade, knows their mission on Sword will be tough. He was told by an intelligence officer at a briefing, 'The Ouistreham end of Sword looks like a hot potato; the town is strongly garrisoned, but please knock out the battery in double quick time.'*

*Lovat will be arriving as part of the second wave, whose job is to push out from the beach and make their way to the bridges over the Caen Canal and the Orne, which he hopes were captured intact by Major John Howard's 6th Airborne Division in the early hours of the morning.*

The South Lancashire Regiment is travelling at a steady four knots towards Sword Beach. Major A D Rouse is shocked by the size of the steel and wooden obstacles emerging from the smoke – he had no sense of their height from the air photographs he studied in England. His landing craft slows and starts to weave around them.

He will say later, 'We seemed to be groping through a grotesque petrified forest.'

In front of them, a Duplex Drive tank – one of the 36 out of 40 that have made it – has its rear in flames and is firing at the German positions. Other tanks are heading up the beach as fast as possible to put their shells at almost point-blank range into the slits of the concrete bunkers, before they themselves are destroyed.

## 'If any of you chaps gets there I'll see you the day after D-Day'

*7.25am*
*H-Hour for Sword Beach*

H-Hour on Gold Beach is in five minutes' time. On Private Joe Minogue's LCT, the driver of his tank is looking at his watch and saying, 'Christ, we're five minutes early – I hope this isn't a bad sign.'

Lieutenant Ivan Dickenson of 77 Assault Squadron has practised clearing obstacles many times on Littlehampton beach. But the sea off the Sussex coast has never been anything like the sea off Sword Beach – the water is rough and the waves are four feet up the stakes he's supposed to clear with his tank. To his horror, contrary to what they've been told, he can see that *every* stake has a mine attached to it.

Utah Beach is already secured. The bunkers that overlook the beach have been cleared of German and conscripted Russian troops – most only too keen to surrender. As a report by the German Army in 1943 predicted, 'We are asking a lot if we expect Russians to fight in France for Germany against the Americans...'

Michael Jennings, an 18-year-old Royal Navy sailor, is sitting on Utah Beach having a large neat tot of rum. His landing craft has been left high and dry by the tide, and as there's nothing else to do now that the troops and equipment have been unloaded, the skipper has opened a bottle for his crew. As Jennings will later recall, 'This seemed to make the day much more pleasant...'

Tom Treanor of the *Los Angeles Times* has hitched a ride on a Higgins Boat to get to Utah Beach. He's amazed at how casual the troops seem. He walks over to the beach defences and is surprised at how ineffective they are – the barbed wire is just four single strands, just the same as he uses on his farm at home.

***War to the uninitiated, is like a Marx Brothers film. Everything is a balls-up.***

***George Saunders, 1st Special Service Brigade***

## *7.30am*
## *H-Hour for Gold Beach*

The British 50th Infantry Division and 8th Armoured Brigade hit Gold Beach.

> *Gold is 10 miles across, but half of it is impossible to land on as it has steep bluffs and a rocky shore. But between Arromanches at the west end and La Rivière to the east, there's a stretch of sandy beach with dunes and holiday homes that before the war were popular with the French middle classes. Behind the dunes are some low bluffs easy for tanks to get over, but nonetheless a good vantage point for German gunners. The British troops' aim is to push off Gold Beach, capture the ancient city of Bayeux by the end of the day and link up with the Americans leaving Omaha Beach.*

Private Joe Minogue's tank is fourth off his LCT and they are advancing slowly out of the water and up the beach. The commander of the tank gives Minogue, who's the gunner, the signal to turn the gun turret 360 degrees to break the waterproof seal around the turret ring. This gives Minogue a unique panoramic view of the beach.

As the turret moves left he can't see any sign of the Germans at the top of the beach, other than the occasional pillbox. Then as it swings round further, Minogue can see the infantry wading ashore, some chest-deep, some waist-deep. Some are falling into the water; others are being dragged by their epaulettes to the safety of the sand dunes. These are the men of the Royal Hampshires and the 1st Dorsets – and they are being cut to pieces. To Minogue the scene is unreal, 'like a cartoon'.

His tank is a Crab flail tank, designed to flog its way through minefields, using long metal chains attached to a revolving drum suspended between two arms in front of a modified Sherman.

*The Crab is just one of a fleet of tanks nicknamed 'Hobart's Funnies' by their crews, after their inventor Major General Percy Hobart. In the 1930s, Hobart had irritated many top brass with his revolutionary ideas about armoured warfare and was forced to retire in 1940. But Churchill brought him out of retirement (he'd joined his local Home Guard platoon as a corporal) and in March 1943, Hobart was given the responsibility of developing specialised armour to break through the concrete, barbed wire and minefields of the Atlantic Wall. After the disaster at Dieppe in 1942, Churchill vowed that engineers trying to demolish beach defences and clear minefields would never again be so exposed. (In fact, Churchill is personally responsible for some of the innovative ideas behind the 'Funnies'.)*

*Hobart formed a secret armoured division – the 79th – to test and ultimately drive his inventions, including Fascines, which carry logs on their fronts to drop into craters and anti-tank ditches to make them passable. His Crocodile tanks throw flames further than an infantryman's flame-thrower (it's hoped they will encourage the Germans to surrender when they see their terrifying 120-yard sheets of flame), and the Bobbin carries a ten-foot-high reel of canvas reinforced with steel poles that unrolls to provide a temporary roadway. The AVRE (Armoured Vehicle Royal Engineers) is a modified Churchill tank with a Petard mortar on the top that fires a high explosive projectile that's so large it's been nicknamed 'the Flying Dustbin'. Most of the 'Funnies' have been tested only on British beaches. Today will be a far tougher trial.*

*The US forces were offered a third of the 'Funnies' but they declined, taking only the Duplex Drive tanks.*

*For every innovation there's a bizarre idea that's quietly dropped. US Admiral Ernest J King suggested to the Joint Chiefs of Staff that large numbers of rabbits should be released on the Normandy beaches before the troops landed, so they could activate trip wires and set off mines.*

As he moves up Gold Beach, Joe Minogue is only too aware of something that Hobart said to him and his crew when they were waterproofing their tank during training near Southampton Water. He'd popped his head under the Sherman and said, 'We're expecting 70 per cent casualties, you know, but if any of you chaps gets there I'll see you the day after D-Day.' (And he does.)

Over the waves 400 yards ahead of him on Gold Beach, Stuart Hills can see two AVRE tanks on fire, and more reassuringly, houses that he recognises from reconnaissance photos. Now it's time for his Duplex Drive tank to leave the landing craft.

'Go, go, go!' he shouts.

The tank inches its way down the ramp. Shells start exploding around him – two men on the LCT are injured. The tank flops into the water and as the sea is rough, the canvas sides are already bending in.

'We're taking water fast!' driver Geoff Storey shouts from below. It's knee-deep and the bilge pump can't cope. A shell must have damaged the underside of the tank and the Sherman is sinking fast. Hills gives the order to abandon it.

Lieutenant Herbert Jalland of the Durham Light Infantry is running onto Gold Beach laden with equipment. Like others in his battalion he is wearing pyjamas underneath his battledress in order to prevent chafing.

There is one panzer force close enough to the coast to take on the Allies – the 21st Panzer Division, who fought with Rommel in North Africa. After six hours of indecision by the German High Command, General Edgar Feuchtinger has had enough and unilaterally orders the 21st Division to attack the Allies' eastern beaches.

### *7.35am*

Wading through the water of Omaha with the 12th Infantry Regiment is 25-year-old Counter-intelligence officer Jerome D Salinger. With him wrapped up securely in his backpack are six chapters of a novel he's writing called *Catcher in the Rye.* He says later he brought the manuscript with him as a lucky charm to help him survive and as a reason to survive.

The boats heading towards Omaha Beach have no idea what's in store for them.

'Look what they're doing to those Germans!' a GI shouts to Ernest Hemingway over the sound of the landing craft's diesel engine.

'I guess there won't be a man alive there!'

But Hemingway isn't so sure. Beyond the surf of Omaha Beach he can see that something is wrong. The tanks that landed some time ago haven't moved up the beach. One of them suddenly explodes.

Back at Southwick House, to the surprise of British officers, the Americans are arriving wearing helmets and sidearms, in solidarity with their colleagues in the invasion forces.

On Gold Beach, further east from Joe Minogue's Crab flail tank, Captain Roger Bell of the Westminster Dragoons is having trouble with his Crab, which has stalled on the landing craft. There are four tanks behind him, eager to get going, their engines revving. Bell grabs the tow cable from the Bobbin tank in front and attaches it to his. The Bobbin's crew are not happy – this is not how they wanted to enter the world's biggest invasion. Fortunately, Bell's engine roars into life, and follows the Bobbin into the sea.

With his head out of the turret, Bell slowly guides his tank through the barbed wire and wooden stakes with their sinister mines. The sand is firm under his tracks. Looking to his right, Bell can see scores of tanks coming ashore – two Crabs close to him take a direct hit. A German gun has their range. An AVRE explodes in front, then Bell's tank suddenly jolts and flames start coming out of its rear. Bell yells at his crew to get out fast. There's a very good reason the Germans call Shermans 'Frying Kettles' and the British call them 'Ronsons' after the cigarette lighter's slogan 'Light First Time'.

Behind Bell, 400 yards offshore, Stuart Hills' Duplex Drive tank is at the bottom of the English Channel. He and his crew of four are squeezed together, soaking wet, in a yellow inflatable dinghy. They have nothing with them, not even a paddle, and the current is pushing them east across Gold Beach. They are using their hands to try and stop themselves drifting out to sea.

'Make it good, men – this is the first time American troops have been here in 25 years!'

First Lieutenant Donald S Newbury of the 115th Regiment is trying to encourage his men as they near the shore of Omaha in their landing craft.

A patrol boat is heading away from Omaha. Ernest Hemingway hears a man call to them, 'Good luck to you fellows.'

Hemingway can tell by the man's tone that things are bad on the beach.

***We were defending ourselves, we wanted to survive. They were not our enemy... We did not know them, and we had no chance to say yes or no to what was happening.***

***Corporal Franz Gockel, Omaha Beach***

*7.40am*

Some progress has been made on Omaha. About 150 men from the 2nd Battalion of the 16th Infantry have crossed their sector of the beach with only two casualties, and are attacking the German forces there. However, the majority of the GIs are still pinned down on the beach. Those who might be able to fight back are discovering that their weapons aren't working as they're full of sand and seawater. Just before they landed they were told to take off their waterproof coverings.

Sergeant John R Slaughter is lying chin-deep in the sea. He's been there for about 40 minutes, surrounded by the living and the dead, all slowly inching in with the tide. Some of the living are pretending to be dead. Slaughter is now in range of the German mortars and decides to run for one of the beach obstacles – he succeeds, but then sees it has a mine attached, so he keeps running as low as his six-foot five frame will allow. Slaughter dives to the ground and sees a man to his right get hit and fall in a small stream – the water runs red. A medic quickly runs over, responding to the man's yells. He too is shot. Both men now lie in the sand, screaming. Slaughter knows that if he goes to them, he too will be cut down. Within a few minutes the two men are silent.

He's determined to get across the beach to the limited protection of a sea wall 100 yards away. Slaughter starts to run and stumbles in a pool of water; his rifle goes off, narrowly missing his foot, but he makes it to the wall. Some other men from his company aren't far behind. Slaughter takes off his jacket and spreads it on the sand so he can clean his rifle. There are bullet holes in the coat. He lights a cigarette, as he suddenly feels very weak.

The Germans realise that men are sheltering behind the sea wall and start using mortars to get at them. As they explode, shingle is sent flying through the air like shrapnel.

Ernest Hemingway's landing craft has been ordered to pick up wounded from a boat that's been hit. The tide is rising and many of the stakes are submerged. The soldiers are pushing them away with their hands, desperately trying not to touch the mines. They manage to collect the wounded, all the time well in range of an anti-tank gun. Hemingway is amazed it never fires at them.

On Gold, to Captain Roger Bell's immense relief, his Crab flail tank isn't on fire. The flames were caused by a huge burning piece of shrapnel that had flown over his head from the shattered AVRE in front and landed on the back of his tank. It tumbled off into the sand just as Bell and his crew were scrambling out of the turret.

Now Bell's tank is heading straight for the German 88mm gun at the top of the beach that's causing so much carnage. He fires two rounds of high-explosive shells at it; the 88 ignores him, firing at targets down by the shore. Bell tries three armour-piercing shells, and then a British tank only 50 yards from the battery passes in front of him, blocking his view. Surely the Germans will take it out, Bell thinks. But the muzzle of the 88 doesn't move. Bell's tank has put it out of action.

BBC newsreader John Snagge, who has been assigned the task of broadcasting the communiqué from SHAEF giving the official announcement of D-Day, is sitting in a tiny radio studio in the Ministry of Information in Central London, waiting for it to arrive. Outside the door is a military policeman, and sitting with Snagge is an RAF commodore, a Royal Navy vice admiral and an American general. Snagge isn't sure why they're here as well. While they wait, the four men are each writing a time on a slip of paper. It's for a two-shilling sweepstake, to guess when they think Snagge will be reading the communiqué.

### *About 7.45am*

Lieutenant Leonard Robertson is one of hundreds of Canadian junior officers who have volunteered to fight with British Army regiments under the so-called Canloan scheme. Robertson is with a platoon of the East Yorkshires on a landing craft off Sword Beach, looking with dismay at barbed wire and wooden defences that are very much intact. British sappers were supposed to have cut exits by now. He decides their only option is to crash through them. The marine corporal in charge of the landing craft isn't so sure, until Robertson threatens to take the wheel himself.

The diesel engine roars, and the landing craft picks up speed.

'Heads down! Here we go!' Robertson shouts.

As the bows hit them, the first set of wires snap like string; then at the second set, the boat scrapes past a post with a mine on top – it doesn't explode. The landing craft ploughs on a few more yards and stops.

The marine corporal thinks that they've beached safely on sand and lowers the ramp. Robertson and two men jump into the water and disappear. In fact, the landing craft is stuck on top of a third set of barbed wire, not the beach. Robertson surfaces, and treading water, shouts for the ramp to be lifted and for the landing craft to reverse and have another go. He and the men in the water get out of the way.

The boat breaks free of the wire and makes it almost to the beach. The rest of the platoon run down the ramp past bodies floating face down in the water. Robertson grabs a soldier who's been hit and pulls him to the shore. Last night he'd said to Robertson, 'If you lead I will follow you anywhere.'

Once on Sword Beach, too many of the East Yorkshire Regiment are digging in; stretched out flat, making themselves an easy target.

In the water off Omaha Beach, Robert Capa is crouching behind a burnt-out amphibious tank. Bodies are in the water around him. He's taking photographs of troops huddled behind obstacles or slowly inching their way to shore. Private Edward K Regan has run out of energy and collapses in the shallows – Capa takes his picture. It will become his most famous photograph. When Regan returns home to Virginia next year his mother will show him the picture, having cut it out of *Life* magazine.

'Look, that's you isn't it?'

As shells fall around him, Capa keeps his eye fixed to the viewfinder of his Contax.

Its load of troops, TNT and bazookas have all been successfully dropped on Omaha Beach, so Ernest Hemingway's landing craft is heading back to the destroyer they left three hours earlier.

A German battery has spotted Sherwood Ranger Stuart Hills

and his tank crew in their yellow inflatable dinghy drifting across the bay off Gold Beach. One shell has exploded a few yards in front of them, another a few yards behind. Now the German gunner has their range. The tank crew are helpless. Suddenly an LCG (Landing Craft, Gun) roars up to them, and the crew pull the men out of the water and speed off. A third shell explodes harmlessly behind them.

## 'Friends are approaching...'

### *7.49am*
### *H-Hour for Juno Beach +14 minutes*

The first landing craft are scraping onto the sand of Juno Beach. H-Hour for Juno was supposed to be 7.35am, but it has been delayed by bad weather.

Now the Allies are on all five beaches. Thousands of men are stumbling and scrambling ashore: farmers from Wyoming, teenagers from the East End of London, Canadians who survived Dieppe, American veterans of Sicily, British veterans of Dunkirk, Frenchmen coming home, conscripts and volunteers, fathers and sons fighting just a few miles apart.

*The assault on Juno is being led by the Canadian 3rd Infantry Division.*

*Task Force J's HMS* Belfast *had started shelling at 5.27am, and was soon followed by the rest of her bombardment group. There had been so much smoke out to sea from the guns that the German defenders couldn't see the Allies' landing craft. At 6.45am they'd reported to their divisional headquarters, 'Purpose of naval bombardment not yet apparent...'*

*The bombardment had stopped at 7.30am, five minutes before Juno's original H-Hour.*

*Now the smoke has cleared, giving the men in the bunkers 20 minutes to get ready for the landing craft they can see clearly in their gunsights.*

*The Canadians had suffered more casualties than the British during the raid on Dieppe in 1942 and are keen to fight back. All the men on Juno Beach are volunteers because although there's been conscription in Canada since 1939, only volunteers are sent to combat zones.*

*Juno Beach, adjacent to the British Gold Beach, stretches from La Rivière to the west to Saint-Aubin-sur-Mer to the east. In the middle, the village of Courseulles is the most heavily defended point of all.*

Juno has been quiet since the naval bombardment stopped.

On an incoming landing craft a Royal Engineer says hopefully, 'Do you think this might be a rehearsal?'

Lieutenant James Doohan of the Winnipeg Rifles, still with £3,600 in winnings tucked into his uniform, is approaching the beach in his landing craft, full of patriotic fervour. He joined up in 1939 to fight Hitler, and Canada's defeat at Dieppe has fuelled that desire even more.

'My God, this is it; it's been five years and I'm in the war; I'm in the damned war...' he thinks.

With the higher than expected tide, most of Juno's beach obstacles are already underwater, and the leading landing craft are trying to pick their way through them. Explosions echo around the beach as one by one they hit mines lashed to the wooden poles and steel spikes.

John Honan of the Royal Engineers is on a landing craft that's stranded on top of a tetrahedron defence. Looking over the side, he can see its mine is only inches away from their hull.

Honan's commanding officer Major Stone shouts, 'I'm going over!'

'Bugger it, I've got to do that too,' Honan thinks.

Honan dumps all his equipment in the water and dives in after the major, who's already trying to cut the mine's wires. Honan wraps his legs around another tetrahedron, to stop himself being knocked off by the waves. Bullets are splashing all around him. He's a sitting duck. With one free hand, Honan manages to unscrew the detonator, then swims round to the stern of the landing craft and joins other men who've jumped into the water to try to push the boat off the obstacle. They succeed.

Elsewhere on Juno, Private Jim Wilkins of the Queen's Own Rifles is lying on his back in the water. He was one of the first men ashore. A bullet has broken his leg and another has passed through his left side. Wilkins has lost his rifle, his helmet and all his ammunition. He's surrounded by five other men, all wounded. He looks up at the sky and is so close to the shore that by tilting his head back he can see the machine-gun nest that shot him firing at the rest of his platoon; the bullets are flying just over his face. The platoon sergeant is hit and drops into the sea.

Wilkins very slowly slips off his backpack and, crawling on his front, starts to make his way up the beach to the sea wall.

Private G W Levers of the Canadian Scottish Regiment has made it to the wall and is taking a moment to update his diary.

'We hit the beach and machine-guns were making us play hopscotch as we crossed it...'

Lieutenant James Doohan and all his 34 men have made it safely across Juno Beach.

### *7.50am*

On Gold Beach the Crab flail tanks are thrashing their way through minefields near the low sand dunes. Behind them, some men from the Royal Hampshire Regiment are waiting to get through. Others from the regiment lie dead in the sand, on fire. Shrapnel has ignited the mortar ammunition that they are carrying on their backs.

### *About 7.55am*

Many of the soldiers on the invasion beaches are friends who have served together in previous campaigns. Major Neville Gill and Captain Ivor Stevens fought together in France in 1940 and both escaped from Dunkirk. Now Neville Gill is lying on his back in the sand of Sword Beach. A bullet has gone right through his chest. He's trying to move his arms and legs but can't. Examining his wound is his friend Ivor Stevens. Stevens gently turns Gill over and sees that he has a large hole between his shoulder blades.

When the bullet first hit him, Gill had just felt numb. Now he's being enveloped by pain. He feels scared and alone. His old comrade Stevens takes his hand, and the fear recedes.

Out of the corner of his eye Stevens spots a Sherman tank close to them, getting into position to blast the German defences.

'Keep your head down, the tank's going to fire its charge,' he says to Gill.

Gill gets as flat as he can.
The Sherman fires, and moves on.

Today happens to be a Red Cross flag day in Britain and a Miss Sullivan is standing outside Hammersmith Underground Station in London. She's been there since 6.30am. Almost everyone is stopping to buy a flag and putting in her tin a shilling or two and sometimes half a crown – most days it's only pennies.

'You'll need all you can get now,' someone says to her as they buy their flag.

### *8.00am/7.00am European Time/3.00am US Eastern War Time*

At BBC Broadcasting House, Frederick Allen is reading the eight o'clock news. German radio has been broadcasting regular bulletins about the invasion for an hour and a half, so the BBC is keen at the very least to announce the fact that an official statement from General Eisenhower will be broadcast soon, but that has been refused by SHAEF.

Allen reads, 'Supreme Allied Headquarters have issued an urgent warning to inhabitants of the enemy-occupied countries living near the coast. The warning said that a new phase of the Allied air offensive had begun.

'Shortly before this warning the Germans reported that Le Havre, Calais and Dunkirk were being bombarded and that German naval units were engaged with Allied landing craft.'

Frederick Allen is beside himself with delight at the news of the invasion. Prudence Neil, one of his fellow announcers, tells colleague Stuart Hibberd that he 'looks like a cat that had swallowed a canary'.

In their secret annexe in Amsterdam, the Frank family is listening with great excitement to Frederick Allen's voice on their radio. Otto and Edith Frank have hidden there with their daughters Margot and Anne, as well as another family, the van Pels, for almost two years.

Later today Anne will write with great delight, '...hope is revived within us; it gives us fresh courage, and makes us strong again... the best part of the invasion is that I have the feeling that friends are approaching...'

Thirteen miles from the coast of Normandy, 14-year-old Leo Harris is crouching in the dark of his parents' kitchen cupboard in the Marina Hotel on the seafront at Havre-des-Pas, Jersey. This is where his father, the hotel's owner, has hidden their small Bush radio. He too is listening to Frederick Allen's momentous news. Since June 1940, the Channel Islands have been occupied by German forces, and for the past two years radios have been illegal – to be caught in possession of one means many months in prison. But the islanders have been constructing their own – every public telephone box on Jersey and Guernsey is out of action as the handsets have been stolen to make headphones. Leo takes delight in small acts of subversion, such as breaking into the local German Army barracks and exposing the live wires on the light switches.

On nearby Guernsey, schoolgirl Marion Tostevin is looking in wonder at a sky that's black with planes heading to France.

'Oh, this is *great*, we'll have our turn soon...' she thinks.

She's been awake since before dawn, watching the fires on the Normandy coast.

*The Channel Islanders have no organised resistance movement. Acts of subversion like Leo's are small, for example 'V' badges made of British coins pinned inside their lapels; one man chalked a 'V' sign on a German soldier's bike saddle so it would leave the mark on his trousers – for which he got 12 months in prison. There is by no means a united front against the German occupiers. At one point in 1943, the police were getting 40 anonymous letters a day denouncing neighbours for owning a radio.*

At Caen Prison, where the Germans keep their political prisoners, Gestapo officer Kurt Geissler has arrived with three other Gestapo men. He has a list of names of prisoners he wants to execute.

'It's got to be done here, and straight away,' he tells the guards.

On Omaha, Robert Capa has stopped taking pictures and is lying as flat as he can in the water, the slope of the beach giving some protection. He's chanting to himself a phrase he learned covering the civil war in Spain, '*Es una cosa muy seria. Es una cosa muy seria...*' 'This is a very serious business. This is a very serious business...'

At the White House, Eleanor Roosevelt's phone is ringing. It's the switchboard operator telling her to wake up her husband the president – the army chief of staff General Marshall wants him on the phone.

In the port of Ouistreham by Sword Beach, a first-aid post has been set up in the town square. Scores of people have been injured by the Allied bombardments and the dead are lined up in rows on the street outside. An elderly doctor is doing what he can, but as he was shot in the hand earlier today, others with only a little medical experience are having to carry out difficult operations such as amputations. The local pharmacist's shop has been destroyed, so medical supplies are limited. Odette Mousset, the owner of the Hôtel de Normandie who was earlier injured by an Allied shell, has been given an injection of morphine to ease her pain, but the doctor fears that she is dying. Her husband Raoul is still trying to get through the German lines to reach her.

The mayor of Ouistreham, Charles Lefauconnier, runs into the first-aid post – he's come from the beach.

'They're landing! They're landing!'

There are cheers, and many weep. Some whisper the news to the wounded to give them hope.

The mayor of nearby Colleville-sur-Orne has decided to greet the British forces personally. Dressed in his full regalia, he is down on Sword Beach smiling and welcoming the bemused assault troops.

> ***[The British submariner] was another one of the unsung heroes of the war. I will never forget the picture of this young sailor with a white scarf flying in the breeze, standing like an avenging god in the shallow water of Normandy with no weapons of any kind, just simply directing traffic of weird vehicles...***
>
> ***Sergeant Leo Gariepy, Canadian 6th Armoured Regiment***

### *8.05am*

GIs are still heading for the American beaches. LCI *91* is approaching Omaha, when a German shell ignites the fuel tank on the back of a soldier holding a flame-thrower. He's catapaulted into the sea and burning fuel sprays all over the ship. Twenty-two soldiers and crew are killed.

Three miles away from Omaha Beach, American combat photographer Seth Shepard on board LCI *92* is looking at the boat's forward gun crew bracing themselves against the waves breaking over the bow. Their faces are streaming with seawater. Ahead of LCI *92* are dozens of small landing craft, and ahead of them columns of smoke drift from vehicles on the beach and from houses beneath the bluffs. Shepard's heart races as he can now make out men running for cover on the shore. Below him, in the pilot house, Edward E Pryzbos, the quartermaster at the helm yells, 'Looks as if we're going to have a rough landing!'

The boat's two pharmacist's mates rush for their medical kits.

Shepard can see their sister ship LCI *91* in flames. LCI *91* will burn for 18 hours.

USS *Corry*'s Ensign Robert Beeman has been in the water off Utah Beach for 45 minutes. He's cold and is running out of strength. Then he sees a raft paddling towards him with eight men hanging onto it. Suddenly a shell falls close by and a piece of shrapnel whizzes past Beeman's ear and takes off the top of the head of a man hanging onto the raft. The water turns red around him, and his shipmates franticly cut the dead man adrift.

The two Royal Navy midget subs *X20* and *X23* are preparing to leave the Normandy beaches; their navigation equipment is now stowed, but their large ensigns are still flying in the wind. Over the past two hours they have guided hundreds of landing craft to the beaches, many of the men aboard grateful to see 'the man on the submarine' clasp his hands above his head to wish them good luck.

The whole midget sub operation had been given the name Operation Gambit. The fact that 'gambit' means sacrificing your pawns had not reassured the crews of the subs, but they have survived.

Lieutenant George Honour is too weak to raise *X23*'s anchor, so he simply cuts the rope.

> ***I saw Army officers pleading with their men to get off as quickly as possible. Some soldiers were jumping overboard and others slid or let themselves down a chain up forward of the damaged ramp. The cries of some of the helpless soldiers in the deep water were pitiful.***
>
> ***Seth Shepard, combat photographer on LCI* 92**

## *8.10am/3.10am US Eastern War Time*

Lord Lovat's LCI *519* is passing an LCT going away from Sword Beach. Lovat asks flotilla officer Rupert Curtis to hail her. Through his megaphone Curtis shouts to a sailor on her quarterdeck.

'How did it go?'

'It was a piece of cake!' he replies, and the sailor gives a 'V' for Victory sign.

Sword Beach does not look like a piece of cake. Piper Bill Millin can see black smoke coming from British tanks on the shore. Standing a few feet in front of Millin, Lord Lovat is also thinking that the beach doesn't look very inviting. He can see infantry with their heads down in the sand, and halfway up the beach others digging in – a certain death trap, Lovat thinks. Lovat had told his men the day before, 'If you wish to live to a ripe old age – keep moving tomorrow.'

President Roosevelt is awake and sitting up in bed wearing a sweater over his pyjamas. Although he seems calm, his wife Eleanor knows he's constantly thinking of his troops on the beaches. The president says to Eleanor that he hopes that Russell Linaka will 'survive the day'. Linaka is a retired naval officer who manages FDR's tree plantations (part of the president's plan when he retires is to get income from thousands of Christmas trees on his estates). Linaka had re-enlisted in 1942 and at this moment is in command of a landing craft off the coast of Normandy.

Linaka will survive D-Day and the war.

Although he doesn't know it, Seth Shepard's Omaha-bound LCI 92, now so close to the beach that the crew can smell gunpowder, is sailing straight towards a mine. Her skipper, Lieutenant Robert M Salmon, is gripping the handrail of the bridge as he speaks down the tube to the quartermaster at the helm, guiding him towards the shore. Seth Shepard is to his left, looking through the viewfinder of his camera.

Suddenly the boat – all 350 feet of her – is lifted out of the water as the bow explodes, sending flames and fragments of steel towards the bridge. Two soldiers are sent flying up through the hatch in the forward hold. Forty-one others are trapped in the flames below. To Shepard the heat feels like a blast furnace. LCI 92's crew have been badly hit – seaman Eugene J Snarski's hair is on fire; Arthur L Lornson Jr is in the sea yelling for help, but no one can hear him; Lester P Phillips is in the water too, but can't shout because his mouth is full of oil.

Shepard staggers to his feet and looks forward, his ears ringing. Smoke and flames are pouring from the hatch, equipment is littered everywhere. LCI 92's ramp is twisted and can't be lowered. The engine room crew are scrambling up on deck, their faces black with smoke.

## 8.15am

For the Canadians and British arriving on Juno, the scene that greets them is not what they'd expected. Hundreds of dead soldiers are being pushed in on the tide and are bumping against wrecked or sinking landing craft.

Nineteen-year-old Anthony Rubenstein of the Royal Marine Commandos has just waded ashore. He looks behind him and can see men from his unit struggling in the water. His friend Yates is drowning. Rubenstein looks away and moves on – his orders are not to help anyone, just to get ashore.

Duplex Drive tanks are rumbling onto Juno out of the sea. Sergeant Leo Gariepy of the Canadian 6th Armoured Regiment and most of his crew can't swim, so they've been particularly determined to get ashore successfully. Only nine out of 18 in their unit made it, so they were lucky.

From his turret, Gariepy watches German machine-gunners standing up in their positions staring, mouths wide open, at these canvas boats turning into tanks. Even to the Allied troops, they are intimidating. To Royal Engineer John Honan, still removing detonators, they look like 'sea monsters coming out of the deep'.

Four miles away at Bénouville, Major John Howard's men spot a squadron of Spitfires flying low and signal to them that the bridges are in British hands. Three of the fighters start circling and perform a series of victory rolls to great cheers. Before they leave, one of the Spitfires drops a package. It's a bundle of the morning papers from England.

Major John Howard recalls, 'Right then, my blokes forgot about the bridge and the war. They were riveted by the *Daily*

*Mirror* and the sight of Jane getting her kit off.'

*After the war, the bridge over the Caen Canal will be renamed Pegasus Bridge, after the symbol of the British airborne forces. The bridge over the River Orne will be renamed Horsa Bridge, after their gliders.*

### *8.20am*

Some Sherman tanks have made it onto Omaha Beach and are firing at the German positions; others are driving up and down the beach to give cover to the troops.

Captain McGrath of the 116th Infantry is trying to get the scores of men huddled by the sea wall at Omaha to advance. Another officer loses patience.

'You guys think you're soldiers?!' he shouts.

The troops refuse to move. One soldier would later call it a 'mass paralysis'.

The men thrown into the water by the explosion on LCI 92 finally have some good fortune. Arthur L Lornson Jr swam through oil to get to a beach defence and after hanging onto it for a while, decided he didn't like the look of its mine and swam away. A shell hit it moments later. Lornson has now made it onto the beach. Lester P Phillips, his mouth clogged with oil, is still alive, kept afloat by his life preserver. He will float for an hour before a landing craft literally scoops him up with its ramp.

Seth Shepard is grabbing film for his camera from the floor of the bridge of LCI 92; no one else is up there, not even the skipper, as they're helping the crew below decks. Shepard feels extremely vulnerable in such an exposed place. A shell explodes on the bridge just after he scrambles down to the signal deck.

Pierre Desoubeaux is a civil servant living in Ouistreham. He's walking the streets of the port looking for wounded to bring to the first-aid post in the town square. He can hear the sound of the Marseillaise being whistled rather badly. Round the corner come a unit of British troops from Sword Beach, and Desoubeaux dissolves into tears and shakes their hands. One soldier, in gratitude, gives him a pipe from his pocket.

Desoubeaux will treasure it for the rest of his life.

### *About 8.25am*

On Gold Beach, the main concern of Sergeant Major H W Bowers of the Hampshire Regiment since he landed almost an hour ago has been to get a new pair of boots, as his own are far too tight and painful. Many of his company have been cut down by fire from a pillbox at the end of a fortified former sanatorium on the seafront. Bowers comes across his commanding officer, who has an injured arm.

'Hello, Bowers, you still living?'

'Yes, sir, just about!'

Bowers tells him about the murderous pillbox.

'Well, go and see what you can do about it... carry on.'

'Christ!' Bowers thinks, 'he must think that I can take on the whole German Army!'

But Bowers, a veteran of the invasions of Sicily and Italy, heads off to see what he can do.

After 15 minutes clinging to tetrahedrons and removing their detonators, Royal Engineer John Honan has had enough, and swims for the shore. Sheltering by the high sea wall above Juno, two soldiers offer him a drink, but he declines.

'You're not a teetotaller, are you?'

'I'm not, I'm just afraid that stuff will make me feel brave or some bloody thing like that...'

Donald Burgett of US 101st Airborne Division landed just after 1am and watched his fellow paratroopers die falling from a Dakota which was flying too low. He has now met up with ten men from the 101st and 82nd Airborne divisions. Similar things are happening all across the countryside – groups of men from different regiments and divisions getting together to attack German positions wherever they can find them and using whatever weapons have survived the drop. Burgett's new unit has assembled outside a village that they've discovered from a local is called Ravenoville. It's about two miles from Utah Beach and 12 miles from their drop zone. The only officer among them, a Lieutenant Muir, has decided on a strategy for taking the village.

'A head-on attack and the sooner the better, so let's go!'

The Americans leap up and run across a field towards some houses, screaming and firing.

Not all the paratroopers are seizing the initiative. One group of men from the 101st and 82nd have found an empty farmhouse near Vierville with a full cellar, and have got roaring drunk.

## 'I am no hero, I did not volunteer for this lot'

### *8.30am*

Albert Speer, Hitler's Armaments Minister, is at the Berghof. An adjutant is telling him about the invasion.

'Has the Führer been woken up?'

'No, he always receives the news after he has eaten breakfast...'

There have been so many false alarms over the past few weeks that no one wants the responsibility of waking Hitler with news of what may be only a small-scale attack.

Twenty-one-year-old ATS driver Evelyn Hyatt is arriving at the base of the US 1st Battalion of the 531st at Bodmin in Cornwall with her regular supply of blankets. Evelyn walks into the first Nissen hut in the camp. It's completely empty. On the tables are dirty plates and bowls and half-drunk mugs of tea. The 531st left the morning before – with barely time to finish their breakfast.

OSS chief, David Bruce, on board USS *Tuscaloosa*, notes in his diary that the vibration of the ship's guns has loosened screws and shattered light bulbs all around the vessel. The most serious casualty so far is a direct hit on his boss William 'Wild Bill' Donovan's toilet.

Ensign Robert Beeman, cold and shivering, is hanging onto the side of one of USS *Corry*'s life rafts, which is full of survivors. The wind is carrying them right over their half-sunken ship. Beeman looks up at the forecastle and the bridge as they drift past. Only two hours before she had been one of the finest ships in the US fleet.

Tea drinking is becoming a feature of the British and Canadian beaches. The regimental history of the South Lancashire Regiment claims that they were brewing tea on Sword Beach by 8.30am, making them the first British unit to do so on French soil.

## *8.31am*

4 Commando is landing on Sword Beach. The Free French are the first down the ramps – a symbolic moment. Their commanding officer Lord Lovat will later recall that in the run-up to D-Day 'their eyes were bright, for they were going home...'

But the French and the British are running through carnage. Private John Mason of 4 Commando is passing bodies that have been 'knocked down like ninepins.' William Spearman, a veteran of the Dieppe raid, thinks it look as if the bodies have 'drowned in their own blood for want of moving'.

No 4's medical officer Joe Patterson passes the body of a commando he recognises. A few days ago he had censored the man's letter to his wife. The commando had written, 'I am no hero, I did not volunteer for this lot.'

Also on Sword Beach is Len Brown, a bugler and stretcher-bearer for the South Lancashires. He'd survived Dunkirk by swimming 600 yards out to sea to reach a ship – unexpectedly his training for the battalion water polo team had turned out to be very useful. Now he's back in France and running up the beach behind a Crab flail tank. Brown has no weapon, only two medical kits. He runs over to a soldier who has strayed from the safe path left by the tank and set off a mine – his leg is hanging off. Brown bandages the man and puts a tourniquet on his leg, then writes 'T' on his forehead and the time he put it on, so the medical team coming behind him will know when to release it.

Brown runs further up the beach to the next injured man. His orders are to keep moving with the leading troops heading off the beach.

Brown is a reassuring presence.

'It's nice to have you up with us', a soldier says to him, as they lie flat on the sand, trying to avoid the bullets.

The assault forces that are landing on the Normandy beaches have the best medical support of any battle in history. At least 70 landing craft have been allocated as 'water ambulances' to ferry the wounded to the larger task force ships out at sea. Stretcher-bearers like Len Brown and doctors and blood transfusion units are setting up dressing stations on the beaches. The British beaches have five blood transfusion units with more than a thousand bottles of refrigerated whole blood.

*The Allies have with them a secret weapon – penicillin. This antibiotic was first tried out on troops in the North African campaign, and was a huge success – the vast majority of wounded who'd been treated with it recovered. Now penicillin is in the backpacks of the medical teams running ashore; the Germans don't have it and Allied wounded are more likely to survive. Penicillin will prove crucial in the next few months of the war.*

***Everyone liked Lord Lovat, although we all thought that at 32 he was a bit too old for the kind of daredevilry he enjoyed. Everyone regarded him as crazy and, in retrospect, I suppose they thought I was pretty crazy too.***

***Piper Bill Millin, 1st Special Service Brigade***

### *8.35am*

'I am going in! Stand by with the ramps!'

Lieutenant Commander Curtis, in charge of Lord Lovat's landing craft, is shouting over the vessel's roaring engines as she starts to bump over the sand.

'Lower away there!'

LCI *519*'s two ramps drop smoothly.

Piper Bill Millin, a few yards behind Lovat, watches the first of their unit of commandos step onto the ramp. One is hit in the face by a piece of shrapnel, holds onto the rail and falls into the sea. Lovat strides on down the ramp regardless, carrying a wading stick that he uses to keep balanced when fly-fishing for salmon. He's wearing highly polished hunting brogues and a white pullover with 'Lovat' embroidered on the collar, and on his beret a 'Fraser Lovat' badge that's glinting in the morning sun.

None of his commandos are wearing helmets, preferring to wear their green berets.

Millin thinks that at six foot, Lovat will give a good indication of how deep the water is. It's not too deep. Millin's kilt spreads around him as, holding his pipes above his head, he jumps in waist high. Millin topples over momentarily from the weight of his rucksack until someone grabs him and pushes him forward. Still wading in the surf, he puts the bagpipes on his shoulder and starts to play 'Highland Laddie', the regimental quick march of Lord Lovat's old regiment the Scots Guards. Lord Lovat turns and smiles.

As they move up the beach, commando Harry Drew shyly comes up behind Lovat and touches his belt, partly out of superstition but also so that if anything happens to him it could be said that he died by his brigadier's side.

Royal Navy sailor Etienne Webb watches the commandos move off the beach, 'chatting and mumbling away as if it was a Sunday afternoon'.

### *About 8.37am*

At the Bénouville bridges, Corporal Wally Parr and Private Charlie Gardner have worked out how to use a captured German anti-tank gun. Early on in their DIY tutorial, Gardner had said, 'What's this?' and pressed a button that fired a shell towards Caen. Parr and Gardner are putting their skills to use by trying to hit German snipers in the trees.

### *About 8.40am*

On Omaha Beach, Robert Capa is shaking 'from toe to hair'. He has had enough. He tried digging a foxhole in the sand but gave up. Holding his cameras above his head, Capa runs into the sea towards LCI *94*, 50 yards out, which is dropping medics off onto the beach. Capa knows deep down that he is running away.

Piper Bill Millin is playing the commandos up the beach. He looks down and sees that he's walking between two dead soldiers, one with his face blown away. He stops playing.

### *8.45am*

Unshaven and weary after his attack on the Allied fleet, Lieutenant Commander Heinrich Hoffmann is back at Le Havre, chain-smoking his favourite English Woodbine cigarettes (captured from Allied shipping) and drinking so-called 'Hoffmann cocktails' – Napoleon Brandy mixed with Grand Marnier liqueur. Hoffmann dictates a short report on the skirmish to the naval chief of staff. He does it as quickly as he can, as he's sure Allied aircraft will attack his base.

On wrecked landing craft LCI 92, Seth Shepard is lying on top of ration boxes, spraying water from a hose into the burning forward hatch where the dead soldiers are. German shells continue to fly overhead, some smacking into the ship and rattling his helmet. Shepard feels scared and lonely.

Free French commando Private Robert Piauge was hit by shrapnel from a mortar just moments after he landed – the third Frenchman to reach the shore. A British medic is checking his wounds. Piauge is aware of him saying '*fini*', injecting him with morphine and moving on. Piauge starts to cry, not because of his injuries, but because he is finally home.

He will later be taken off the beach and will recover.

*8.50am*

On Gold Beach, Sergeant Major H W Bowers' boots are still very painful. He's lying flat on top of the pillbox by the old sanatorium that's been slaughtering so many of his regiment. He's being given covering fire by two marine commandos with tommy guns who asked to join him on his mission 'for a bit of fun'.

Bowers leans over the edge of the pillbox with a grenade in his hand. A white flag emerges from the slit below him.

'Hell with you mate, after all this trouble!' Bowers thinks, and slips it inside. There's an explosion, and after a pause, men come running out with their hands up, shouting, 'Russkis! Russkis!'

Bowers isn't interested in their nationality – all he can see is their nice, soft boots.

On Sword, while the Free French Commandos attack the casino overlooking the beach at Ouistreham (where Count Guy de

Montlaur lost so much money), the British Commandos attack the batteries that block their route to the town.

By now, five exits from Sword beach have been cleared by engineers and Hobart's 'Funnies', and now infantry from the East Yorkshires and South Lancashires, who have both suffered heavy losses, are gratefully heading inland.

On Utah Beach, the invasion continues to proceed smoothly. Lieutenant Richard Bird is watching American troops run across the beach. Their professionalism and their spirit reminds him of Errol Flynn.

One soldier running onto Omaha Beach thinks that the bodies in the water look like waxworks from Madame Tussaud's.

Robert Capa has not been able to flee bloody Omaha yet. He's on LCI *94*, putting fresh film in his camera, when the craft is hit by a German shell. Feathers from dead soldiers' kapok jackets are flying everywhere. The skipper is covered in the blood and flesh of one of his crew, and weeps in shock. Capa darts below deck to the engine room, cleans his hands and tries to put fresh film in the cameras. When he gets back on deck, LCI *94* is slowly pulling away. Capa looks back towards Normandy and takes one last picture of Omaha.

### *9.00am*

At the Berghof, Hitler has woken up and is standing in his dressing gown being told about the invasion. He is triumphant.

'The news couldn't be better. As long as they were in Britain we couldn't get at them. Now we have them where we can get at them! Do you recall? Among the reports we've received there was one that exactly predicted the landing site and the day and the hour. That only confirms my opinion that this is not the real invasion yet.'

Operation Fortitude has done its work well, Hitler is convinced that the landings in Normandy are just a diversion for the real invasion in the Pas-de-Calais.

He calls for a military conference.

### *About 9.10am*

Over breakfast in their secret annexe, the Frank family is discussing whether the invasion is the real thing, or just a trial run like the raid on Dieppe. They are desperate for more information.

Major von der Heydte of the German 6th Paratroop Regiment is at the top of the church tower at Saint-Côme-du-Mont, about nine miles from Utah Beach. He wants to assess the situation before he plans a counter-attack. What he sees through his field glasses makes him go pale. Later he writes, 'Thirty-six ships were peacefully unloading. The bustling shuttle of small boats between the transport ships and beaches reminded one of a peaceful summer's day on the Wannsee' [a Berlin boating lake].

The South Lancashires are now off Sword Beach and have taken the inland village of Hermanville.

The tea drinking continues on the British and Canadian beaches. In the middle of the battle for Sword, 'Slim' Wileman of the Royal Hussars is surprised to see the crew of one of their tanks brewing up beside their wrecked vehicle. When Wileman asks them what they are doing they reply, 'We're not infantry. We're not equipped to fight. What else could we do?'

On Juno, men from the 2nd Canadian Armoured Brigade are brewing tea over a petrol fire and discussing the weather with a group of locals. Later on in the day, brothers Bill and Stanley Dudka, both in the Nova Scotia Highlanders, bump into each other in a village not far from Juno and have a cup of tea and a chat, and 'caution each other to be careful, as brothers do'.

All gas, water and electricity supplies have been cut off in Caen.

## 'How about a tune?'

*9.15am*

The crew of LCI 92 are abandoning ship. But Seth Shepard, still fighting the fire, and hidden from view, doesn't know.

The BBC transmitters to Europe are giving a countdown to the ten o'clock speech by General Eisenhower in a number of languages, heightening the tension for the Corporation's millions of secret listeners.

*'In fünfundvierzig Minuten wird General Eisenhower sprechen...'*

*'En quarante-cinq minutes, General Eisenhower...'*

For most of the morning, General Omar Bradley has been on the bridge of the cruiser USS *Augusta*, watching events on Omaha Beach through binoculars, and wearing ear plugs to protect his hearing from the noise of the ship's guns. (He also has a plaster covering up a large boil on his nose.)

Bradley has sent a gunnery officer out in a patrol boat to get an eyewitness account of the battle for Omaha Beach. But he can see, even from his anchorage in the Channel, that the situation is chaotic. The congestion on the beach from troops, jeeps, tanks, half-tracks and wreckage is so bad that he's given orders for no more boats to land until it's cleared.

The patrol boat radios in its report: 'Boats and vehicles piled up on the beach. Troops dug in on beach. Enemy holds fire until craft beaches. Enemy appears to concentrate fire on officers and non-commissioned officers.'

General Bradley is contemplating a drastic move – to divert forces from Utah to help the troops on Omaha.

Bill Ryan of 116th Regiment is lying with his back against a small embankment on Omaha Beach. His landing craft was hit by a shell and he was knocked unconscious. Ryan was then dragged ashore by members of his platoon. He's now come to, and wishes he had his movie camera as he has a front-row seat for the unfolding drama on the beach. Ryan is amazed by the bravery of a US Navy destroyer (probably USS *Harding*) that's come in close to fire on the gun emplacements that hadn't been knocked out during the pre-invasion bombardment.

Ryan is just one of many men watching the horrors of the beach from the sea wall. Melvin Farrell of the 121st Combat Battalion can't tear his eyes away from the infantry running up the beach, 'the dead and the dying piling up behind them...'

Things are different on Sword Beach. Lord Lovat is making himself at home. As each unit comes ashore he greets them, saying coolly, 'Good morning, gentlemen...'

George Saunders, of Lovat's 1st Special Service Brigade, is watching him and thinking that he looks as if he's at a grouse shoot on his Scottish estate. Every now and then Lovat calmly brushes sand from his polished brogues when bursts of machine-gun fire get too close.

*Twenty-one-year-old Saunders was born Georg Saloschin, in Munich, and as a boy was in the Hitler Youth (as was his whole school), just one of the reasons why he was refused a commission in the British Army. In 1938 the Saloschins fled the Nazis (Georg's father Victor is half Jewish and the family owned a liberal newspaper) and moved to Scotland, where his father got a job teaching at Gordonstoun School.*

*The commandos were more than happy to take Georg on as an intelligence officer and translator in 'X Troop' of 10 Commando, part of the 1st Special Service Brigade. X Troop is mostly made up of Austrian and German Jews, who have been given new names and new histories, even a new faith – their dog tags are stamped 'Church of England'. If they were captured and their identity discovered, they and any surviving relatives in occupied Europe would be executed.*

*In April, a member of X Troop came face to face with Rommel. George Lane (real name Gyorgy Lanyi) was sent on a mission to look at what British Intelligence feared was a new hyper-sensitive mine on the Normandy beaches. An RAF bomb had set off a chain of explosions, but it turned out the mines were merely inadequately waterproofed.*

*Lane was captured and taken to La Roche-Guyon where Rommel asked him, 'How is my old friend Montgomery?'*

*'Very well, sir, as far as I know,' Lane replied, disguising his Hungarian accent by pretending to be Welsh.*

*'You really think there is going to be an invasion?'*

*'I don't know anything more than I read in* The Times.*'*

*Lane was later interrogated by the Gestapo, but they'd clearly been told by Rommel to go easy on him. Lane will spend the rest of the war as a POW.*

At the top of Sword Beach, 22-year-old Corporal Peter Masters, an intelligence officer and translator also with X Troop, who fled Nazi persecution in Austria (real name Peter Arany), walks past a soldier sweeping for mines using a detector and headphones.

'Hey, what are you doing?' the soldier yells. Masters and his unit keep going as they have their instructions to get off the beach as soon as possible. His family came to England in 1938 and at the outbreak of war were briefly interned. In 1940, as soon as he turned 18, Peter Arany enlisted in the British Army, and two years later joined X Troop. Masters sees his skipper, Captain Brian Hilton-Jones, and instinctively salutes. Years later, Masters will think it must have been the only salute on the D-Day beaches.

Piper Bill Millin has also made it to the top of Sword Beach, and joins Lord Lovat in time to hear their bridgade major telling him that Major Howard's audacious glider raid has succeeded and the bridges have been taken intact. Lovat tells the brigade major that he estimates he's lost about 60 men coming up Sword Beach.

Seeing Millin, Lovat's tone brightens. 'Good show, the piper,' he says. 'How about a tune?'

Millin can't believe his ears and says sarcastically, 'What should I play then, sir?'

'The Road to the Isles.'

'Would you prefer me to walk up and down the beach, sir?'

'Yes, that would be fine.'

Millin places the pipes on his shoulder once more. Soldiers by the sea wall cheer him as he heads to the shore at a brisk pace. But Millin feels awkward playing while bodies wash back and forth in the waves.

### *About 9.20am*

On the top of Juno Beach, Captain Daniel Flunder of 48 Commando is looking back towards the sea. He can see scores of Canadian and British wounded on the sand. Suddenly he sees that a tank with its turret closed is blindly running over wounded men. 48 Commando's padre is lying injured and can't move, and the tank is heading his way.

Flunder sprints down the beach shouting, 'They're my men! They're my men!'

He reaches the tank and starts bashing it with his walking stick to try and get it to stop, but it keeps going. In desperation, Flunders pulls the pin out of an anti-tank grenade and wedges it in the sprockets of one of the wheels. Flunders backs away, and the grenade blows the tank's track off. It comes to a halt before it hits the helpless padre.

Lieutenant George Finn, the engineering officer for LCI 92 spots Seth Shepard, still at his post, trying to put out the fire, and yells at him to abandon ship.

### *9.25am*

Instead of heading overboard, Shepard is now sliding down a ladder to get below decks. He grabs some film and camera equipment from his bunk and some bread from the mess table as he's had no breakfast. There's no fire or smoke down here – everything is as they left it at 4am.

Most of the crew are swimming for the shore, but some have made it into life rafts.

Bill Millin's playing is not going down well with all the troops on Sword Beach. He feels a hand on his left shoulder.

'What are you playing at, piper? You mad bastard! Don't you think there's enough going on here without you attracting every German in France?'

### *9.30am*

Shepard is climbing down a rope ladder on the starboard side and LCI *92* is starting to heel over under him. He jumps into the sea and instantly his helmet and boots begin to drag him down, but he kicks, swims and struggles his way to the shore.

Nearby, the LCI's motor machinist mate Vincent DiFalco is trying to swim with burnt hands towards something dark in the water that he hopes will hold him up. Gunner Michael Zaley, also in the water, sees what he's about to do and yells at him to stop. DiFalco was about to grab onto a mine.

Seth Shepard and Robert Capa are not the only photographers on the invasion beaches. Carter Barber is an American war correspondent based with US Coast Guard boat CG *16*. He's been with the landing craft heading to Utah Beach, taking pictures with a borrowed camera; he's also helped pull drowning men from the water and assisted in a burial at sea.

The skipper, Lieutenant R V McPhail, calls out to him, 'What time do you think it is, Barber?'

'Way past noon, at least. Maybe four o'clock.'

'No! It's only nine-thirty in the morning...'

USS *Corry*'s Ensign Robert Beeman is dry and safe and in a bunk on board USS *Fitch*. He's drinking black coffee. For the rest of his life the taste will remind him of the sinking of the *Corry*.

At the Bénouville bridges, two German gunboats, fleeing 4 Commando's attack on Ouistreham, are approaching up the canal at speed, the lead boat firing its 20mm gun. Wally Parr's anti-tank gun is in the wrong position, but Corporal Godbolt has the PIAT. Its projectile hits the gunboat's wheelhouse and it veers out of control. The crew readily surrender, but the gunboat's young skipper rants and raves so loudly in English about how the British are going to be driven into the sea that Major Howard has him gagged. The second gunboat heads back towards Ouistreham.

### *9.32am*

From the small Ministry of Information studio, John Snagge is reading the official communiqué giving confirmation of the invasion, on the BBC's Home, Overseas and European Services.

'Under the command of General Eisenhower, Allied Naval Forces, supported by strong Air Forces, began landing Allied Armies this morning on the northern coast of France...'

Stuart Hills and the crew of his Duplex Drive are listening to the broadcast below decks of the LCG that pulled them out of the water off Gold Beach almost two hours ago. Whisky, chocolate bars and blankets are helping them recover from their ordeal.

*The original plan was to have an American colonel read the introduction to the communiqué, but the BBC director general, Sir William Haley, vetoed it, saying that the listeners needed to hear such vital news from a voice they knew and trusted.*

***Everybody was shooting at us. I don't think they liked us very much. We came under a hell of a lot of fire and we lost 18 tanks within about the first 12 minutes we***

***were ashore. Don't forget the Germans had been in those positions for about four years, so they must have known the range to every pebble on the beach.***

**Sam Pezaro, tank commander, 1st Northamptonshire Yeomanry**

*9.40am*

In among the wreckage of the tanks and dead bodies on Sword Beach is an 18-year-old French girl named Jacqueline Noel. She's a Red Cross volunteer, and is helping the injured as best she can. Wolf whistles accompany her efforts. Jacqueline hadn't planned to help; earlier she'd cycled to the coast to go to one of the beach huts to retrieve a bathing suit that her twin sister had given her as a present. Her sister had died in an air raid on Caen two weeks ago and Jacqueline wanted to make sure the costume wasn't stolen.

As well as nursing the injured she's also helping to bring bodies out of the water.

## 'This is the Allies' big day'

*About 9.50am*

Minefields are still a deadly hazard on the beaches. Captain Albert H Smith and Captain Hank Hangsterfer of the 1st Infantry are on the edge of a minefield on Omaha. They decide the safest route is to walk over the bodies of two dead GIs who have been blown up by a mine.

On Juno, R S Haig-Brown of the Royal Artillery believes he understands how to interpret the German signs warning of minefields. If the writing slopes down to the left it's a dummy field; if it slopes to the right it's an anti-personnel field; if the writing's level there are anti-tank mines buried there. However, Haig-Brown is completely thrown by the fact that so many of the mines he has deactivated have turned out to be British, captured at Dunkirk four years before. Many of the dummy minefields in Normandy were laid out by German officers in order to fool Rommel that they were keeping up with his strict timetable for the Atlantic Wall.

First Lieutenant Martin Pöppel, a paratrooper with the German 6th Parachute Regiment, is updating his diary.

'It turns out that this is the Allies' big day – which unfortunately means that it's ours too.'

Much of the German response to the Allied paratroopers creating havoc in the countryside behind the beaches has been fragmented and disorganised, partly because many of their commanding officers are in Rennes for the map exercise, but also because a large number of phone lines have been cut. Pöppel's 6th Parachute Regiment, numbering 3,500 men, is scattered across the countryside and still struggling to coordinate a counter-attack.

### *10.00am*

General Eisenhower's pre-recorded announcement is being broadcast by the BBC.

'People of Western Europe, a landing was made this morning on the coast of France by troops of the Allied Expeditionary Force. This landing is part of the concerted United Nations' plan for the liberation of Europe made in conjunction with our great Russian allies. I have this message for all of you: although the initial assault may not have been made in your own country, the hour of your liberation is approaching...'

In their hiding place in Amsterdam, for Anne Frank and her family this is the confirmation they've longed for.

Ben Smith Jr, a radio operator-gunner with the 8th US Air Force, is listening to Eisenhower's address at his base in Cambridgeshire. He thinks Churchill would do it with a lot more class.

On Gold Beach, in a sandbagged shelter close to the sea wall, Sergeant John Bosworth is sharing some rum with men from the Royal Pioneer Corps who've been on the beach for an hour. Bosworth's job is to clear Gold of any remaining obstacles with his armoured bulldozer, parked just outside the shelter.

Bosworth takes off his gloves and notices for the first time that his palm has been pierced by a piece of shrapnel. A navy beachmaster (whose job is to marshal troops and equipment) spots his injury.

'You had better get that fixed up. The FAP [First Aid Post] is over there. Take my dog with you. The walk will do her good.'

Bosworth puts on a steel helmet and heads for the medics, taking a dog for a walk in the middle of the invasion of Normandy.

Juno Beach also has a beachmaster with a dog. Captain Colin Maud greets each new unit holding a stick in one hand and his Alsatian's lead in the other, saying, 'I'm the chairman of the reception committee and of this party, so get a move on!'

### *10.15am*

Fifty Royal Marine Commandos are having a humiliating D-Day. An LCT found them struggling in the water 200 yards off Juno Beach. They'd assumed it would take them ashore, but the skipper has orders to return to port, and so the men are heading, wet and cold, back to England without firing a shot.

### *10.20am*

The hydrogen-filled barrage balloons that have been flying above Sword Beach to deter the Luftwaffe have all been cut adrift and are floating away. They had inadvertently been acting as markers for German artillery inland. The RAF crews manning the balloons had been getting a great deal of abuse.

Churchill is in the underground Map Room in Great George Street, not far from No 10, monitoring the progress of the troops on the beaches.

### *10.30am*

Lord Lovat and his men are on an eight-mile forced march to the two bridges at Bénouville captured earlier by Howard's men. Marching reluctantly with them at gunpoint is a German officer whom Lovat spotted sitting at the bottom of a shell hole on Sword Beach, trying to avoid the fighting. The fact that he was calmly smoking a pipe had especially irritated Lovat.

Intelligence officer Corporal Peter Masters is part of a unit cycling through the village of Colleville-sur-Orne, a mile from Sword Beach. The locals are cheering and waving.

'*Vive les Tommies*! *Vive la France*!'

His unit went down the ramps of the landing craft laden down not only with their bicycles, but also backpacks, 200 feet of rope to help cross the Orne if the bridge hasn't been taken, two days' rations and a spade.

Rommel has heard enough reports over the last few hours from his chief of staff General Speidel to know that he must leave home and head to Normandy. He's already cancelled his meeting with Hitler to ask for the panzer regiments to be moved to the coast. Rommel kisses Lucie and puts his hand on his son's head.

'Well Manfred, you and I will try and win the war.'

At Caen Prison, the Gestapo have finished their first wave of executions of political prisoners. They included farmers, policemen, fishermen, railway workers and a dentist. They are being buried in flowerbeds outside the prison, and soldiers are washing away the blood. They will be back to shoot more this afternoon.

### *10.45am*

After the initial bloodbath on Gold Beach in which the Royal Hampshires, the 1st Dorsets and the Green Howards especially suffered high casualties, seven exits have now been cleared, and after stubborn resistance by the German forces in the hamlet of La Rivière, the eastern end of the beach is almost secure.

German POWs are trudging towards the seashore. Twenty-two-year-old Private Francis Williams of the Green Howards had earlier helped capture six of them in a machine gun nest. He notices that one has a band on his sleeve saying 'Afrika Korps'. Williams had fought them as part of Monty's desert army.

'You Rommel's man?' Williams says to him.

'Ja,' the soldier says with a nod.

Williams points to his Africa Star campaign ribbon.

'Me 8th Army,' and he shakes the German's hand, then goes to rejoin the remnant of his platoon.

On Juno, a group of German POWs blinded by Crocodile flamethrowers are being treated by British medics. They are seated in seaside deckchairs.

### *11.00am*

Major 'Tubby' Barton, Ted Roosevelt's commanding officer, has arrived on Utah Beach. He had initially refused Roosevelt's request to be a part of the invasion force. Roosevelt is giving Barton a report on the situation on the beach.

Barton will write later, 'I loved Ted. When I finally agreed to his landing with the first wave, I felt sure he would be killed. When I had bade him goodbye, I never expected to see him alive. You can imagine then the emotion with which I greeted him when he came out to meet me.'

Second Lieutenant Arthur Jahnke and a few of his men are still holding out on the dunes above Utah. Through his binoculars he can see an American assault team studying a captured German Goliath – a small remote-controlled tank. The Americans are intrigued but amused by its size. One of the soldiers places a hand grenade inside the Goliath and runs off. What the GIs don't know is that it contains a huge quantity of explosives, and it detonates, killing all of them.

In the centre of Omaha Beach, the 16th Infantry Regiment

has progressed about half a mile inland, but elsewhere they are still pinned down.

At the west end of the beach, Private Ray Moon of the 116th has managed to reach the top of a bluff and is looking back towards the sea.

'The view was unforgettable. The beach was a shooting gallery for machine-gunners. The scene below reminded me of the Chicago stockyard cattle pens and its slaughter house...'

On Juno Beach, Royal Navy telegraphist Ronald Seaborne has climbed over the sea wall and is trying to make contact by radio with HMS *Belfast* to tell her that the beachhead is secured. There's no reply. Seaborne wonders if she's been sunk.

Count Guy de Montlaur and the other Free French Commandos have taken the casino at Sword Beach.

Sheets that were put out to dry first thing this morning near airfields in the south of England are covered in black oily grease from the steady stream of planes flying overhead.

### *11.05am*

The British plan to advance from Sword Beach and capture the city of Caen by nightfall has stalled. The infantry of the South Lancashires have the village of Hermanville but they're now waiting for tank support from the Staffordshire Yeomanry before they can take the road to Caen.

A German strongpoint nearby, which is also the headquarters of the 736th Grenadier Regiment and code-named Hillman by the British, is also halting the advance. (The well-protected strongpoints around Sword have been named, rather light-heartedly, after cars or fish, hence Daimler, Morris, Sole, Cod.)

Hillman is a formidable 600 yards wide, with 12 gun emplacements, concrete walls nine feet thick, and defended by 300 men. The 1st Battalion of the Suffolk Regiment is struggling to take it.

Morris surrendered after an hour, and Daimler, with four lethal 77mm guns facing Sword Beach, is being slowly overrun by the East Yorkshire Regiment. Private Lionel Roebuck of the Yorkshires ran into an empty Daimler pillbox and was confronted by a large picture of Hitler. Angry at 'all the trouble that chap had caused us', he smashed its glass with his rifle, then grabbed a couple of fountain pens from a desk and left.

Seventy of Daimler's defenders are being led away. One of them is trying to ingratiate himself with his captors by showing off his collection of pornography. Another shouts in perfect English, 'This is only a raid, ay?'

The men of the East Yorkshires shout back in unison:

'This is the invasion!'

As on Juno and Gold, the men manning the bunkers are very happy to surrender. A captain from the Royal Artillery comes across four Germans with their suitcases already packed.

Inland, a unit from 4 Commando is walking past a field of strawberries. For some the temptation is too great, and they start eating them. The farmer protests to their commanding officer, Major Pat Porteous.

'For four years the Germans were here, and they never ate one...'

Some of the fighting has moved into the surrounding fields. The battle has echoes of the recent past. Private E Evans of the Royal Norfolk Regiment will write later, 'That was the day that I first saw the red poppies of France in the cornfields, diving to the ground out of the machine-gun fire. My nose was stuck right amongst them! They reminded me of the hell and horrors of the 1914 war which my father had talked about so often.'

'The invasion? What about the invasion!?'

General Eisenhower's wife Mamie has just been woken up by a phone call from a reporter from the *New York Post*, and this is the first she's heard about it. She's staying in a hotel room in West Point ahead of their son's graduation ceremony.

***11.10am***

Two miles from Utah Beach and four and a half hours after he landed, Captain George Mabry is outside the village of Pouppeville with soldiers he's collected since leaving the beach. They can hear gunfire – some of it must be from US paratroopers, as no one else from Utah Beach has come this far out, and so Mabry hoists a small identification flag. Some paratroopers of the 101st Airborne appear and head towards Mabry and his men.

'They stared at me as though I were the first American they had ever seen – because I came from the sea!' he will write later.

The US infantry have linked up with the US airborne.

Royal Engineer John Honan is sitting in a barber's chair having a shave in a village close to Juno Beach. For the moment, his perilous job of removing the detonators on Rommel's defences is over. The barber had offered him a cognac but Honan asked for a trim instead. Honan's battledress is soaking wet and water from the English Channel is squelching in his boots.

### 11.20am

The House of Commons is packed as MPs wait eagerly for the arrival of the prime minister, who is running late. In the meantime, a junior treasury minister is listening to a question from a Labour MP asking for office cleaners in future to no longer be referred to as 'charwomen' or 'charladies'. This would be very much appreciated by the Association of Office Cleaners. The minister is happy to oblige.

At St Paul's Cathedral an impromptu service is taking place. The congregation mostly consists of office workers who have just heard the news that today is D-Day. They have sung 'Oh God Our Help in Ages Past' and 'Soldiers of Christ Arise'. Women in the congregation who came to work without a hat are using handkerchiefs to cover their heads.

St Ann's Church in the centre of Manchester is holding short services every half-hour, ending with the National Anthem; queues are already forming for the midday service.

Photographer Seth Shepard has been on Omaha Beach for almost two hours. After swimming ashore, he and some other members of the crew of LCI 92 slowly crawled to a low sea wall at the top of the beach – the only place they could find protection from the bullets and shells. Shivering with cold, he's watching a team of navy men trying to set up a signal light – every time they start to flash out a message a German sniper shoots it out. Shepard is shocked by the sight of mangled bodies on the sand and in the surf, and is amazed that the wounded lie so quietly, knowing that there's no use in calling for help, as every man is needed to fight.

There are approximately 3,000 dead or seriously wounded lying on Omaha Beach.

## 'How do you say 'I'm sorry' in German?'

### *11.30am*

From a command post on the Normandy cliffs, Lieutenant Commander Heinrich Hoffmann is looking over the waters, where six hours ago he was fighting the Allies in his E-boat. With him is Admiral Herman von Bredow, the commander of the Le Havre base.

Hoffmann is startled by what he can see – the bay is filled with Allied ships; he can count almost 200. He is amazed that the Luftwaffe is nowhere to be seen.

'It is a miracle that you're here. We were convinced that none of you would ever make it back,' the admiral says.

When they return to Le Havre, there will be a message for Hoffmann from Admiral Dönitz, the commander in chief of the German Navy, commending him and his crew for their bravery, and allowing them double food rations.

On a grassy knoll above Omaha Beach, Captain Albert H Smith suggests to Captain Hank Hangsterfer that they 'have a little break'. Smith gets out a bottle of Johnnie Walker Red that was a gift from an old lady in Lyme Regis, and the two men have an apple and a nip of Scotch as the battle rages below them.

'It was,' Smith will later recall, 'the most pleasant five-minute break of my military career.'

General Omar Bradley on USS *Augusta* receives a message that on Omaha Beach 'things look better'.

### *About 11.45am*

'Everybody out! Come out! You are totally surrounded! Give yourselves up! The war is over for you! You don't have a chance unless you surrender now!'

Corporal Peter Masters of X Troop is shouting in German (while trying to disguise his Austrian accent) as he walks down a road towards a machine-gun nest. He's attempting something he saw Cary Grant do in the 1939 film *Gunga Din*, when he was hopelessly outnumbered by Indian rebels.

Masters is part of a commando troop whose advance towards the Bénouville bridges has been hindered by the machine-gun that has already killed one of their men. His commanding officer, Captain 'Robbo' Robinson, has sent him on a mission to reconnoitre the German position.

'How many men do I take?' Masters had asked.

'No, Masters, just you.'

'Very good, sir. I'll approach those houses from the left and make my way back in a sweep around the right.'

'You don't seem to understand what I want you to do. Go down this road and see what's going on in the village,' Robinson said.

The penny dropped. Robinson doesn't know Masters, and clearly feels this young man with the strange accent is expendable – he wants him to draw the Germans' fire so the commandos can see where they're hiding.

It works – suddenly a German soldier stands up from behind a wall and he and Masters fire at each other, both missing. Behind Masters, the entire troop of commandos take this as their cue to storm the machine-gun. The Germans flee, leaving two wounded men behind.

The commando who shot them is mortified – he's never shot anyone before.

'How do you say "I'm sorry" in German?' he asks Masters. '*Verzeihung – es tut mir leid*,' Masters tells him.

> ***On the morning of 6th June, we saw the full might of the English and Americans. At sea close inshore the fleet was drawn up, limitless ships small and great as if for a parade, a grandiose spectacle. No one who did not see it could have believed it. The whistling of the shells and shattering explosions around us created the worst kind of music. Our unit has suffered terribly – you and the children will be glad I survived.***
>
> ***A letter found on the body of a German soldier, summer 1944***

*Midday/11.00am European Time/7.00am US Eastern War Time*

With no news from Normandy, the BBC midday bulletin says only that 'no details have yet come in from the Allied side of the progress of the operations'.

In the United States, the mayor of Philadelphia, Bernard Samuel, is tapping the Liberty Bell 12 times with a wooden mallet, and the chimes are being broadcast live to radios across the country.

The New York *Daily News* has scrapped its leading articles and printed the Lord's Prayer instead. In a couple of hours the New York Stock Exchange will stop for a two-minute silence, and today all Major League baseball games will be cancelled. In Dallas, a newborn baby girl has been named Invasia Mae.

In Canada later today special church services will be held, and in the House of Commons in Ottawa, MPs will sing the Marseillaise and 'God Save the King'.

The entire 3rd Canadian Division has now landed on Juno Beach. Some regiments are a mile inland.

Hitler is chairing a military conference at Schloss Klessheim, an hour's drive from the Berghof.

'So we're off!' he chuckles to his High Command as he walks in.

Hitler tells them that the weather is on Germany's side and that the Allied troops will be easily repulsed. He wants them 'annihilated' by the end of the day, as there is a danger of further sea and airborne landings.

Watching him, Goebbels thinks that Hitler seems almost relieved that the invasion has finally happened.

### *12.05pm*

Donald Burgett of US 101st Airborne Division is on raised ground near Ravenoville, a village he and a small band of paratroopers took a couple of hours earlier. He can see Utah Beach and the exits from it crammed full of troops, and an American battleship making its way across the bay. Suddenly she opens fire, and Burgett watches as explosions slam into an apple orchard close by, sending whole trees into the air. Someone in Burgett's makeshift unit sends up orange smoke as a signal that friendly troops are in the area. The warship stops firing and in turn sends up an orange smoke flare in acknowledgement.

## *12.10pm*

General Montgomery is spending the day at Southwick House, reading reports from the beaches, consulting with the officers in the Map Room and taking walks in the gardens.

Churchill is addressing the House of Commons about the successes of the Italian campaign. He is teasing his audience, who are desperate for news of the invasion. They'd been concerned when he'd arrived, as he'd looked deathly pale. The prime minister finally gives them what they want.

'I have also to announce to the House that during the night and the early hours of this morning, the first of the series of landings in force upon the European Continent has taken place... So far the commanders who are engaged report that everything is proceeding according to plan. And what a plan! This vast operation is undoubtedly the most complicated and difficult that has ever taken place. It involves tides, wind, waves, visibility, both from the air and the sea standpoint, and the combined employment of land, air and sea forces in the highest degree of intimacy and in contact with conditions which could not and cannot be fully foreseen...'

*Churchill thought that by including the phrase 'the first of the series of landings' he was carrying out a simple but effective deception. In fact, he's posed a major problem for British Intelligence. Their double agent Garbo told his German minders a few weeks ago that he'd got a job at the Ministry of Information and had even signed the Official Secrets Act, as the material he'd be reading was so sensitive. Garbo said that the Ministry was determined that after an invasion there should be no reference to 'further attacks and diversions', because that is exactly what the Allies are planning. Because Churchill has unwittingly contradicted that false intelligence, Garbo's German minders might start to doubt his credibility as a spy, and therefore doubt the whole of Operation Fortitude. To save the situation, MI5 must come up with a plan by the end of the day.*

Peter Masters' wounded prisoners turn out to be only 15 and 17. They deny that they killed anyone from his commando troop. But Masters can see their half-empty machine-gun belts, and so knows they are lying. They are also keen to be prisoners of war in England.

'Can we be evacuated right now?'

'Give us a chance, we've only just got here,' Masters replies.

## 'Now they'll know how our boys felt on the beaches of Dunkirk'

### *12.15pm*

The prime minister is wrapping up his statement to the Commons.

'It is, therefore, a most serious time that we enter upon. Thank God, we enter upon it with our great Allies all in good heart and all in good friendship.'

As he sits down, Churchill is greeted by enthusiastic cheers. He leaves the House for lunch with the King.

Across Britain, people are queuing to give blood and buy newspapers. Teenager Veronica Smith has queued for a quarter of an hour for the midday edition of the *London Evening Standard*. No sooner has she bought it than a woman dashes up and offers her four times the money for it.

Journalist Mollie Panter-Downes is on the streets of London, looking up at the planes overheard. Someone by her says, 'Now they'll know how our boys felt on the beaches of Dunkirk.'

Mollie will write later that day in her weekly column for the *New Yorker*, 'For the English, D-Day might well have stood for Dunkirk Day. The tremendous news that British soldiers were back on French soil seemed suddenly to reveal exactly how much it had rankled when they were beaten off it four years ago.'

At one stage Churchill had pushed for Overlord to include a sort of 'reverse Dunkirk' – small boats piloted by civilians, as had been the case in May 1940, but this time landing infantry on the Normandy beaches. Churchill's military aides, who could no doubt see the psychology at play here, managed to persuade him it was not a good idea.

George Saunders of 10 Commando's X Troop, is in the cellar of a farmhouse not far from Sword Beach. His leg is injured after a German grenade exploded close by, and he didn't move quickly enough to escape its shrapnel. Saunders' injury is not stopping him enjoying a lunch of Camembert washed down with a bottle of Château d'Yquem that he's found in the cellar. He hasn't had a lunch like this in years.

### *12.30pm*

Lord Lovat and his brigade of commandos are walking in single file along a poplar-lined road on the outskirts of the village of Bénouville. They aren't far now from the captured bridges. Bill Millin is out in front playing 'Lochan Side', with Lovat just behind him. Suddenly Millin spots a sniper in a tree ahead and a second later a flash from his rifle. Half a dozen commandos rush past Millin firing into the tree. The sniper tumbles down and runs into a field – his head bobbing up and down over the corn. Lovat drops to one knee and fires his rifle. The sniper falls, and Lovat sends in some men to retrieve his body.

'Well, start playing your pipes again, piper,' Lovat says. The brigade continues along the road.

### *12.43pm*

After the initial confusion when the Utah troops landed in the wrong place, the assault on the beach has gone almost exactly as planned. Its three transport ships the *Empire Gauntlet*, the *Dickman* and the *Barnett* have unloaded their troops and landing craft and are heading back to Portland Harbour for more.

Second Lieutenant Jahnke is sitting on the anti-tank wall of Utah beach, desperate for a cigarette. After six hours of fighting he's been captured, not before being almost buried alive by a tank shell. An American officer calls him over.

'How many guns do you have? How strong was your complement of men?'

Jahnke shakes his head and says nothing. The officer then produces a map printed on silk that has a complete layout of Strongpoint W5 – even including the old Renault tank. On top of the map is written 'Utah'.

'Do you come from there?' Jahnke asks, mystified.

Throughout the morning, at Rommel's headquarters at La Roche-Guyon, the mood has been remarkably optimistic. They'd expected Allied air attacks on the chateau, but so far there have been none. They remain convinced that the Allies will be thrown back into the sea. Yet there is a feeling of annoyance that Rommel, '*Der Chef*', isn't here.

At this moment, Rommel is being driven at 90mph in his black Horch convertible by his driver Corporal Daniel. Occasionally Rommel encourages him to go faster, '*Tempo*! *Tempo*! *Tempo*!'

The car has no escort as Rommel believes he doesn't need protection – he likes and trusts the French. On 4th June when they were travelling down from Normandy, a tyre had punctured. While Corporal Daniel was changing the tyre a woman passed with a child and said, 'Look, there's Field Marshal Rommel.'

Rommel had held the child in his arms and turned to his aide Captain Hellmuth Lang and said, 'Lang, you see they really do like me.'

> ***Though death had no attractions, and would distress a happy family, I regarded such risk as the luck of the draw. People who enjoy life are seldom troubled by thoughts of departure...***
>
> ***Lord 'Shimi' Lovat***

### *1.00pm*

John Snagge is reading the one o'clock news on the BBC.

*The following May, BBC newsreaders will start to receive letters from grateful listeners in occupied Europe. Like H Bloemraad from Larwik in Norway.*

*'The optimistic sound in your voices was undeniable when the news was good. That was the case when the Germans began to retreat in Russia, and when the invasion took place on D-Day... It did not last long before we were forbidden to listen to your stations by our 'protectors' as we called the Germans, but this prohibition with all the threatenings did not keep us from listening. As soon*

*as the Germans are in their cages I'll bring this letter to the post office...'*

Anne Frank is listening to John Snagge's bulletin. It gives her hope that their ordeal could soon be over.

'Perhaps, Margot [Anne's sister] says, I may be able to go back to school in September or October, ' she writes later.

*Sadly, it will prove to be a false hope. On 4th August, almost two months to the day, the Franks will be betrayed, and their secret annexe discovered by the Gestapo. Her mother Edith will die in Auschwitz, Anne and Margot in Bergen-Belsen, just days before the camp is liberated. Her father Otto will survive.*

Lieutenant 'Tod' Sweeney is part of the successful mission by the Oxfordshire and Buckinghamshire Light Infantry to capture the Bénouville bridges. He's lying on the east side of the bridges, exhausted. He nudges Lieutenant Dennis Fox next to him.

'Listen! You know, Dennis, I can hear pipes!'

'Don't be stupid, Tod, we're in the middle of France...'

Before they left for France, Lord Lovat, Lieutenant Colonel Geoffrey Pine-Coffin of the 1st Airborne and Major John Howard, the leader of the Oxford and Buckinghamshire Light Infantry, had agreed on some signals. When Lovat and his men approach the bridges over the Orne and the Caen Canal, Millin will play his pipes to let Pine-Coffin and Howard know they're coming; Pine-Coffin's bugler will reply – one blast meaning that the road is clear, another that it is being fought over.

One of Howard's men asked him this morning, 'Is Pine-Coffin a code name, sir?'

A few hundred yards from the bridge, Bill Millin hears two blasts from a bugle. He can also hear bullets hitting the side of the metal bridge and see wounded being carried into the Café Gondrée.

Ever since Major Howard's men took the bridges at Bénouville just after midnight, they've been fending off German attempts to retake them. At around 3am reinforcements arrived – Pine-Coffin and his unit of paratroopers – but their ammunition is beginning to run out, and help from the beaches was supposed to have come at noon.

'Quiet! Quiet!' Major Howard shouts.

Over the other side of the bridge he can see Lovat walking two paces behind a piper, with his trademark white pullover and walking stick, and with a rifle over his shoulder, looking 'as if he were on exercise back in Scotland'. To Lovat, the scene in front of him looks like something from a Western, and to the beleaguered defenders it certainly feels as if the commandos are the cavalry.

Georges Gondrée runs out of his café towards Lord Lovat with a tray carrying a bottle of champagne and a couple of glasses, but Lovat waves him away and marches on. Paratrooper Corporal Wally Parr, who 12 hours ago had been shouting, 'Come out and fight, you square-headed bastards!' as he stormed the bridge, accepts a glass with a grateful, '*Oui*, *oui*, *oui*!'

Bill Millin, tired and thirsty, looks over his shoulder longingly as Parr drinks the champagne. Many of the tired paratroopers are hugging the commandos, tears running down their cheeks.

Lovat is crossing the first bridge with Millin still playing. When they reach the other side, Major Howard steps forward and puts out his hand. Lovat takes it.

'John, today history is being made,' he says.

Howard briefs Lovat about the situation and warns him about bringing his men across the bridges because of snipers.

'Hi, you, German!'

On Utah Beach, Second Lieutenant Jahnke is being told to stand in the presence of an American officer. The officer is General Roosevelt. Jahnke raises his hand to his forehead in salute. Roosevelt instinctively starts to raise his, but then thinks better of it.

### *1.02pm*

Piper Millin and Lovat are walking across the second bridge – the bridge over the River Orne. It's narrower, with open sides, and Millin can see two paratroopers in a trench motioning to them to go back. Millin turns to Lovat, who is walking casually behind him.

'Carry on, carry on…' Lovat says.

'Blue Bonnets Over the Border' echoes around the bridge.

When the two men have crossed, Lieutenant 'Tod' Sweeney comes up to Lovat and says, 'Very pleased to see you, old boy.'

'And we are very pleased to see you, old boy. Sorry we are two and half minutes late.'

Millin shakes hands with the two amazed paratroopers in the trench.

General Hermann von Oppeln-Bronikowski is in charge of the 22nd Panzer Regiment of the 21st Panzer Division. He's trying to get his tanks through Caen so that he can get to the western

British beaches, but the Allied bombers have created so much devastation, the roads are blocked with rubble. Fleeing civilians are also getting in the way. Earlier he received orders to attack the eastern beaches, but they were countermanded by General Marcks, who wanted his regiment to attack further west. This meant von Oppeln-Bronikowski had to turn his convoy around and go through Caen, a far longer route, which also made him vulnerable to air attack. Although the regimental commander, von Oppeln-Bronikowski is now at the rear of his line of tanks.

Von Oppeln-Bronikowski is watching three German soldiers totter down the rubble-filled street. Their faces and uniforms are dirty – they are clearly drunk. At the top of their voices they are singing '*Deutschland Über Alles*'. Far from being angry at their ill discipline, von Oppeln-Bronikowski feels that the scene is tragically humourous – it is how they all feel. The war is lost already.

*He himself has let discipline slide. On 11th May, Rommel had turned up at 7am at von Oppeln-Bronikowski's headquarters to find him not there. Half an hour later von Oppeln-Bronikowski turned up drunk, muttering, 'What a disaster…' when he saw the field marshal. Rommel let it go, as von Oppeln-Bronikowski is such an excellent soldier.*

*Von Oppeln-Bronikowski is a legend to his men. In the First World War he won an Iron Cross, and in 1936 he represented Germany at the Olympic Games in dressage, and won gold. On the Eastern Front he commanded a tank that destroyed 25 Russian tanks. On the battlefield von Oppeln-Bronikowski chooses to sleep under his tank, rather than seek the more comfortable accommodation usually preferred by officers.*

### *1.05pm*

General de Gaulle has finally agreed to make a speech to the French people, and is at the BBC's Bush House recording it. The speech will be broadcast at 6pm this evening.

Lovat's commandos are now running in twos and threes past the Gondrées' café and over the first of the two bridges. Sniper fire rings out. The Oxfordshire and Buckinghamshire's medical officer Dr John Vaughan steps out to greet a young commando. The man drops down dead in front of him and rolls into a ditch, shot in the head. A dozen men are killed before they get across the bridges – most shot in the head, their green berets no protection. Lovat believes that going into war with a steel helmet is like 'having a piano on your head'.

The commandos that follow later decide to swim across the river and the canal.

Sitting on the far side of the second bridge are three German POWs. One of them is calling out for water. A commando, who has just witnessed one of his colleagues getting killed, shouts, 'I'll give you water!'

Then kills all three.

### *1.15pm*

Corporal Franz Gockel had been firing his machine-gun at the GIs on Omaha Beach for almost five hours. Then his gun was hit so he resorted to firing single shots from his pistol. Now he's darting up a zigzag trench at the rear of his bunker to get something to eat for his commanding officer and his colleagues. Suddenly he sees some American soldiers and turns to run. There are shots and a violent pain stabs his hand. Gockel looks down and sees three fingers dangling only by their tendons. He manages to get back to his bunker.

Looking at the wound a colleague says, 'Gockel, you should be glad; that is your ticket home; we don't know how we are going to get there...'

### *1.30pm*

On board USS *Augusta*, General Omar Bradley is receiving another update from Omaha Beach.

'Troops formerly pinned down on beaches... advancing up heights beyond beaches.'

The battle for Omaha is beginning to go the Americans' way, in part due to the skilled gunnery of the destroyers ordered to sail closer to the shore to support the beleaguered troops. They sailed so close that some of the ships' keels scraped the seabed, and their guns had to be constantly hosed to cool them down. It is also due to the overwhelming numbers of men and machinery landing every hour (18,772 men have arrived so far on Omaha). But mostly the GIs are winning the battle thanks to the bravery of the officers and men of the 1st and the 29th divisions.

The GIs stuck behind beach obstacles, sea walls and wrecked vehicles have a stark choice, summed up by Colonel George Taylor of 1st Division's 16th Infantry Regiment.

'The only people on this beach are the dead and those that are going to die – now let's get the hell out of here!'

Taylor's prediction in the run-up to D-Day, that only by 'throwing stuff onto the beaches until something breaks' would they prevail, has proved to be correct on Omaha.

Fifty-one-year-old Brigadier-General Norman 'Dutch' Cota typifies the courage of Omaha. He'd been under no illusions how difficult the landings would be. A few days ago he'd warned his officers that there would be 'confusion... people are going to be landed in the wrong place... but we must improvise, carry on, not lose our heads.'

Since he arrived on the beach at 7.30am, Cota has been urging his men forward and even leading a charge himself up one of the gullies. For hours he's moved up and down the gully urging men through the minefields. C Company of the 116th met Cota and a unit of his men as they headed towards the village of Vierville. Cota was calmly twirling his pistol on his finger.

'Where have you been, boys?' Cota asked.

Lacking the correct equipment, engineers have cleared some minefields by crawling on their stomachs and gently digging with a knife. One path was cleared by forcing a German prisoner to walk through a minefield first, the Americans then following in his footsteps.

> ***[On the bus] we sang our heads off – mostly the dirtiest ditties we knew – it was our compliment to the boys in the battles to come... Even the most notorious slackers were working like hell that morning... I think we all said a prayer as we worked...***
>
> ***Anonymous female war production worker, Cheshire***

### *About 1.30pm*

'Taking you off. POW camp. War over!' a sergeant says to Second Lieutenant Jahnke.

Jahnke takes off his boots and socks and wades out to a landing craft off Utah Beach.

Many British factories and offices have been running sweepstakes on when D-day will be. At Airspeed Ltd in Portsmouth (who make Horsa gliders) 17-year-old draughtswoman Dorothy Hinde is celebrating her winnings of £12, 12 shillings and sixpence. She's decided to donate it to the Salute the Soldier fundraising campaign. News bulletins are being relayed by speakers into the offices at Airspeed, keeping the staff up to date on the progress of the Allies. The streets around their building are strangely quiet now all the trucks and tanks are gone.

To Wren Joan Carr-Jones in nearby Southampton, the day feels 'suddenly empty and dead, as if all life had been sucked out of it'.

At a factory in Wales where she's a supervisor, Sylvia Ogden-Smith, whose husband Bruce has been making nighttime trips to Normandy for the last few months to get sand samples, and is currently in a boat off Omaha Beach, has heard that it's D-Day. Now she knows why Bruce couldn't be at Buckingham Palace today to receive his Military Medal from the King.

***1.45pm***

Early this morning the Special Leaflet Squadron, the American 422nd, had dropped leaflets over Caen warning the civilians that its railway station, electricity plant and other key buildings would be attacked and that they should flee to the countryside. Few people have done so. Many people, like the family of Resistance member André Heintz, have heard on the radio that the invasion is in 'the north of France' and assume that must mean the Pas-de-Calais. They think there's no reason to leave. But now 600 heavy bombers of the USAAF are above the city, and their bomb doors are opening. The Allies' aim is to destroy Caen as a communications centre for the Germans, and to inhibit their retreat by blocking the roads with even more rubble.

### *2.00pm*

Sixteen-year-old Naina Cox is working in the accounts department of Chapman's Laundry in Portsmouth, when Miss Hobbs, the commandant of her Red Cross Detachment, rushes in saying that they have so many D-Day wounded at nearby Queen Alexandra's Hospital that they need help from volunteers. Naina, who has taken and passed every Red Cross exam that she can, drops everything and follows Miss Hobbs out of the door.

Fourteen-year-old Leo Harris and his parents are on the balcony of their hotel on the seafront at Havre-des-Pas in Jersey. They have listened to the BBC this morning, and are watching with great delight the German occupiers' reaction to the news of D-Day. Great coils of barbed wire are being pulled across the street, and machine-gun nests are being constructed out of sandbags, some already armed and manned. Looking to his right, Leo can see a small gun, freshly cleaned and lubricated and with a stack of ammunition next to it.

Later that day in the pages of the *Jersey Evening Post*, military commander Colonel Siegfried Heine will issue a stark warning to the Channel Islanders.

'I expect the population of Jersey to keep its head. At the first sight of unrest or trouble I will close the streets to traffic and will secure hostages. Attacks against the German Forces will be punished by death.'

With the tide going out on Omaha Beach, LCI *92* is now high and dry. She has a massive hole on her starboard side close to the bows, where she hit a mine. Some of her crew, including photographer Seth Shepard, are now back on board and are chucking cans of pea soup and army blankets onto the sand. Machine-gun bullets rattle against the hull.

Electrician's mate Gaylord Jones grabs his fishing rod, clambers over the side and then weaves and dodges along the beach.

## *About 2.15pm*

Martha Gellhorn, Ernest Hemingway's wife and a distinguished correspondent in her own right, is having trouble persuading a London cabbie that today is D-Day. He's a member of the Home Guard and he's insisting that the invasion could not possibly have started without him knowing. It's not a good day for cabbies in London – their worst in months. There are few takers on the streets.

Gellhorn currently has no press credentials, so in order to get to Normandy in a few days' time she'll smuggle herself aboard a hospital ship and hide in a toilet for the duration of the voyage.

Nineteen-year-old Bill Davey of the Commando Combined Operations Unit is in a landing craft off Gold Beach having his hair cut by his mate Eddie. They were supposed to land this morning to help shift or repair anything obstructing landing craft or troops, but the bad weather and the loss of 34 LCTs has put everything behind schedule, so the two men are passing the time playing cards and cutting each other's hair.

General von Oppeln-Bronikowski has successfully made it through Caen with his 22nd Panzer Regiment, with the loss of only six tanks from attacks by RAF Typhoons. He's rendezvoused with the 192nd Infantry Regiment – their target is the British beaches, but first they must climb and hold the gently sloping hills that overlook them. General Marcks, the one-eyed, one-legged 84th Corps commander, who at midnight had been celebrating his birthday in Saint-Lô, has come to oversee the battle for himself.

Marcks says to him, 'Oppeln, if you don't succeed in throwing the British into the sea we shall have lost the war.'

Von Oppeln-Bronikowski salutes and says, 'I shall attack now.'

But he's thinking, 'Victory or defeat will depend on my 98 tanks? A mere 98?'

At Caen Prison, the Gestapo have returned with a new list of people to execute, most of them members of the Resistance – both men and women.

### *2.45pm*

Red Cross volunteer Naina Cox is walking down the corridors of Queen Alexandra's Hospital in Portsmouth, looking for the ward she's been assigned to. It's slow work as the corridors are filled with hundreds of wounded men on stretchers who have come straight up from the docks in lorries.

### *2.50pm*

Rommel is being driven as fast as possible to his headquarters in La Roche-Guyon. He says to his aide Captain Hellmuth Lang as he punches a gloved fist into his hand, 'God, I hope there isn't a second landing right now in the Mediterranean. If Montgomery only knew what a mess we're in, he would have no worries tonight.'

## 'It seems to be the beginning of a new phase of history...'

*3.00pm*

Naina Cox has found the ward and together with her friend Win has been assigned the task of cleaning the soldiers and giving them water and cold milk. Those soldiers who are conscious are suffering from exhaustion. Many have soiled themselves from fear.

'How long will it go on? If I come tomorrow and the next day, will I still be doing this?' Naina thinks.

Two nurses come into the ward.

'We have a lot of German prisoners – they were picked up very early from the beaches. A lot of people won't work with them; they are either walking out or refusing to treat them. Will you do what you're doing, for them..?'

Nina says nothing.

Then Win says, 'Oh, come on, Naina. My Eddie is out there and if somebody said they wouldn't clean him up, Mum would feel terrible.'

Naina resolves that if Win is going to do it, she will do it.

A few hours ago, Second Lieutenant Arthur Jahnke was fighting for his life in Stronghold W5 on Utah Beach; now he's on a US destroyer, wounded and holding his boots and socks. He is kicked from behind, and a group of sailors laugh as he falls on the deck. From the bridge an officer shouts something Jahnke can't understand, and he's helped up.

At Caen Prison, members of the Resistance are being killed six at a time. One man with a wooden leg slips in the blood and is shot as he lies on the ground.

In all, 69 are executed on D-Day. Their bodies will never be found as the Gestapo return to painstakingly remove all evidence of their crime.

The news of D-Day has reached the Auschwitz death camp in Poland. Earlier today a Dutch-Jewish teenager named Rita Boas-Koupmann arrived at the camp. She was instantly overwhelmed by a terrible sweet smell that reminded her of Fridays at home when her mother cooks chicken.

One of the prisoners says to her, 'You're unlucky, because even though today the English landed in France, you're going to the crematorium.'

'What crematorium?'

'Look.' She pointed. 'You are going up the chimney, that's where you go through...'

In fact, Rita will survive Auschwitz.

### *3.15pm*

Some parts of Caen are ablaze. Hundreds of people have been killed and injured by the bombardment – and it's still going on. Scores of children have died with their parents, as schools were closed this morning.

André Heintz is trying to get to the Red Cross centre where his sister Danielle works. A house explodes behind him and he's amazed to see two girls tumble out of a cupboard where they'd been hiding, unharmed.

> *In July, the body of a man will be found in a cellar. With him is a note.*
>
> *'I feel that I am dying. It is terrible to know that I'm going to die because I have been expecting the liberation for so long. But I know that, because of my death, other people will be liberated. Long live France, long live the Allies.'*

### *3.30pm*

Jean Layton, a pupil at Bedales School in Petersfield, is starting a diary in an exercise book during a school 'siesta', which she's calling 'Diary of Invasion'.

'No French conversation class, Eileen [a language teacher] is upset. Her husband is in the French Navy, so presumably he's gone. This is the first difference the invasion has made to school life today. Poor Eileen, and there must be millions in her position... We've been waiting for the invasion for so long, that now it's happened one feels, not that it's all over, but what will the confusion be like when it is. It seems to be the beginning of a new phase of history...'

### *4.00pm*

Hitler finally gives his consent for extra panzer divisions to be moved to the coast to assist the 21st Panzer Division.

Second Lieutenant Jahnke is sitting in the wardroom of the US destroyer. He's being treated with respect by her officers, who are intrigued by the Knight's Cross around his neck. Jahnke is enjoying his first real coffee for a long time.

Naina and her friend Win are in a Nissen hut full of German prisoners. Four armed guards on the door have checked their papers and then a nurse says to them bluntly, 'You know what you are here for, don't you? Get on with it.'

Naina is shocked at how the German prisoners look – they are pale, dirty and they smell. They look like tramps. What Naina will always remember is the silence of that Nissen hut, and the German soldiers' glazed, staring eyes.

The whole of Operation Overlord is being photographed by a squadron of reconnaissance aircraft. Tonight the photographic laboratory of the 10th Reconnaissance Group will process almost 10,000 negatives.

Winston Churchill has returned to the House of Commons and is breaking the news about the successful capture by British airborne forces of the Bénouville bridges.

'It is a most serious time that we enter upon. Thank God we enter upon it with our great Allies all in good heart and all in good friendship.'

On board USS *Tuscaloosa*, Colonel David Bruce, the London chief of the Office of Strategic Services, is making the latest entry in his diary. As an intelligence officer he has heard of the 'rocket projectiles' that the Germans have developed, and he's writing that he's mystified why the Germans haven't retaliated by launching them on London and other cities. In fact, about now, Hitler is giving the order for the flying-bomb offensive to begin.

*The first V1 attacks will take place on the morning of the 16th June. Initially, the jet flames from their tails lead to cheering, as people think it is a German plane in flames. But soon people begin to recognise their sinister shape and sound. London taxi drivers will hoot their horn as a warning when they spot one. For many, the summer of 1944 will be more terrifying than the Blitz. In all 10,500 flying bombs will target England.*

David Bruce's Office of Strategic Services agents in France are proving to be invaluable. Earlier today, one of their teams, code-named Vitrail, located the crack Panzer Lehr Division south-west of Caen, as it was about to head to the beaches.

The Vitrail team radioed the division's position, and since then the tanks have been under attack from the RAF and USAAF, and unable to move.

Evelyn Waugh has been working all day on the last chapter of his novel *Brideshead Revisited.* He's recuperating in Devon on unpaid leave, having broken his leg while training to be a paratrooper. Waugh puts down his pen – the book is finished. Now he has to catch the last post to get it to the typist in Sussex. Waugh is worried about the last chapter ('the dialogue's poor') and whether the manuscript will get to the typist safely, and if he will be distracted by the news of the invasion.

> ***Of course we felt patriotic. We were fighting for Germany; the Nazis could go to hell! You separated your country from who was running it and we knew that it was a bunch of criminals but there was nothing we could do about it.***
>
> ***Lieutenant Heinrich Fürst, 706/8 Festungsdivision***

### *About 4.30pm*

Navy telegraphist Ronald Seaborne is hiding behind a gravestone in a churchyard in Crépon, not far from Juno Beach, and sending back situation reports for HMS *Belfast*. He was walking through the churchyard a moment ago, when a bullet whistled past his head. Seaborne peers round the gravestone and catches a glimpse of a steel helmet before another bullet comes his way. He fires back, thinking, 'This is real cowboys and Indians stuff.'

Soon, Seaborne fires his last bullet. It ricochets off a grave and hits the German soldier, who tumbles into view.

Seaborne gets up and walks over to the soldier. He is just a young boy, one of the Hitler Youth. Seaborne feels sick.

A staff officer of the American 29th Division is scribbling an entry in his diary, 'Prayed for the fourth time today, asking God, "Why do these things have to be visited upon men?"'

### *About 5.00pm*

Seth Shepard, the photographer on LCI 92, and some of the other surviving crew are digging with their hands in the sand and rocks of Omaha Beach. Their knuckles are scratched and bloody. The Germans, although retreating, are still bombarding the beach. Shepard and the others have realised that if they are going to survive the night, they will have to dig a foxhole. (Engineers will discover later that if the crew of LCI 92 had dug any deeper, buried German booby traps would have killed them.)

Shepard can see German POWs being marched down the beach, hands on heads. When they hear the sound of their own shells, they fall flat on the sand.

Earlier on Omaha, a GI was marching five German prisoners at gunpoint, when two were shot dead by machine-gun fire from their own men up on the cliffs. The remaining three fell to their knees towards their countrymen, begging not to be shot. But the machine-gunner opened fire once more and another soldier fell dead.

Commando medic Percy 'Shock' Kendrick (so-called because so many of his patients are shell-shocked) is treating an old lady he found crying by the roadside, who's been wounded in the arm. He tries to tell her in broken French that she should be in bed. Misunderstanding him, she slaps him across the face.

Kendrick apologises, gives her some morphine and carries on down the road a little wiser.

### *5.15pm*

André Heintz has reached the Bon Sauveur convent where his sister Danielle works. It's been hit by Allied bombs. The former psychiatric home had been turned into a temporary Red Cross hospital wing but has been reduced to rubble, burying nuns, nurses and patients. Mothers from the maternity wing cling onto their newborn babies and weep and hug each other for comfort.

A nun at the convent will write later, 'Not even the most pessimistic imagined the horrors we witnessed.'

André finds Danielle, and they decide they need somehow to let the Allied pilots know that the hospital is not a target.

### *5.21pm*

On Omaha Beach, Colonel Benjamin Talley signals to the fleet offshore that the beach is now safe enough to receive 'wheeled and tracked vehicular traffic'.

### *About 5.30pm*

Robert Capa wakes up naked under a rough blanket. He is back on USS *Samuel Chase*. He has a note around his neck that says, 'Exhaustion case. No dog tags.' Capa can see his camera bag with its two rolls of film safe on a table nearby.

In a bunk next to him, a young man is staring at the ceiling. He too has a note around his neck saying 'Exhaustion case'.

'I'm a coward,' he says to Capa.

The man is the sole survivor of one of the Duplex Drive tanks that sank long before they got to Omaha. He managed to swim onto the beach, but feels he should have stayed there and fought. Capa insists that of the two of them, he is the coward.

*Capa's photographs will show the world the carnage and chaos of Omaha. They are collected from him at Weymouth on 7th June, and by late that evening they are with a 16-year-old dark-room assistant named Dennis Banks. Banks puts them in a drying cabinet, but at a too high temperature, so the film begins to melt. Of the 72 shots, only 11 frames survive. When they are published by* Life *magazine on 19th June, the caption says they are blurred because the 'intense excitement' made Capa move his camera.*

### *5.45pm*

D-Day is just beginning for some. More waves of troops are on their way to the Normandy beaches. On LCT *7073*, Royal Navy officer J A C Hugill is watching HMS *Roberts* sail past on her way back from Sword Beach. He thinks that she has a smug look about her, 'such as you'd expect to see on the face of a cat after a successful raid on the larder'.

The German and Allied armies are burying their dead. British officer Lieutenant E G G Williams has had to bury a dozen of his men. He will always remember how his sergeant's gold fillings shone in the sun.

## 'You great tub of lard, have you no sentiment?'

### *6.00pm*

General de Gaulle's pre-recorded speech is being broadcast by the BBC European Service.

'The battle has begun and France will fight it with fury. For the sons of France, wherever and whoever they may be, there is a simple and sacred duty to fight with all the means at their disposal.'

Churchill is listening to the broadcast, and when he hears de Gaulle say that a huge attack has been launched from 'old England' he bursts into tears.

His chief of staff Sir Hastings Ismay looks at him in surprise.

Churchill retorts, 'You great tub of lard, have you no sentiment?'

De Gaulle's address is finishing.

'Behind the heavy cloud of our blood and our tears, the sun of our greatness is shining again.'

At Brévands, a few miles from Utah Beach, Captain Ernst Düring of the 352nd Infantry Division (who earlier in the day had befriended a terrified American paratrooper) has received orders to pull out.

Düring has enjoyed his time in Brévands as his quarters were in the comfortable home of the village schoolteacher Monsieur Le Chevalier and his family. Düring is a veteran of the hardships of the Russian Front and has appreciated the comfortable bed at the schoolhouse.

Düring has come to the Le Chevaliers' to say his farewells. He has brought with him some real coffee, and Simone, the teaching assistant has provided a bowl of freshly picked strawberries. Mme Le Chevalier has found some whipped cream. Düring tells Monsieur Le Chevalier that they must all shelter in an anti-tank ditch he's built outside, as he's convinced that the Allies will soon attack the village.

### *6.15pm*

The North Nova Highlanders are marching past the German barracks in the village of Beny-sur-Mer, three miles from Juno Beach. The villagers are helping themselves to furniture, food, boots, sheets, pillows and chickens. Even the parish priest is carrying a set of dishes.

US radio correspondent Bill Herbert is recording a dispatch from the outskirts of Caen.

'The results of this visual bombing attack are really terrific... This is an attack in a big way. The whole target area is a seething mass of smoke. In the growing darkness I can see the first dull red outline of the fire that is apparently raging in Caen. It will be a big bonfire soon...'

André and Danielle Heintz have had an idea that they hope will stop the Allies bombing the hospital at the convent. They are in the vegetable garden of Bon Sauveur, dipping bed sheets in buckets of blood from the hospital's operating room. They then place the sheets in the shape of a large red cross.

As they are spreading the last sheet to make the fourth arm of the cross, an aircraft flies low overhead, heading right for them. André and Danielle are tempted to run, but then see that the plane is waggling its wings. It's an Allied reconnaissance aircraft and it's got the message.

### *6.45pm/5.45pm European Time*

At Oflag IV-C, better known as Colditz, the prisoner-of-war camp for those considered '*deutschfeindlich*' or hostile to the Germans, commando Micky Burn and Captain Jimmy Yule of the Royal Signals are pushing open a steel door that leads to the huge, dusty, empty attic overlooking the castle's courtyard. They are one of three teams who take it turns to listen to the BBC's seven o'clock bulletin. They are wearing shoes without any tread. The Germans sometimes search the attic and look for any sign of footprints in the dust. They know that the prisoners have a radio – their mood changes after significant events in the war.

### *7.00pm/6.00pm European Time*

Micky Burn and Jimmy Yule are sitting in the Colditz radio hide waiting for the BBC news bulletin to begin. The hide was built in 1943 by French officers shortly before they were moved to a different camp. It's hidden under the floor joists of the attic roof, and is an amazingly sophisticated operation. Yule operates the radio while Burn, a former journalist, uses his shorthand skills to write down the latest news of the war. Blankets line the walls to keep drafts out and light in. Pinned to the blankets are charts and maps of Europe. The radio is powered by the castle's electricity supply.

The two of them sit at a table, in front of the radio. Micky Burn has a pencil and paper ready. In the early 1930s he had been a supporter of National Socialism and had even met Hitler at a Nuremburg rally, and got him to sign his copy of *Mein Kampf*. But Burn soon became disillusioned, and in 1938 joined the British Army so he could fight the Nazis in a war that he knew was inevitable. Burn was captured during the amphibious raid on Saint-Nazaire in 1942.

Usually the two men arrive in the attic early, and Yule catches the end of the previous programme. Once he listened to a tennis commentary from Wimbledon, which he found rather surreal. Yule, a POW for four years, plays the piano in the Colditz band and organises revues and pantomimes – the music and the applause often masks the sound of an escape.

John Snagge's voice fills Burn's headphones: 'This is London Calling...'

*The hide will be discovered in 1993 by workmen building a museum at Colditz. On the table they'll find Jimmy Yule's notebook full of codes and directions to help escapees.*

> ***[The German soldier's] slogan is 'Ich oder Du!' 'Me or you!' 'My life or yours!' There he stands. What are you going to do about it?***
>
> ***US* Army Talks *magazine, 'Enemy and You', 3rd May 1944***

George Saunders of 10 Commando's X Troop is cycling towards the British lines, having enjoyed his lunch of Camembert and wine in the farmhouse cellar. He can see a group of soldiers standing around a road junction. They are wearing camouflage and have twigs in their helmets. Saunders waves at them, thinking they're British.

'*Das ist ein Engländer*!' one of them shouts, and they start shooting. Saunders dives into a ditch.

### *About 7.05pm/2.05pm US Eastern War Time*

Churchill will say after the war, 'No lover ever studied the whims of his mistress as I did those of President Roosevelt.'

But FDR is keen to keep the prime minister happy too if he can. He is writing a note to Churchill to accompany a gift of two typewriters. The prime minister had admired the 'squared serif' typeface used by the typewriters in a letter sent to him by General McNarney.

'The two electric typewriters are being shipped without delay which I hope you will accept as a gift from me and as a symbol of the strong bond between the people of America and Great Britain.'

Ronald Seaborne is climbing a tall tree in the middle of a village green in a village a few miles south of Juno Beach. The village is so quiet and idyllic it's as if the war has passed it by. Seaborne's job as a navy telegraphist is to send signals back to HMS *Belfast*, giving her targets to aim at and to inform the ship of her accuracy. But so far he's failed to make contact. With him climbing the tree is an army captain and another navy telegraphist.

They've been told by a group of Russians conscripted into the German Army that there's an airfield nearby. The captain suggested they might see it from the tree.

Suddenly there is a rumbling noise and the three men see a German half-track enter the village and park right under their tree. Two men in the front consult a map; the remaining four get out and urinate against the tree.

### *7.10pm*

Beneath Ronald Seaborne, all six Germans are now back in their half-track. But to the dismay of the three Britons in the tree, they show no signs of moving. Then two other half-tracks arrive and the Germans start a lengthy discussion. The British Army captain decides to do something. He whispers to Seaborne, 'Send a signal to *Belfast* – "Cut off in Daedalus"' (the code name for the village.)

'Don't be daft' the other telegraphist hisses back. 'What bloody good will that do? Jerry will hear the morse key for sure!'

The captain is furious.

'This is mutiny in the face of the enemy! I'll have you shot.'

'Belt up, or you'll get us all killed...'

Seaborne doesn't make the signal.

Captain Ernst Düring and his men are pulling out of Brévands in a column of trucks and half-tracks, and have got about 300 yards along the road heading west. The half-tracks are in front – they're noisy and sound like tanks, which at night might deter Allied paratroopers from attacking them. Suddenly a series of explosions rocks the village – Düring can see Allied warships bombarding Brévands. His column speeds away. Düring wonders if his friends the Le Chevaliers and Simone are safe.

### *7.15pm*

Bill Davey of the Commando Combined Operations Unit was supposed to land on Gold Beach this morning to help shift or repair anything obstructing landing. His unit only managed to land a few hours ago. They have been given a new, grim task – digging bodies out of the sand and rolling them in grey army blankets. They've been ordered to cover up British soldiers but to leave German soldiers where they fell 'for morale purposes'.

### *7.30pm*

In Colditz, Micky Burn and Jimmy Yule have made their way down from the attic and back to their quarters, while a team of 'dust layers' are scattering dust over the attic floor to hide any trace of the men's footsteps. Burn, in a state of high excitement, is reading his shorthand notes of the BBC bulletin, and representatives of each officers' mess are scribbling down their own version.

Flight Lieutenant 'Checko' Chaloupka hears the news of D-Day and like many others is now convinced that the war will be over by Christmas. If it isn't, he declares, on Christmas Eve he will run around the courtyard naked – twice.

*At 4pm on 24th December 1944, to much applause from his fellow prisoners, Chaloupka will run around the courtyard of Oflag IV-C Colditz without his clothes on. The temperature will be -7 degrees C.*

### *About 7.35pm*

The two navy telegraphists and the army captain are still up the tree in the middle of the village green. The Germans below them have made a decision – the crew of one half-track are splitting up and getting into the other two. One half-track turns left out of the village, the other turns right, leaving one half-track behind empty.

Seaborne watches as the other telegraphist immediately slides down the trunk of the tree and into the driver's seat. Seaborne follows him down. The telegraphist gets the engine started so quickly (Seaborne never works out how) they're moving away before the army captain is out of the tree – he has to run to catch them up.

The captured half-track heads down the main road towards the advancing British troops – and safety. Ronald Seaborne had packed all his spare kit and possessions in a truck that sank earlier this morning. For the rest of the month he'll wear what he wore running ashore on D-Day.

## 'Queuing up for fish, getting haircuts, and scrambling for lunch'

### *7.45pm*

George Saunders of X Troop is still hiding from his German pursuers in the ditch. They've been hunting for him for almost an hour. Saunders' advantage, being born in Munich, is that he can understand what they're saying. He knows they are scared and demoralised.

'Aren't you ashamed? It's only one Englishman!' an officer shouts.

'Then why don't you go, *Leutnant*?'

Saunders has grenades and a tommy gun, and he's well trained in commando tactics – he's killed four already.

In England, journalist Mollie Panter-Downes is on the train home from Waterloo to Haslemere. She's spent the day walking around London, gathering impressions and thoughts for her column for the *New Yorker*. Mollie was struck by the sight of typists in summer dresses kneeling by the Tomb of the Unknown Soldier at Westminster Abbey next to old couples in tweeds, and people buying little Red Cross flags and looking thoughtfully at the symbol before pinning them to their lapels.

'There was also a slightly bemused expression on most D-Day faces, because the event wasn't working out quite the way anybody had expected. Londoners seemed to imagine that there would be some immediate, miraculous change, that the heavens would open, that something like the last trumpet would sound. What they definitely hadn't expected was that the greatest day of our times would be just the same old London day, with men and women going to the office, queuing up for fish, getting haircuts, and scrambling for lunch.'

### *8.00pm*

Rommel is pulling up outside his headquarters at La Roche-Guyon, having driven non-stop since 10.30am. The return trip has taken him almost two hours less than his journey south on Sunday.

Rommel's aide Captain Lang runs inside the chateau and can hear opera coming from a gramophone in General Speidel's office.

Lang, incredulous, says to the chief of staff,

'General Speidel, the invasion has begun and you're able to listen to Wagner?'

Speidel replies coolly, 'My dear Lang, do you honestly believe that my listening to Wagner will make any difference whatsoever to the course of the invasion?'

Rommel walks into Speidel's office without making a reference to the music. Watching him start to take control, Lang remembers something that the field marshal said in the car as they drove back to La Roche-Guyon.

'Lang, just imagine, the invasion has begun and we didn't even know about it. No reconnaissance aircraft – and this is the way they want me to win the war...'

Lang has an overwhelming feeling of depression.

On Gold Beach, in an abandoned German bunker, medics from the Essex Yeomanry are treating their wounded. Around them are remains of the German gunners' breakfast, and their wine from the night before. Someone has found a note from a French girl to 'Hans chéri' saying that she'll meet him at the bunker at 8pm. The British troops half hope she'll turn up.

The British 50th Division, which landed on Gold Beach today, is about three miles short of its D-Day objective – Bayeux. Nevertheless 20,000 men and 21,000 vehicles are ashore, and they have secured a beachhead of almost 30 square miles. Although they've failed to link up with the American 1st Division at Omaha, they have joined up with the Canadians at Juno. At the west end of the beach, the hard-pressed

Hampshires have finally taken Arromanches (a key location for a Mulberry harbour) and the hamlet of Le Hamel; the East Yorkshires had a tough battle to win La Rivière on the east side of Gold, but succeeded. Together with the 69th Brigade, they are now pushing south.

In his suburban house in Hendon, north London, double agent Garbo is sending a radio message to his German Intelligence minder in Madrid. He is trying to resolve the security issue created by Churchill's Commons statement that today's assault was 'the first in a series of landings'. This had posed a problem for MI5 who, through Garbo, had earlier told the Germans that after an invasion there would be no further reference to 'further attacks and diversions'.

The credibility of Garbo and Operation Fortitude is on the line – the Germans must believe that the invasion of Normandy is merely a prelude to the invasion at the Pas-de-Calais.

In his message Garbo is saying that he has spoken to a government official who is mortified that Churchill ignored their advice, but that the prime minister had felt obliged not to distort the facts. 'Great men and leaders of countries are bound to tell the truth to their people, even if the truth is damaging to security.' It's risky to praise Churchill to German Intelligence, but they accept his report.

### *About 8.15pm*

Signaller John Raaen from the 5th Ranger Battalion has been ordered to take all papers from German POWs captured on Omaha Beach. He's holding onto any official documents but putting their family photos back in their pockets. The soldiers give Raeen a grateful '*Danke*'. Not all POWs have fared as well today. Near the top of the Vierville gully two US Rangers circling a machine-gun nest were spotted by the three Germans manning it.

One of them suddenly yelled, '*Bitte*! *Bitte*! *Bitte*!'

One of the Rangers opened fire. After the three lay dead he turned and said, 'I wonder what '*bitte*' means?'

### *8.30pm*

In Blandford, Dorset, a number of Land Girls have volunteered to help with the casualties recently brought into the US Army camp. One GI who Land Girl Patricia Gent is helping is so grateful he insists on giving her his Purple Heart, awarded when he was wounded on a previous campaign.

'It's something to remember D-Day by,' he says to her.

A single British soldier is arriving by ambulance at Basingstoke Hospital in Hampshire. The ward is empty, having being cleared of civilian patients. Irish nurse Nancy O'Sullivan is stunned to see that the soldier is still covered in wet Normandy sand.

Whenever he gets a moment at 'Action Stations' in a gun magazine on HMS *Glasgow*, Able Seaman Leslie Sherman updates a diary he's keeping called 'The Second Front.' He's been writing it since Friday. Sherman is writing the entry for today.

'There is only one thing we want when we get back and for the little part we played in this big scene – we hope that they will grant us leave, the sailor's delight. So I must leave you once again with a motto that we lads in the Navy can never forget: "a job worth doing is worth doing well."'

***We lay on our backs and fired, and fired, and fired at those gliders, until we could not work the bolts of our***

***rifles any more. Our flak troop shot some down and damaged many more, but with such masses it seemed to make little difference.***

***Lieutenant Hans Höller, 192nd Panzer Grenadier Regiment***

### *9.00pm*

From Buckingham Palace, via the BBC, King George VI is addressing Britain and the Empire in his familiar faltering delivery.

'Once more... a supreme... test has to be faced. This time, the challenge is not to fight to survive... but to fight the final victory for the good cause...'

In some houses, cafés and pubs people are standing as they listen.

Captain Kenneth Wright of 4 Commando was wounded at about 8am this morning. He's lying on a stretcher by the edge of the water on Sword Beach. His pain has been eased by morphine and some Calvados brought to him by two locals. The beach is still being occasionally shelled. Wright is watching hundreds of aircraft flying over the coast – Dakota transport planes and Stirlings and Halifaxes towing gliders. Parachutes start falling. It is, he thinks, 'a very fine sight indeed'.

An officer with the Suffolk Regiment is watching the reaction of their POWs to the hundreds of planes in the sky.

'It equally impressed the German prisoners but in a different way. They did not seem to think it was quite fair...'

In one of the gliders are hundreds of copies of the *London Evening Standard* with the headline 'Skymen Land In Europe'. An officer in the 6th Airborne bought them from a paper-seller on the street this afternoon so that the first wave of D-Day paratroopers could read about their exploits.

Just above the sand dunes on Sword Beach, BBC reporter Alan Melville is recording a dispatch on his midget portable disc recorder.

'This is Alan Melville, dispatch thirteen, 21.00 hours, 6th of June, from the beach west of Ouistreham. The paratroops are landing! They're landing all around me as I speak – red, white and blue parachutes fluttering down and they're just about the best thing we've seen for a good many hours... I can still see the signs of a typical panzer battle being raged on the slightly raised ground ahead of me...'

What Melville can see is the end of the 21st Panzer Division's attack on the slopes above the beaches near Biéville. General Hermann von Oppeln-Bronikowski, in charge of the 22nd Panzer Regiment, had to wait all day to engage the enemy, and they were waiting for him. As he neared the top of the ridge, the Shermans of the Staffordshire Yeomanry attacked. Within a few minutes, von Oppeln-Bronikowski lost six tanks. Outgunned, he's retreating.

The few Germans still defending the remaining strongholds on the invasion beaches, and the panzer crews who've successfully advanced north, are also looking at the sky in amazement. To the Germans it looks like a rapid response to their counter-attack – an attempt to cut them off. In fact, it's the planned drop by the British 6th Airborne of more men, supplies and heavy equipment to the troops inland.

### *9.15pm*

On the BBC Home Service, announcer Joseph Macleod is introducing the first *War Report*.

'*War Report*! Night by night at this time, this programme will bring you news of the war from correspondents and fighting men; it will contain live broadcasts and recordings made in the field...'

There is a report from Frank Gillard in a landing craft:

'It's coming up to time... the moment when the assault craft are to set off from their assembly area to the beaches...'

An RAF observer in a Mitchell bomber over Normandy:

'We're just getting ready to go in and bomb, and I'd better shut up. Hold it! My God, there's some nasty flak round this place – very nasty flak, blast it!'

Guy Byam reporting from an airfield 'somewhere in England' where he's about to take off with paratroopers heading for Normandy (and he's jumping with them):

'As they knelt round their padre in prayer, with bent heads and on one knee, the men with their equipment and camouflaged faces looked like some strange creatures from another world...'

*Guy Byam will be killed reporting from a bomber over Berlin the following February.* War Report *will run until 5th May 1945. One of its most memorable moments will be when reporter Stanley Maxted in France greets a paratrooper with the words 'Hello son' – and it is his son.*

Outside the Café Gondrée Major Nigel Taylor of the Oxfordshire and Buckinghamshire is enjoying a glass of champagne brought to him by Georges Gondrée and watching the planes and the parachutes of the reinforcements. When the paratroopers arrive shortly after, they are heckled by the tired and weary men who took the bridge that morning.

'Where have you been?'

'A bit late for parade, chaps!'

All day Raoul Mousset has been trying to get to his wife Odette in Ouistreham. All he knows is that their hotel has been destroyed, but he doesn't know if she's survived. He's been repeatedly turned back by German roadblocks, but now he's on a bike that he found next to a dead German soldier, and he's pedalling as fast as he can down the main road to Ouistreham, no longer caring if anyone tries to stop him.

Odette is alive – just. She is still in the first-aid post in the town square, and the British medics treating her think that she will die in the next 24 hours unless she can get proper treatment.

*9.30pm*

An American infantry regiment is setting up camp in a farmer's field in Baynes, a village two miles from Omaha Beach. It's owned by the Hardy family, who all day have been listening to the gunfire and thunder-like explosions coming from the beach. Monsieur Hardy and his four daughters are bringing the exhausted soldiers milk and cheese. 15-year-old Madelaine has noticed that all day there's been no bird song, 'as if nature had simply stopped'.

Peter Masters of X Troop has been part of a commando unit that's made its way off Sword Beach and beyond the Bénouville bridges. His *Gunga Din* heroics were just part of an extraordinary day for the 22-year-old.

Their wireless operator has managed to tune into a BBC

broadcast in German. Masters is translating the news updates for his comrades. When he translates Eisenhower's address to the people of Europe, they all cheer.

## 'Invaded Normandy; left Portsmouth 10.30'

*10.00pm*

General Montgomery, who has been desperate to get to France all day, is finally boarding HMS *Faulknor* at Portsmouth, which will take him to the beaches. Monty won't return to England for six months.

*About 10.15pm*

Raoul Mousset has finally made it through the German and British lines to Ouistreham. He is relieved to discover that Odette is still alive, but the medics break it to him just how seriously injured his wife is.

*10.30pm*

There's a party going on at the Berghof. The Propaganda Minister Joseph Goebbels is playing a piano duet with the Countess Faber-Castell.

He is drunk.

Piper Bill Millin is waking up in a trench after an hour's sleep. His bagpipes are with him, patched up after being hit by shrapnel shortly after he crossed the Orne Bridge.

In the trench with him is fellow commando, Corporal MacGill. Earlier the two of them had taken a walk in the dark around a nearby field and enjoyed the smell of its cornflowers. Their stroll was cut short when mortar bombs started flying through the air, and the two men had dashed back to their trench, MacGill landing feet first.

They'd agreed beforehand that MacGill would take the first watch and so Millin promptly went to sleep.

Now wide awake, Millin wonders why he can't hear a sound from MacGill, not even snoring. He reaches out his hand and pulls it back covered in blood. MacGill has been hit by several pieces of shrapnel and has been dead for an hour.

> ***I think it was about another four to six weeks before we got to Caen eventually, but, if we'd had another infantry regiment that day, we could have done it. Still, there we are. That's war, isn't it?***
>
> ***Lieutenant Lionel Knight, tank commander, Staffordshire Yeomanry***

### *10.45pm*

The D-Day wounded are being treated by medical teams, some of whom who have been working non-stop for 15 hours. Many are taking Benzedrine tablets (supplied in their regular rations) to keep awake. The wounded are being taken out to troop ships that have been converted into temporary hospital ships for the journey back to England. Some confused and shell-shocked casualties think that the nurses and doctors are German medics and are refusing to say anything other than their rank and serial number. On USS *Bayfield* the dead are being put in the ship's refrigerator.

Almost from the start of the fighting on Sword Beach, 18-year-old Jacqueline Noel has been helping the injured and the dying. Since midday she's been helping out at a temporary hospital set up in a shell crater in the sand dunes. In fact, she will remain on Sword Beach for another two days.

For many years after D-Day, soldiers whom Jacqueline helped return to Normandy to say thank you.

By now, six square miles of Sword Beach are under British control. Almost 29,000 men have been landed, and there have been approximately 1,000 casualties. The whole of the British 3rd Division is ashore, including the 27th Armoured Brigade. Units from the 3rd Division are three miles from Caen, but as the (unrealistic) aim of Montgomery was to capture the city by nightfall, in that regard the Sword forces have failed.

Stuart Hills and his tank crew have spent all day on the LCG that had picked them up off Gold Beach this morning after their tank sank. The LCG has been patrolling the beach, firing its main gun and twin machine-guns in support of the second wave of tanks and infantry going ashore. In the gloom, Hills can see that there's still smoke drifting off the beach and the occasional explosion, but the battle has moved inland.

Tomorrow the crew of the LCG will retrieve a dinghy from the sea and put Hills and his four men in it. Armed only with a revolver, and with a helmet each, they slowly paddle towards Gold, watched by a beachmaster on the shore. As they tumble out he says with a smile, 'This will swing the balance in Montgomery's favour; there'll be consternation in Berlin…'

> ***All Commanders… are required to submit after-action reports covering 6th June, to be shown to the Führer, in which questions of surprise and the rapidity of the break-in and penetration are to be carefully addressed.***
>
> ***Field Marshal Rommel***

### *11.00pm/10.00pm European Time/6.00pm US Eastern War Time*

At the Berghof, Hitler holds his second situation conference of the day. He tells his High Command that he remains convinced that the landings are a diversionary attack.

The *Sicherheitsdienst*, Hitler's security service, issues a memo on the mood of the German public.

'The onset of the invasion is widely experienced as a deliverance from unbearable tension and oppressive uncertainty. It constitutes the only topic of conversation.'

The text of an address by President Roosevelt to be broadcast at 10pm Eastern War Time has been published in the afternoon editions of US newspapers. It takes the form of a prayer that people can read out loud with their president.

'Almighty God, our sons, pride of our Nation, this day have set upon a mighty endeavour, a struggle to preserve our Republic, our religion, and our civilization, and to set free a suffering humanity. Lead them straight and true; give strength to their arms, stoutness to their hearts, steadfastness in their faith. Their road will be long and hard. For the enemy is strong... We know that by Thy grace, and by the righteousness of our cause, our sons will triumph...'

Roosevelt ends the prayer by looking ahead to the post-war world.

'Help us to conquer the apostles of greed and racial arrogancies. Lead us to the saving of our country, and with our sister Nations into a world unity that will spell a sure peace. A peace invulnerable to the schemings of unworthy men, and a peace that will let all of men live in freedom, reaping the just rewards of their honest toil. Thy will be done, Almighty God. Amen.'

Roosevelt will have the prayer bound in leather and sent to Churchill.

### *11.15pm*

Piper Bill Millin is lying in his trench in the dark looking at the flashes of artillery fire as the Germans try to recapture the two bridges. Corporal MacGill's body has been taken away by medics and Millin is thinking of all the men who have died today.

'Yesterday evening we were all sipping pints in the canteen in Southampton, talking about wives and girlfriends. Now they're lying dead in a ditch having soil thrown over them...'

All day at an RAF listening station on the Channel coast, Wren Rosemary Geddes has been monitoring the wireless transmissions of the German gun emplacements on the Normandy beaches. In fact, over the past few weeks she's been listening to their rehearsals in the event of an invasion and feels in a strange way that she's got to know them. As D-Day progresses and the Allies destroy the guns, they've been falling silent. Rosemary will write later, 'Each call sign had developed a personality, and one was aware of the sad madness of war, as one by one the messages ceased.'

On Omaha Beach, Seth Shepard, the photographer on LCI 92, and other members of her crew are looking anxiously at the advancing waves – in less than an hour it will be high tide. In the shelter of a sea wall they are in a shallow foxhole they've dug with their bare hands. Soon they'll have to clamber over the wall and be exposed to German snipers. The sound of the pebbles being rolled back and forth by the waves sounds to Shepard just like machine-gun fire, adding to his unease.

In the Channel, HMS *Faulknor* is making good progress. In his cabin Monty is writing his entry for 6th June in his pocket diary.

'Invaded Normandy; left Portsmouth 10.30.'

By the end of D-Day, the Americans had hoped to have a bridgehead 16 miles wide and five miles deep on Omaha Beach. In fact, the bridgehead is barely the width of the beach and although some units are two miles inland, most are still below the cliffs. The casualties on Omaha are the highest of all the beaches. Nearly 40,000 men came ashore but the 29th Division has 2,440 casualties, and the 1st Division 1,744. Most men were killed in the first two hours.

Thirty years later, General Omar Bradley will write, 'Omaha Beach was a nightmare. Even now it brings pain to recall what happened there on June 6th 1944... Every man who set foot on Omaha Beach was a hero.'

Three LCMs have landed on Omaha Beach to collect survivors. Seth Shepard and other crew members are walking gratefully towards them. The full moon is shining an eerie light on the bodies on the beach. Some are stacked, Shepard thinks, 'like lumber'.

Many US paratroopers who landed in the countryside behind Utah and Omaha beaches in the early hours of D-Day are hunkered down in hedgerows and ditches, farmhouses and orchards, and wondering if the invasion has been a success. Very few have linked up with the infantry from the beaches. Donald Burgett of US 101st Airborne has spent the day fighting with a unit made up of men from his division and the 82nd, and they are hearing rumours that the assault troops have been pushed back onto the beaches, leaving them stranded.

However, Utah's beachhead has been secured, over 23,000 troops have landed and some have pushed four miles inland. About 900 men died fighting for Utah Beach today, that's fewer than at the rehearsal at Slapton Sands on 28th April when German torpedo boats attacked the Force U landing craft.

### *About 11.20pm*

Audacious E-boat commander Heinrich Hoffmann is back among the Allied fleet – his D-Day isn't over…

Earlier, he asked his commanding officer for full tactical freedom – and got it. Under cover of darkness, with just two boats, he sailed north and swung round to join the Allied ships sailing towards Normandy. For the last hour he's been carefully sailing at the same speed as them, and because the fleet is so vast, so far this small German flotilla has been undetected.

Then Hoffmann gives the order for all 12 of his torpedoes to be fired at once. He watches in amazement as the night is lit 'as if it was day' by three powerful explosions. The Allied fleet responds by firing into the air, thinking the ships must have been hit by bombs from a Luftwaffe attack, as there are no enemy ships on the radar. To remain undetected the two German E-boats join in and fire into the air too.

Juno Beach is illuminated by burning seafront houses. An ammunition truck that was hit by a shell in the early evening is still on fire, and every now and then sends up fireworks of exploding ammunition.

The troops on the beach are cold and unable to relax – they fully expect a German counter-attack from the land or from the air.

The Canadians who landed at Juno Beach have progressed further than anyone else: 21,400 men of the 3rd Canadian Division and 2nd Armoured Brigade are ashore, having suffered 359 losses and seen 715 wounded. By nightfall two battalions which landed at Juno are only three miles from Caen's outskirts.

### *11.30pm*

First Lieutenant Martin Pöppel of the German 6th Parachute Regiment is updating his war diary. Early this morning he witnessed the capture of scores of US paratroopers, but since then his regiment has failed to engage the enemy, thanks to indecision and confusion from their headquarters.

Pöppel has his unit camped in the open air, some using the protection of shell craters, so they can be ready for action. But Pöppel is frustrated.

'Every day is crucial... in fact every hour – the enemy is bringing his reinforcements ashore. Only by destroying the landing craft, the enemy fleet involved in the whole operation, can we destroy the enemy's supplies and give ourselves a chance to drive him back into the sea...'

George Saunders is in the back of a German truck heading to an army field hospital. He managed to escape from the Germans hunting him by hiding in a ditch, but was later captured on patrol. So far the Germans haven't discovered that Saunders is one of their countrymen. If they do, he'll be shot as a deserter. Before the start of the war, Saunders had received his German Army call-up papers, in his real name of Georg Saloschin.

Odette Mousset has been carried on a stretcher from the first-aid post in Ouistreham to the seashore and carefully put in a landing craft. Now both Odette and Raoul are heading away from France, and tomorrow her urgently needed treatment will begin in an English hospital. After 11 months' care, Odette and Raoul will return home to rebuild their life in Ouistreham.

### *11.40pm*

Lieutenant James Doohan of the Winnipeg Rifles, who'd run onto Juno Beach with £3,600 in gambling winnings in his pocket, is being treated in a first-aid post. His unit has survived the day unscathed, and Doohan hasn't even fired a shot. But at 11.30pm, when he was patrolling the top of the beach with fellow officer Tommy O'Brennan, he was hit by machine-gun fire. A medic is examining Doohan's right hand and right leg, which have been hit a number of times.

Doohan spots a bullet hole in his shirt. Could he have been hit in the chest? Nervously, he reaches inside his breast pocket and pulls out a silver cigarette case his brother gave him when he was his best man. The case has a dent in it. It stopped the bullet.

*Doohan will leave Juno Beach in the morning on order to receive specialist treatment in England. Tommy Brennan takes over command of their unit, including a tank which has Doohan's £3,600 in it. The tank and the money are later blown up.*

*Doohan's middle finger is amputated in Colchester Hospital, and after VE Day, he leaves the army and pursues a career in acting.*

*The fact that he lost a finger on D-Day doesn't stop James Doohan getting the part of Scotty, the engineer on USS* Enterprise *in the TV series* Star Trek *– but he hides his right hand whenever possible.*

### *11.45pm*

Lieutenant Donald Holman of the Royal Army Service Corps is walking alone on Sword Beach. He thinks he's treading on soft seaweed but when he looks down, he realises it's the bodies of British soldiers which have come in on the tide.

Hoffmann's E-boat crew are nervous. They've stopped firing in the air at imaginary aircraft. They want their commander to give the order to leave the convoy now. But Hoffmann is in no rush. He'll wait another 15 minutes before ordering the E-boats to peel away from the Allied fleet. The two E-boats will arrive at Le Havre almost without a scratch.

> ***My father was tremendously impressed with the organisation and the imagination involved. It was a glorious battle for the Allies, and as a soldier, he admired them greatly. Father knew from North Africa that the British were good soldiers. But, as he said, Normandy showed him they were better than he had presumed. He knew by then that Germany could not win the war.***
>
> **Manfred Rommel**

### *Midnight*

Since 6.30am 59,900 personnel, 8,900 vehicles and 1,900 tons of stores have been landed in France. All five Normandy beachheads are established along a 50-mile front. Operation Overlord is a success.

In Caen, at the headquarters of Major General Wilhelm Richter, commander of the 716th Infantry Division, the phone is ringing. It's hardly rung all day. Scores of wounded men lie in the corridors. General Richter answers the phone. It's Colonel Krug of the 736th Grenadier Regiment, who is in command of the strongpoint on the Périers ridge the British have code-named Hillman.

'*Herr General*, the enemy are on top of my bunker. I have no means of resisting, and no communication with my own men. What shall I do?'

General Richter hesitates, then says slowly, 'Colonel, I can no longer give you any orders. You must make your own decisions now. Goodbye.'

And he puts down the receiver.

Meteorologist Group Captain James Stagg's weather forecast has been vindicated. Tuesday 6th is the only day in June in which D-Day could have been successfully launched. The fortnight that follows will be the stormiest of the whole month.

The contribution to D-Day by the two employees of the toy firm Chad Valley isn't over. Although D-Day is done, the fact that Normandy is the Allies' only invasion point, as shown on their map, has to stay secret. The men must be kept at Southwick House for a few weeks more.

*A French civilian gives an American officer details of German troop movements*

# After D-Day...

For the majority of those who took part in the Normandy landings, D-Day was just the first of many days they had to survive. For those at home, joy that the Second Front had finally started soon gave way to anxiety and frustration. Land Girl Muriel Green wrote in her diary in September 1944, 'We all thought the war was so nearly over and now we hear of such sacrifice of lives, it makes me miserable...'

Some troops would not return home for a year.

In the weeks after D-Day, the British got bogged down trying to capture Caen, and the Americans in the so-called 'battle for the hedgerows' or *bocages*.

The US Army chief of staff, General George C Marshall, admitted to his biographer that they didn't know Normandy's patchwork of fields made defending easier for the Germans. 'We had to pay in blood for our lack of knowledge. Don't print that.'

French civilian casualties, already high, increased after D-Day – 20,000 died as the Allied armies moved through north-west France. Montgomery was not entirely sympathetic:

'When they chucked their hand in in 1940 they thought that they could avoid all this – they cannot.'

On 25th August the German garrison in Paris surrendered, and the Allies moved east into Belgium, Luxembourg and the Netherlands. However, the bitter winter that followed slowed the Allied advance, and the Germans took the opportunity to regroup. During a last-ditch offensive in December that became known as the 'Battle of Bulge' they pushed through the American lines at their weakest point – the US First Army in the Ardennes. Until the German forces were repulsed, at the cost of 80,000 casualties, for a few alarming days it seemed possible that the Allies might be pushed back to the beaches. Many German units fought to the last man. One British brigadier wrote, 'I have often wondered how we ever beat them...'

As they moved through occupied Europe and into Germany, the front-line troops discovered what some had heard from captured conscripted Poles in Normandy, but could not believe possible – atrocities on an industrial scale. When General Patton visited the Ohrdruf concentration camp in Germany, the first to be liberated, he was physically sick, and ordered that as many of his men as possible should see what he saw.

Meanwhile, the Russians had been moving steadily through Bulgaria, Romania, Yugoslavia, Poland and Hungary, their tanks outnumbering the Germans' by ten to one, and their aircraft by eight to one. On 30th April, with the Russians above his bunker in Berlin, Hitler committed suicide by simultaneously biting on a cyanide capsule and shooting himself in the head. German military leaders signed unconditional surrender agreements on 4th and 7th May 1945.

## Winston Churchill

Having been advised against going to Normandy on D-Day itself, Churchill finally got to the beaches on D+6, and would visit them twice more. He continued to monitor every aspect of the war but from 16th June, the V1 menace occupied a great deal of his time.

In the general election of July 1945, a war-weary Britain voted for Clement Attlee's Labour Party rather than Churchill's caretaker Conservative government. On the afternoon of the result, Churchill's doctor Lord Moran told him he thought the British people were ungrateful. 'Oh no, I wouldn't call it that,' Churchill replied. 'They have had a very hard time.' In 1951, Churchill bounced back, winning office once more. He served as an MP until 1964, dying, aged 90, a year later.

At his funeral a *New York Times* reporter spoke to a man in the crowd, who said he'd been, 'PBI – Poor Bloody Infantry – France, Africa, Italy – the lot. I tell you, we wouldn't have got through if it hadn't been for him.'

## President Franklin D Roosevelt

In November 1944, President Roosevelt won an unprecedented fourth election with 53 per cent of the vote, but his health had declined to such an extent that his inauguration in January 1945 had to be held on the White House lawn. FDR managed to stand for a five-minute speech:

'We have learned that we cannot live alone, at peace; that our own well-being is dependent upon the well-being of other nations, far away.'

On 12th April 1945, President Roosevelt died, and Vice President Harry S Truman took over as the 33rd president of the United States.

## General Bernard Montgomery

For the rest of the war, Monty frustrated SHAEF with both his caution in battle and his tendency to mislead them with his 'successes'. He always tried to keep 'Winston's podgy finger' out of his campaigns, much to the prime minister's frustration (Churchill came close to sacking Monty in July 1944).

By the autumn of 1944 the Allies were confident of a swift victory. In September, Montgomery launched Operation Market Garden, an attempt by 20,000 airborne troops to secure the bridge over the Rhine at Arnhem. He'd ignored, or didn't receive intelligence that warned of German panzer units close by. Prince Bernhard of the Netherlands said sarcastically, 'My country can never again afford the luxury of a Montgomery success.' Nevertheless, Montgomery's troops continued a slow and steady advance through Belgium and Holland, reaching the Baltic port of Lübeck on 2nd May, successfully detering the Russians from moving into Denmark.

On 3rd May, Admiral von Friedeburg arrived unexpectedly at Monty's German headquarters, offering the surrender of all the forces in the north of Europe. Monty greeted von Friedeburg by saying, 'Who are you and what do you want? I've never heard of you!' He then lectured von Friedeburg about the bombing of Coventry and the mass murder of Jews. The surrender was signed the next day.

In the 1946 New Year's Honours list, Montgomery was named a viscount. His staff already knew, as he'd been practising his signature for weeks. He retired from the army in 1958, and died on 24th March 1976.

## Field Marshal Erwin Rommel

A week after the Normandy landings, Rommel knew the war was lost. He and Field Marshal von Rundstedt met with Hitler to try and make him realise the gravity of the military situation in France, and that 'the whole world stands together against Germany'. Hitler furiously ordered Rommel to leave the room.

Rommel was working on a plan to allow the Allies to pass through his lines and therefore get to Berlin before the Russians, but on 17th July his car was attacked by a Spitfire (ironically near the village of Sainte-Foy-de-Montgommery) and he was flung onto the road and suffered a quadruple skull fracture.

Recovering at home, Rommel was informed by two army generals that he'd been implicated in a failed plot to assassinate the Führer. Rommel was offered the choice of a public trial or suicide – he chose suicide. Rommel broke the news to Lucie and Manfred ('I shall be dead in a quarter of an hour...') and then drove with the generals to a quiet road, where he took the poison they'd brought with them.

Rommel was given a state funeral, and Hitler sent his condolences to Lucie Rommel.

### General Dwight D Eisenhower

For the rest of the war, Eisenhower had to manage the competing egos of Patton and Montgomery – each wanting their army to be the first to break through the German lines and reach Berlin. After the war ended, Eisenhower became the army chief of staff, then the president of Columbia University. In 1950 he was appointed NATO's Supreme Commander of Allied Forces in Europe. In 1953, still hugely popular with the public, Eisenhower, as the Republican Party candidate, was elected the 34th president of the United States, and he went on to serve two terms. He was succeeded by another Second World War veteran, John F Kennedy. Kennedy once asked Eisenhower what gave him the edge over the Germans on D-Day. 'I think we had better weather forecasters,' Eisenhower replied.

## General George Patton

Patton arrived in France in command of the US Third Army in August 1944. 'I'm going in there to kick someone's ass,' he declared.

Armed with Michelin maps (and in relatively under-defended areas) his army progressed at high speed through France, until they met tough German resistance at Metz. By March, the Third Army had crossed the River Rhine (Patton boasted he urinated in it as he crossed).

After Germany surrendered in May 1945, Patton was made military governor of Bavaria, but was soon criticised for allowing former Nazis to run the civil government. Patton was deeply hostile to the Russians who he feared would overrun Europe, and believed if he was given the chance he could 'kick them back home in three months'.

On 9th December 1945, the car in which he was a passenger hit a truck, and Patton was paralysed from the neck down. He died in his sleep on 21st December.

General Patton was buried in the American military cemetery at Hamm in Luxembourg. He had told his wife Beatrice, 'If I should conk, it would be far more pleasant for my ghostly future to lie among my soldiers than to rest in the sanctimonious precincts of a civilian cemetery.'

## General Charles de Gaulle

De Gaulle entered Paris on 25th August 1944, and in October the following year was elected head of the provisional government of France. In 1958 he became president of the new Fifth Republic and remained in office for 11 years. He died in 1970.

### Kay Summersby

Eisenhower flew home to Washington on 10th November 1945, and Kay expected to follow him. Ten days later she received a telegram telling her she'd been dropped from the roster of military staff due to leave for the US. Although she and Eisenhower met two further times (she hung around Columbia when she found out he'd become president of the university) their affair had ended. Eisenhower was very ambitious, and a mistress would have been an embarrassment.

In an interview in 1974, President Truman claimed that Eisenhower intended to divorce his wife Mamie and marry Kay, but that US Army chief of staff George Marshall threatened to 'run Eisenhower out of the army' if he did.

Shortly before she died of cancer on Long Island in January 1975, Kay published a memoir of her affair with Eisenhower called *Past Forgetting.*

### Major General Hans Speidel

Rommel's chief of staff was implicated in the July 1944 plot to kill Hitler, and was imprisoned for seven months before managing to escape. After the war he worked for NATO and in the late 1950s became Commander of Allied Land Forces in Europe, often dealing with Eisenhower, who was by then president of the United States. Speidel was viewed with suspicion by many; when he visited Oslo, buses and trams stopped for two minutes in protest. Demonstrators greeted him with banners saying, 'We have forgiven the German people but not Hitler's generals.' Hans Speidel died in 1984 aged 87.

### Lord 'Shimi' Lovat

A few days after D-Day, Lord Lovat was severely injured by

a shell burst. Piper Bill Millin sent someone to find a priest to give him the last rites. 'Not a foot back,' Lovat kept repeating. He survived, but that was the end of his military career.

Working in 1961 as an advisor on the D-Day film *The Longest Day*, Lord Lovat fell asleep in a cab heading into Caen. He woke up to find the car heading towards a group of German soldiers. Instinctively, he dived out of the moving car and into a ditch. Emerging from the ditch, he realised they were just film extras.

Lord Lovat died in 1995, after a career in politics, and the funeral lament was played by Bill Millin.

### Bill Millin

When the war ended, instead of going home to his parents, Millin went straight to Fort William to see a girl he'd met and fallen in love with while training there. Millin was told that she had died of cancer while he was in Normandy. He then worked for a while on Lord Lovat's estate before joining a theatre company, playing his pipes on stage. In the 1950s he trained as a mental health nurse and moved to Devon, where he died aged 88 in August 2010. A statue near Sword Beach of Bill playing his pipes was unveiled by his son John in 2013.

### Brigadier General Theodore 'Ted' Roosevelt Jr

Five weeks after surviving and sorting out the confusion on Utah Beach, Ted Roosevelt died of a heart attack near Sainte-Mère-Église on 12th July 1944. He was 56. Roosevelt was posthumously awarded the Medal of Honour for his attack on Utah Beach.

## Lieutenant Colonel Terence Otway

Two days after capturing the Merville Battery, Otway was injured by a stray shell and was graded unfit for active service. He left the army in 1948 and had a variety of careers, from running a toyshop in Knightsbridge to working in life insurance.

In 1993, he returned to Merville and met the German commander of the battery, and reluctantly shook his hand; the loss of so many of his men, shot as they hung in trees, was still painful. Otway rebuked tourists for picnicking: 'I don't like people eating and drinking where my men died.'

## André Heintz

Seventy per cent of the city of Caen was destroyed in the Allied bombing; only two landmarks survived – the abbey, and thanks to André and his sister's bloody red cross, the hospital. After Caen was liberated, André worked as an interpreter for the British Army for five months, then moved to Scotland to teach French at the University of Edinburgh.

He returned to Caen, and for the next 36 years he taught languages at the university's Institute of Technology. For many years André gave guided tours of the D-Day beaches and Caen Museum, where his radio is displayed, hidden in an old bean tin.

## 'Garbo'/Juan Pujol

Double agent 'Garbo' was awarded an MBE and £17,500 in December 1944. Hitler ordered that the agent he knew as 'Arabel' be awarded an Iron Cross, and that his fictitious network of agents in Britain be given a total of £31,000 as a reward for their service to the Reich.

In 1949, MI6 faked Juan Pujol's death, and he settled in Venezuela, where he worked as a language teacher for Shell Oil. In 1984 he was finally presented with his MBE, by the Duke of Edinburgh. Juan Pujol died in Caracas in 1988.

### Robert Capa

Capa was one of the founders of the influential photo agency Magnum in 1947. On assignment in Vietnam in 1957, he stepped on a landmine and was killed. He was 40 years old.

### Seth Shepard

Shepard, the photographer on LCI 92, was taken by landing craft to a troop ship off Omaha Beach. For four days until it made it back to England he helped tend the sick and wounded. On Sunday 11th June he arrived at a survivors' base in Plymouth where he wrote an account of D-Day.

### Lieutenant Commander Heinrich Hoffmann

Hoffmann was decorated by Hitler with the Knight's Cross with Oak Leaves for his daring E-boat attacks on the Allied fleets. After the war he became an officer in the West German Navy, based in the Defence Ministry in Bonn. He retired in 1968 after 40 years in the navy.

### Corporal Franz Gockel

Shot in the hand on Omaha Beach, Gockel was taken to Paris to recover. He was considered fit enough in the autumn of 1944 to be sent back to the Western Front, but was soon captured by the Americans. After the war Gockel met up with some of the

GIs who had been his enemies on the beaches of Normandy. He has received awards for his attempts at reconciliation.

### Second Lieutenant Stuart Hills

Tank commander Hills took his crew all the way from Normandy, through Belgium, the Netherlands, where they saw action at Arnhem, and into Germany. When the war ended, Captain Hills was awarded the Military Cross. He joined the Malayan Civil Service and later returned to England and worked for Shell Oil. He died in May 2008, aged 80.

### Major John Howard

Shortly after capturing the bridges at Bénouville, Howard was injured in a road accident and returned home, leaving the army in 1945. In 1954 he was awarded the Croix de Guerre avec Palme by the French government. After he retired, Howard gave talks to army cadets in NATO countries and lectures in the US. Every 6th June he would return to the Pegasus Bridge and lay a wreath in memory of fallen comrades. Major Howard died in May 1999.

### Meteorologist Group Captain James Stagg

In 1945 Stagg was made an OBE and given the Legion of Merit by the US government. He was knighted in 1954. Stagg served as the director of services at the Meteorological Office until 1960. In 1971 he published *Forecast for Overlord*, his memoirs about the crucial D-day forecasts. He died in June 1975, aged 74.

## George Saunders/Georg Saloschin

After being captured, X Troop commando Saunders was taken to a Luftwaffe hospital where he was well looked after. On his way to a POW camp he leapt from the train into a cornfield. When his guards threatened to set fire to the field, he gave himself up. Saunders was a POW for the rest of the war, but attempted to escape many times. The Germans never discovered his true identity.

When Saunders' camp was overrun by the Russians, they forced the POWs to build them a bridge, which he saw as little more than slave labour. He escaped again and hitchhiked his way to Odessa, where he found a British ship to take him home. George Saunders died in Oxfordshire in 2008.

## Peter Masters/ Peter Arany

Impressed by their capture of the Pegasus Bridge, Masters joined the Oxfordshire and Buckinghamshire Light Infantry. After the war he became an art student in London and had a highly successful career as a graphic designer in American television and for the federal government. In 1997 he published a memoir called *Fighting Back*, in which he described the D-Day campaign as 'a truly holy war fought against a monstrous system bent on destroying us...' Peter Masters died of a heart attack while playing tennis at the age of 83.

## *Acknowledgements*

In 1972 the Imperial War Museum started a programme of recording interviews with Second World War veterans, and that collection has proved to be a treasure trove for me. Many of the stories and quotations in this book come from those interviews; my thanks to the staff in the IWM research department. The D-Day Museum in Portsmouth has some remarkable D-Day memoirs from local people and sailors and soldiers; they also have the full text of the German interviews made by researchers for Cornelius Ryan's classic D-Day book *The Longest Day* – all were extremely useful. I'm grateful to Andrew Whitmarsh at the D-Day Museum for his help.

My thanks also to George Batts of the Normandy Veterans Association, Mary James, Sir Nicholas Mosley and Eve Cherry for their stories, and for providing background to the period.

Phil Critchlow at TBI, who has produced with me our Minute by Minute programmes for BBC Radio 2, is the hardest working man in the media, and remains one of the good guys.

I very much appreciate the encouragement of Bob Shennan, the controller of Radio 2, and of Robert Gallagher, its commissioning editor, both supporters of the Minute by Minute format.

The team at Short Books has been a tremendous help once again: Rebecca Nicolson, Aurea Carpenter and Paul Bougourd, and I couldn't ask for a wiser editor in Emma Craigie.

Finally, grateful thanks to my wife Hannah and son Charlie, who have had to put up with a big part of my head being in 1944 while I wrote this book (I had to set an alarm to remind me to collect Charlie from school...). I couldn't have received more love, support and encouragement.

# Bibliography

Ambrose, Stephen E, *D-Day: 6 June 1944 – The Climactic Battle of World War II* (Simon and Schuster, 1994)
Ambrose, Stephen E, *Pegagus Bridge: D-Day – the Daring British Airborne Raid* (Simon and Schuster, 2003)
Arthur, Max, *Forgotten Voices of the Second World War* (Ebury Press, 2005)
Bailey, Roderick, *Forgotten Voices of D-Day* (Ebury Press, 2009)
Bailey, Roderick, *Forgotten Voices of the Secret War* (Ebury Press, 2009)
Balkoski, Joseph, *Omaha Beach: D-Day, June 6, 1944* (Stackpole Books, 2006)
Balkoski, Joseph, *Utah Beach: The Amphibious Landing and Airborne Operations on D-Day, June 6, 1944* (Stackpole Books, 2005)
Bastable, Jonathan, *Voices from D-Day: Eye-Witness Accounts of 6th June 1944* (David and Charles, 2004)
Beevor, Anthony, *D-Day: The Battle for Normandy* (Viking , 2009)
Blair, Clay and Bradley, General Omar, *A General's Life* (Simon and Schuster, 1983)
Bowman, Martin W, *Remembering D-Day: Personal Histories of Everyday Heroes* (Harper Collins, 2004)
Briggs, Asa, *The BBC : A Short Story of the First Fifty Years* (OUP, 1985)
Bruce, Colin John, *Invaders: British and American Experience of Seaborne Landings 1939-1945* (Caxton Editions, 1999)
Burgett, Donald R, *Currahee!: A Screaming Eagle at Normandy* (Dell Publishing, 1967)
Calder, Angus, *The People's War: Britain 1939-1945* (Jonathan Cape, 1969)
Capa, Robert, *Slightly Out of Focus* (Modern Library, 2001)
Carell, Paul, *Invasion!: They're Coming!* (Harrap and Co., 1962)
Chancellor, Henry, *Colditz* (Hodder and Stoughton, 2001)
Chandler,. David G eds, *The D-Day Encyclopedia* (Simon and Schuster, 1994)
Delaforce, Patrick, *Marching to the Sound of Gunfire: Northwest Europe 1944-5* (Wrens Park, 1999)
Doohan, James, *Beam Me Up, Scotty* (Pocket Books, 1996)
Durnford-Slater, Brigadier John, *Commando: Memoirs of a Fighting Commando in World War II* (Tandem, 1973)
Foot, M R D, *SOE* (BBC, 1984)
Frank, Anne, *The Diary of a Young Girl* (Pan Books, 1954)
Gardiner, Juliet, *Wartime: Britain 1939-1945* (Headline, 2004)
Harris, Carol, *D-Day Diary: Life on the Front Line in the Second World War* (The History Press, 2013)
Harris, Leo, *A Boy Remembers* (Apache Guides, 2000)
Hastings, Max, *All Hell Let Loose: The World at War 1939-1945* (Harper Press, 2011)
Hastings, Max, *Overlord: D-Day and the Battle for Normandy* (Pan Military Classics, 1984)
Hawkins, Desmond eds, *War Report: From D-Day to VE-Day* (BBC Books, 1994)
Hibberd, Stuart, *This is London* (MacDonald and Evans, 1950)
Hills, Stuart, *By Tank Into Normandy* (Cassell, 2002)
Holmes, Richard, *The World at War* (Ebury, 2007)
Horne, Alistair and Montgomery, David, *The Lonely Leader: Monty 1944-1945* (Pan Macmillan, 1994)
Howard, Michael, *Strategic Deceptions in the Second World War* (Pimlico, 1990)
Howarth, David, *Dawn of D-Day* (Greenhill Books, 2001)
Keegan, John, *Six Armies in Normandy* (Pimlico, 1992)
Kemp, Paul, *Underwater Warriors* (Brockhampton Press, 1999)

Kershaw, Robert, *D-Day Piercing the Atlantic Wall* (Ian Allan, 1993)
Lefebvre, Laurent, *They Were On Omaha Beach* (American D-Day Edition, 2003)
Lewis, Jon E eds, *D-Day: The Normandy Landings In The Words Of Those Who Took Part* (Magpie Books, 2010)
Lewis, Jon E, *World War II: The Autobiography* (Robinson, 2009)
Longmate, Norman, *How We Lived Then: A History of Everyday Life During the Second World War* (Pimlico, 2002)
Lovat, Lord, *March Past* (Weidenfeld and Nicolson, 1978)
Masters, Peter, *Striking Back: A Jewish Commando's War Against the Nazis* (Presido, 1997)
McDonough, Frank, *Hitler and Nazi Germany* (Cambridge University Press, 1999)
McDougall, Murdoch C, *Swiftly They Struck: The Story of No. 4 Commando* (Grafton Books, 1954)
McKee, Alexander, *Caen: Anvil of Victory* (Souvenir Press, 1964)
Meacham, Jon, *Franklin and Winston: A Portrait of a Friendship* (Random House, 2003)
Miller, Russell, *Nothing Less Than Victory* (Michael Joseph, 1993)
Montgomery, Bernard Law, *The Memoirs of Field-Marshal the Viscount Montgomery of Alamein* (Collins, 1958)
Moorehead, Alan, *Eclipse* (Hamish Hamilton, 1946)
Nichol, John and Rennell, Tony, *Medic: Saving Lives – From Dunkirk to Afghanistan* (Penguin, 2009)
Nicholson, Virginia, *Millions Like Us* (Penguin, 2011)
Owen, James, *Commando: Winning World War II Behind Enemy Lines* (Little, Brown, 2012)
Parker, John, *Commandos* (Bounty Books, 2005)
Parry, Dan, *D-Day: 6.6.44* (BBC Books, 2004)
Poppel, Martin, *Heaven and Hell: The War Diary of a German Paratrooper* (Spellmount, 1988)
Roberts, Andrew, *Masters and Commanders: How Roosevelt, Churchill, Marshall and Alanbrooke Won the War in the West* (Allen Lane, 2008)
Ruge, Friedrich, *Rommel in Normandy* (MacDonald and Jane's, 1979)
Ryan, Cornelius, *The Longest Day* (New Orchard, 1994)
Smith, Lyn, *Young Voices: British Children Remember the Second World War* (Viking, 2007)
Speer, Albert, *Inside the Third Reich* (Phoenix, 1995)
Stafford, David, *Ten Days to D-Day* (Abacus, 2003)
Summersby Morgan, Kay, *Past Forgetting: My Love Affair With Dwight D Eisenhower* (Collins, 1977)
Turner, Barry, *Outpost of Occupation: The Nazi Occupation of the Channel Islands 1940-45* (Aurum, 2010)

## *Other Sources*

D-Day & Normandy Fellowship, 'D-Day Memories'
http://www.ddnf.org.uk/memories
Goldstein, Richard, 'Obituary of Jimmy Yule', *New York Times*, 15th January 2001
Hemingway, Ernest, 'Voyage to Victory', *Collier's Weekly* (22nd July 1944)
Home Page of the USS Corry
http://www.uss-corry-dd463.com
Shepard, Seth, 'The Story of the LCI (L) 92 in the Invasion of Normandy on June 6, 1944.', *US Coast Guard*
http://www.uscg.mil/history/docs/LCI92.asp

# Index